Lineberger Memorial Library

Lutheran Theological Southern Seminary   Columbia, S. C.

GAY, STRAIGHT, AND
IN-BETWEEN

GAY, STRAIGHT, AND IN-BETWEEN

The Sexology of Erotic Orientation

John Money

Johns Hopkins University and Hospital
Baltimore, Maryland

New York   Oxford
OXFORD UNIVERSITY PRESS
1988

Oxford University Press

Oxford   New York   Toronto
Delhi   Bombay   Calcutta   Madras   Karachi
Petaling Jaya   Singapore   Hong Kong   Tokyo
Nairobi   Dar es Salaam   Cape Town
Melbourne   Auckland

and associated companies in
Berlin   Ibadan

Library of Congress Cataloging-in-Publication Data
Money, John, 1921–
Gay, straight, and in-between.
Bibliography: p.   Includes indexes. 1. Sex differentiation.
2. Sex determination, Genetic. 3. Psychosexual disorders. 4. Sex (Psychology)
I. Title. [DNLM: 1. Brain—physiology. 2. Homosexuality.
3. Identification (Psychology) 4. Paraphilias. 5. Sex
Hormones—physiology. WM 610 M742g]
QP278.M66 1988   155.3   87-24751
ISBN 0-19-505407-5

1 3 5 7 9 8 6 4 2

Printed in the United States of America
on acid-free paper

For Libby Hopkins and all other members of my extended family together with all other morally sane people everywhere who bestow equality on others regardless of whether they are heterosexual, homosexual, or bisexual.

Acknowledgments

During the period when this book was written, the author's Psycho-hormonal Research Unit at the Johns Hopkins University and Hospital was supported by USPHS Grant #HD00325 and Grant 83086900 from the William T. Grant Foundation. The manuscript was word-processed by Sandra Aamodt, who also assisted with editing. H. T. Walker, Cecilia Lobato, and other members of the psychohormonal research staff assisted in proofreading. Sally Hopkins, my niece, designed the background for the dust jacket. Material from Chapter 1 has appeared in the *American Psychologist* (Vol. 42, No. 4, 1987); and from Chapter 2 in *Balcones* (Vol. 1, 1987). J.C.G. Conniff of New Jersey initiated the etymological search recorded in the Introduction, to which M. Aston and C.J. Migeon, both of Baltimore, contributed additional information.

Contents

GAY, STRAIGHT, AND
IN-BETWEEN

Introduction

In New Zealand's forestry business, exotic evergreen species from the Northern Hemisphere mature more rapidly than in their colder, native habitat, and are ready for harvesting in thirty to thirty-five years. One of these exotic forests is the image that I see in my mind's eye when I view the manuscript of this book. It is a down-under image, for I left New Zealand in 1947 at the age of twenty-six, and in 1950, while a doctoral student at Harvard, began planting the seedlings of intersex research that are now harvested in this book, over thirty years later. It has been evident to me for some time that this particular harvest time was due, since an unending succession of people, especially those from the print and electronic media, request an account by telephone, or on camera, of the significance of my sexological and psychohormonal research publications for today's understanding of homosexuality. "Is it nature or nurture? Biological or psychological?" These are the commonest questions. Their response has required a semester's course condensed into an hour!

The impetus to write a complete account of the significance of my clinical sexological research for the theory of homosexuality—and, therefore, of bisexuality and heterosexuality as well—instead of continually repeating an hour's course, was launched by the American Psychological Association (APA), when it notified me that, at its ninety-third Annual Meeting in Los Angeles, I would receive its 1985 Distinguished Scientific Award for the Applications of Psychology. Then, on August 25th, 1986, at the ninety-fourth Annual Meeting in Washington, D.C., I would deliver the award-winner's address. The title of my address, I decided, would be "Sin, Sickness, or Status? Homosexual Gender Identity and Psychoneuroendocrinology." I would summarize the significance for homosexual theory of my long-term, outcome studies of selected endocrine syndromes, many of them of prenatal onset. It immediately became obvious that I would, in the fifty minutes allocated, be able to deliver only a very abridged version of what I would write for publication in the *American Psychologist* (Money, 1987c). Even so, the written version would itself be heavily condensed; and it would also omit syndromes that, although relevant, are primarily cytogenetic rather than hormonogenic in prenatal origin. These considerations notwithstanding, the

3

written version would have its own coherency and unity. Since I had an overabundance of other commitments, it might well have to stand alone, and on its own merits. However, fate would decide otherwise.

In the spring of 1986 I was delivered an edict: the space allocated to the Psychohormonal Research Unit in the building that houses the Department of Psychiatry and Behavioral Sciences would be reallocated. The new space would be away from the hospital campus in a commercial building. No further explanation would be given. There would be no appeal. The distance of the new location from the hospital would, I knew, prevent continued synchronization of patients' psychohormonal schedules with their other inpatient and outpatient schedules. I envisioned myself in a position reminiscent of that of my illustrious forebear at Johns Hopkins, John B. Watson, the founder of the school of behaviorism in psychology. In 1920, for reasons not fully disclosed at the time, he too had been evicted not only from his space, but also from his job (Magoun, 1981; Pauly, 1979). My reaction was to write this book.

In May 1986, I had been the discussant for the opening session of The Second Kinsey Symposium, "Homosexuality/Heterosexuality: The Kinsey Scale and Current Research" (McWhirter, Sanders, and Reinisch, 1988). I discussed the need for a criterion of what is male and what is female, so as to put some constraints on the chaos of undisciplined cultural relativity, while at the same time respecting cultural diversity and accommodating also the incongruities of hermaphroditism. Even in cases of infertility, I said, the basic criterion of the male/female distinction, acceptable in all branches of biology, is the male/female difference in procreation. In the overall context of homosexuality, this criterion is not as straightforward as it seems. It was not acceptable to some of the scholars in humanities and social science present at the symposium. Their discontent, and their lack of an alternative, warned me that I should, perhaps, deal in more detail with the criteria of male and female, homosexual and heterosexual, in what I was preparing for the APA. Such discursiveness would, however, lead me far from my original intention of writing a paper into writing this book.

In the early stage of planning, I considered the possibility of having a book in three parts. Part One would be a narrative survey. Part Two would be an anthology of those of my own clinical research publications surveyed in Part One. Part Three would be a portfolio of matched pairs of psycho-hormonal biographies in which each member of the pair was diagnostically concordant for intersexual prenatal history, and discordant for postnatal history as male or female by rearing; or concordant for rearing but discordant for prenatal diagnostic history. For reasons of time, space, and cost, Parts Two and Three were put on hold, and Part One was expanded to become the present book.

If there were a single term with which to denote the sexology of homosexuality, heterosexuality, and bisexuality, that would be the term for the title of this book, for the understanding and explanation of any one of the three applies to the other two as well. Homosexology fails to qualify as signifying the sexology of mankind, for according to its other etymology it signifies also the sexology of same-sexed partners, that is of homosexuals. The term sexology itself also fails to qualify, as its meaning is already established as encompassing more than the science of sexual orientation as homo-, hetero-, or bisexual.

One way around this terminological impasse would be to have a word like fuckology, used in everyday, vernacular English to signify the science of what it is that people actually do under the cover of polite expressions like making love or having sex. To love does not mean to fuck, and to sex is not even a verb, except when it means to determine the sex of, for instance, newly hatched chicks. The polite synonyms for fuck as a noun are coitus, copulation, and sexual intercourse, but no one who speaks English as a native language would invite a partner of either sex to coit, to copulate, or to intercourse. Nor would the two say they had a good coition, copulation, or intercourse.

Dictionaries are of no help in providing a polite synonym for the term that still exists in disgrace, debased and dishonored. A dictionary search a few years ago yielded two quasi-archaic words that survive in bawdy verse (Money, 1982). Quim, of Welsh origin, signifies what a woman does to a man when she takes charge of his quim stick, or quim wedge. Swive, of Anglo-Saxon origin, signifies what a man does to a woman. But there is no corresponding word of non-Latin origin for what two people do together, mutually, either heterosexually or homosexually, other than fuck—except, perhaps, that by de-Anglicizing the spelling and the pronunciation, they phuck (pronounced fook). The derivation of this neologism is from the Greek verb, *phuteuein*, to sow or plant in the ground; hence, to beget, and thus to impregnate. The aorist passive of this verb is *ephuchthen*, the gerund *phuktos*, and the gerundive *phukteos*. For this etymological Greek connection, I am indebted to James C. G. Conniff (personal communication, based on the 8th edition, p. 1702, of Liddell and Scott's *Greek Dictionary*, American Book Co., New York, 1897). He recalled that Sophocles used the term in Antigone with its meaning of impregnate, as had Aeschylus before him. He quoted from Shakespeare's *Julius Caesar*: "He ploughed her, and she cropped"; and from Aldous Huxley's *Devils of Loudun* (p.186), Sister Claire, one of the nuns accused of devil possession, went into a hysterical seizure and cried out repeatedly, "*Venez donc, foutez-moi*," which in French signifies the same lewd abandon as does "Come on, fuck me," in English. The modern spelling of *foutez* is *foutrez*, the infinitive of the verb being *foutrer*, from which is derived the noun, *le foutre*, a contemporary vulgarism for the ejaculate. These French words are derived through the Greek from the Latin, *futuere*, to have connection with a female. Lewis and Short, in their *Latin Dictionary* Oxford, 1879), say that usage of the word is rare; and an undated edition of last century's *Ainsworth's Dictionary* abridged for use in American schools gives no definition and specifies only that the word is obscene.

There is a corresponding implication of obscenity or, at least, of vulgarity in the modern Italian equivalent of the Latin *futuere*, namely *fottere*, which is used with the same significance as the English, *to fuck*. The polite Italian synonym for *fottere* is *figere*, which corresponds to the French *ficher*. Both mean to drive or thrust into. Both are soundalikes of the German, *fichen*, the term that is applied to the copulation of pigs and dogs and that is not acceptable in polite company. The English pronunciation of the German *fichen* would be ficken—and, indeed, in the working-class slang of Devon in the southwest of England, *ficky-ficky* is the term used instead of *fuck* as the noun for sexual intercourse.

In Greek, the first-person singular of the verb meaning to sow, plant, or beget is *phitio*. Thus it is likely that ficky-ficky and fuck have a shared ancestry either in Greek, or in an antecedent Indo-European linguistic stock shared by Greek, Latin, and the Teutonic languages.

Eric Partridge, in his *Origins: A Short Etymological Dictionary of Modern English* (London, Routledge and Kegan Paul, 1958), attributes the first printed appearance of the word *fuck* to Dunbar in 1503: "By his feiris he wald have fukkit" (Poem 75, line 13). Lyndsay is quoted (*Satyre* No. 1363, 1535) thus: "Bishops . . . may fuck their fill and be vnmaryit (unmarried)." John Wilmot, Earl of Rochester, in 1680 wrote:

"Much wine had passed with grave discourse
Of he who fucks who, and who does worse"

(*Poems on Several Occasions*. Poem No. 14, line 1). In the *Origins*, Partridge entered the forbidden term as f..k, and said that f..k and c..t were the two words that, throughout the English-speaking world, never appeared, fully spelled, in print.

Etymology was not productive as a way to find a title for this book. I abandoned a one-word title: *Homosexology*, or *Homosexuology*. I used a working title: *Gay and Lesbian Sexology*, and abandoned it at the behest of one of the three referees of the manuscript. In this anonymous referee's opinion, this title was too restrictive for a book that applies as much to heterosexuality as homosexuality. I gave thought to a title that would very literally mirror the book conceptually: *Genes, Genitals, Hormones, and Gender*—and then settled temporarily on the title: *Genes to Gender: The Sexology of Being Homosexual, Bisexual and Heterosexual*, so that the book would be included in all the computer-indexing services where it legitimately belongs. There were too many sexes in that title. Hence the final revision to *Gay, Straight, and In-Between: The Sexology of Erotic Orientation*.

The title announces that this book is addressed to those who would like to know the present state of knowledge regarding what determines that some children grow up to become homosexual, whereas others become bisexual or heterosexual. Each reader will find a story of his/her own sexological development and, at the same time, recognize that the book is designed to explain homosexuality to homosexuals themselves, as well as to other people, and likewise for heterosexuality and bisexuality.

People become homosexual, bisexual, or heterosexual because of what happens to them partly in their prenatal history, and partly in their postnatal history. Scientific investigation of prenatal causes is done predominantly in experiments on animals that yield valuable ideas that may or may not apply to human beings. It is ethically forbidden to experiment on human beings. Therefore, one must rely on nature's own experiments, which are the various conditions of birth defect of the sex organs. That is why most of Chapter 1, "Prenatal Hormones and Brain Dimorphism," consists of a comprehensive survey of what has been learned from long-term, follow-up studies of people born with defective sex organs. With the support of Lawson Wilkins, the world's first pediatric endocrinologist, these long-term studies began in 1951 and have continued until the present day in my Psychohormonal Research Unit of the Pediatric Endocrine Clinic at the Johns Hopkins Hospital and University. The findings of these studies have never before been brought together for comparison with one another and with the work of others, so that their full significance can be systematically recognized and evaluated.

Chapter 2, "Gender Coding," bridges the gap between prenatal history and postnatal history, and spells out the principles of identification and complementation by which masculine and feminine become differentiated in the childhood years. Chapter 2 prepares the way for the gender discrepancies of Chapter 3, "Gender Crosscoding," in which masculinizing and feminizing develop at cross-purposes with the sex of the external genitalia. Biological determinants are not set off against social and psychological determinants because at critical developmental periods all prior determinants are recognized as being able to influence those that follow, and their influence becomes biologically incorporated into the organism, especially into the brain. The important consideration is not biology versus nonbiology, but whether a particular outcome of development becomes fixed and immutable, or loose and easily changed. The different crosscoded phenomena or syndromes in Chapter 3 include, among others, transexualism, transvestism, homosexuality, and bisexuality, each differing from the others on the criteria of duration and extent or degree of crosscoding. Chapter 3 concludes with a review of today's knowledge of the relationship between hormones and homosexuality in adulthood.

Chapter 4, "Lovemaps and Paraphilia," introduces and explains the new concept of *lovemaps*, which may be healthy or pathological in their development. Whereas a homosexual lovemap is not pathological, per se, it also is not exempt from possible pathology any more than is a bisexual or heterosexual lovemap. Developmentally, lovemaps of all three types are able to incorporate a paraphilia. Paraphilias are legally defined as perversions and, on the street, as kinky or bizarre sex. The relationship of paraphilia to homosexuality has been neglected in gay politics and scholarship in general. In this book, paraphilia is examined in relationship to the cleavage between love and lust, to opponent-process theory, to addiction to various sexual stimuli, to pornography, and to prevention and treatment. There is a list of the forty-odd known paraphilias, each of which is defined in the glossary.

This is a book that should appeal to anyone, animal sexologists included, who is interested in the whys and wherefores of human sexuality in general, as well as to students and scholars of human homosexuality in particular. It is meant for physicians, psychologists, and other health care practitioners; for professionals in sex therapy and counseling; for sex educators and social workers; and for legislators, lawyers, police, and others in the judicial system who specialize in sex. It is written so as to be intelligible to not only the professional, but also the layperson. Unfamiliar and technical terms are defined in the glossary, so that the book will be understandable not only to professionals, but also to readers of literary and news magazines with a widespread national circulation, and to readers of periodicals with a specialty circulation, like the *New York Native, Christopher Street,* or *The Advocate,* and various regional and foreign publications for the gay community.

CHAPTER
ONE

Prenatal Hormones and Brain Dimorphism

1 HISTORICAL AND CULTURAL RELATIVITY

The phenomenon that is today named homosexuality did not have that name until is was coined by K.M. Benkert, writing under the pseudonym of Kertbeny, in 1869 (Bullough, 1976). Although he applied the term homosexuality to both males and females, he defined it on the criterion of erectile failure:

> In addition to the normal sexual urge in men and women, Nature in her sovereign mood has endowed at birth certain male and female individuals with the homosexual urge, thus placing them in a sexual bondage which renders them physically and psychically incapable—even with the best intention—of normal erection. This urge creates in advance a direct horror of the opposite sex, and the victim of this passion finds it impossible to suppress the feeling which individuals of his own sex exercise upon him.

Instead of the criterion of genital sexuality, as in homo*sexual*, Benkert could have used the criterion of falling in love, as in homo*philic*, or the criterion of being attracted to those of the same sex, as in homo*genic*. Both terms were proposed by others, but homosexual won the day, probably because it was taken up in the early years of the twentieth century by Havelock Ellis and Magnus Hirschfeld (Ellis, 1942; Hirschfeld, 1948). Neither of these two writers recognized that the ethnocentricity of Benkert's

9

definition of homosexuality as a sickness, though freeing it from being a sin or a crime, confines it too narrowly to pathological deviancy. It leaves no place for homosexuality as a status that is culturally ordained to be normal and healthy, as it is in societies that, since time immemorial, have institutionalized bisexuality. In bisexuality, homosexuality and heterosexuality may coexist concurrently, or they may be sequential, with a homosexual phase of development antecedent to heterosexuality and marriage. Concurrent bisexuality was exemplified in classical Athenian culture (Bullough, 1976). Sequential bisexuality is exemplified in various tribal Melanesian and related cultures.

There is a vast area of the world, stretching from the northwestern tip of Sumatra through Papua New Guinea to the outlying islands of Melanesia in the Pacific, in which the social institutionalization of homosexuality is shared by various ethnic and tribal people (Money and Ehrhardt, 1972b; Herdt, 1984). More precisely, it is sequential bisexuality that is institutionalized in these societies. Their cultural tradition dictates that males between the ages of nine and nineteen reside no longer with their families but in the single longhouse in the village center where males congregate. Until the age of nineteen, the prescribed age of marriage, they all participate in homosexual activities. After marriage homosexual activity either ceases or is sporadic.

The Sambia people (Herdt, 1981) of the eastern highlands of New Guinea are among those who traditional folk wisdom provided a rationale for the policy of prepubertal homosexuality. According to this wisdom, a prepubertal boy must leave the society of his mother and sisters and enter the secret society of men, in order to achieve the fierce manhood of a headhunter. Whereas in infancy he must have been fed woman's milk in order to grow, in the secret society of men he must be fed men's milk, that is, the semen of mature youths and unmarried men, in order to become pubertal and grow mature himself. It is the duty of the young bachelors to feed him their semen. They are obliged to practice institutionalized pedophilia. For them to give their semen to another who could already ejaculate his own is forbidden, for it robs a prepubertal boy of the substance he requires to become an adult. When a bachelor reaches the marrying age, his family negotiates the procurement of a wife and arranges the marriage. He then embarks on the heterosexual phase of his career. He could not, however, have become a complete man on the basis of heterosexual experience alone. Full manhood necessitates a prior phase of exclusively homosexual experience. Thus, homosexuality is universalized and is a defining characteristic of head-hunting, macho manhood.

In Sambia culture, omission of, rather than participation in the homosexual developmental phase would be classified as sporadic in occurrence, if it occurred at all, and would stigmatize a man as deviant. In our own culture, by contrast, it is homosexual participation that is classified as sporadic, and stigmatized as a deviancy in need of explanation. For us, heterosexuality, like health, is taken as a verity that needs no explanation, other than being attributed to the immutability of the natural order of things. Since heterosexuality needs no explanation, then in bisexuality the homosexual component alone needs explanation. Consequently, there has been no satisfactory place for bisexuality in theoretical sexology. The universalization of sequential bisexuality, as in the Sambia tradition, is unexplainable in homosexual theory that is based exclusively on the concept of homosexuality as sporadic in occurrence and pathologically deviant (Stoller and Herdt, 1985).

Institutionalized homosexuality, in serial sequence with institutionalized heterosexuality and marriage, as among the Sambia and other tribal peoples, must be taken into account in any theory that proposes to explain homosexuality. The theory will be deficient unless it takes heterosexuality into account also. Culturally institutionalized bisexuality signifies either that bisexuality is a universal potential to which any member of the human species could be acculturated; or that bisexuality is a unique potential of those cultures whose members have become selectively inbred for it. There are no data that give conclusive and absolute support to either alternative. However, genetically pure inbred strains are an ideal of animal husbandry, not of human social and sexual interaction. Therefore, it is likely that acculturation to bisexuality is less a concomitant of inbreeding than it is of the bisexual plasticity of all members of the human species. It is possible that bisexual plasticity may vary over the life span. Later in life it may give way to exclusive monosexuality—or it may not.

2 PREFERENCES VERSUS STATUS OR ORIENTATION

A heterosexual man or woman does not become heterosexual by preference. There is no option, no plan. Becoming heterosexual is something that happens—an example of the way things are, like being tall or short, left-handed or right-handed, color-blind or color-seeing. Being homosexual is no more a preference than being heterosexual. No one, boy or girl, man or woman, prefers to be homosexual instead of heterosexual. Likewise, no one prefers to be bisexual instead of monosexual. One either is or is not bisexual, homosexual, or heterosexual.

Sexual preference is a moral and political term. Conceptually it implies voluntary choice, that is, that one chooses, or prefers, to be homosexual instead of heterosexual or bisexual, and vice versa. Politically, sexual preference is a dangerous term, for it implies that if homosexuals choose their preference, then they can be legally forced, under threat of punishment, to choose to be heterosexual.

The concept of voluntary choice is as much in error here as in its application to handedness, or to native language. You do not choose your native language as a preference, even though you are born without it. You assimilate it into a brain prenatally made ready to receive a native language from those who constitute your primate troop and who speak it to you and listen to you when you speak it. Once assimilated through the ears into the brain, a native language becomes securely locked in—as securely as if it had been phylogenetically preordained to be locked in prenatally by a process of genetic determinism, or by the determinism of fetal hormonal or other brain chemistries. So also with sexual status or orientation, which—whatever its genesis—also may become assimilated and locked into the brain as monosexually homosexual or heterosexual or as bisexually a mixture of both.

A sexual status (or orientation) is not the same as a sexual act. It is possible to participate in homosexual acts, and even to be cajoled or coerced into participation, without becoming predestined to have a permanently homosexual status—and vice versa for heterosexuality. The Skyscraper Test exemplifies the difference between sexual act and sexual status. One of the versions of this test applies to a tourist with a homosexual status who is atop the Empire State Building or another high building and is pushed to the edge of the parapet by a gun-toting, crazed sex terrorist with a heterosexual status. Suppose the homosexual is a man and the terrorist a woman who demands that he perform oral sex with her or go over the edge. To save his life, he might do it. If so, he would have performed a heterosexual act, but he would not have changed to have a heterosexual status. The same would apply, vice versa, if the tourist were a straight man and the terrorist a gay man, and so on.

This Skyscraper Test, by dramatizing the difference between act and status, points to the criterion of falling in love as the definitive criterion of homosexual, heterosexual, and bisexual status. A person with a homosexual status is one who has the potential to fall in love only with someone who has the same body sex—the same genital and body morphology—as the self. For a heterosexual, the morphology must be that of a person of the other sex. For the bisexual it may be either.

It is not necessary for the body sex of the partner to be in agreement with the chromosomal sex, the gonadal sex (testicles or ovaries), or the sex of the internal reproductive anatomy. For example, a male-to-female, sex-reassigned transexual with the body morphology transformed to be female in appearance is responded to as a woman—and vice versa in female-to-male transexualism.

Discordance between the body morphology and other variables of sex occurs also in some cases of intersexuality (see Section 3, this chapter). For example, it is possible to be born with a penis and empty scrotum and to grow up with a fully virilized body and mentality, both discordant with the genetic sex (46,XX), the gonadal sex (two normal ovaries), and the internal sexual structures (uterus and oviducts) (Figures 1-1 and 1-2). Conversely, it is possible to be born with a female vulva and to grow up with a fully feminized body and mentality, both discordant with the genetic sex (46,XY), the gonadal sex (two testes), and the internal sexual structures (vestigiated feminine müllerian duct structures and differentiated masculine wolffian duct structures) (Figures 1-3 and 1-4). Clinical photographic examples of these syndromes, and many others, are reproduced in Money (1968b, 1974).

The aforesaid type of 46,XX intersexed man who falls in love with and has a sex life with a 46,XX normal woman is regarded by everyone as

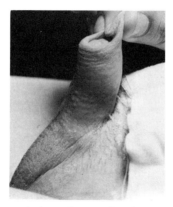

Figure 1-1. 46,XX Adrenogenital syndrome showing complete masculinization of the external genitalia; the scrotum is empty and the intraabdominal gonads are ovaries.

heterosexual, and so is his partner. The criterion of their heterosexuality is the sexual morphology of their bodies and the masculinity or femininity of their mentality and behavior, not the sex of their chromosomes, gonads, or internal organs. The same principle applies conversely in the case of the aforesaid type of feminized 46,XY intersexed woman whose sex life is with a normal 46,XY man.

3 EVOLUTIONARY BISEXUALITY

Any theory of the genesis of either exclusive homosexuality or exclusive heterosexuality must address primarily the genesis of bisexuality. Monosexuality, whether homosexual or heterosexual, is secondary and a derivative of the primary bisexual or ambisexual potential. Ambisexuality has its origins in evolutionary sexology and in the embryology of sexual differentiation.

Ambisexuality has many manifestations in evolutionary sexology. Oysters, garden worms, and snails, for example, are ambisexual. They are also classified as bisexual and as hermaphroditic. There are many species of fish capable of changing their sex from female to male, or male to female, in some species more than once (Chan, 1977). The change is so complete that the fish spends part of its life breeding as a male with testicles that make sperms, and part as a female with ovaries that make eggs—an exceptionally thorough degree of sequential bisexuality.

There is a species of whiptail lizard from the Southwest, *Cnemedophorus uniparens,* that offers a unique contribution to bisexual theory (Crews, 1982, 1987a,b). This species has neither males nor females and so is said to be monecious or one-sexed. It is also said to be parthenogenic, meaning that procreation does not require male sperms. Nonetheless, as judged by comparison with closely related two-sexed whiptail species, each individual

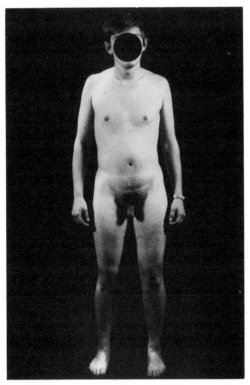

Figure 1-2. 46,XX Adrenogenital syndrome showing complete masculinization of the body at puberty, independently of treatment.

lizard is able at different times to behave as if a male, and as if a female in mating. The one in whom a clutch of eggs is ripening, ready to be laid in the sand for sun-hatching, is mounted by a mate whose ovaries are in a dormant, nonovulatory phase (Figure 1-5). This enactment is believed to affect the hormonal function of the pituitary of the ovulating lizard, and to facilitate reproduction. At a later date, their roles reverse.

In this parthenogenic reptilian species, the brain is bisexual or ambisexual, even though the pelvic reproductive anatomy is not. According to MacLean's evolutionary theory of the triune brain, the mammalian brain is made up of an evolutionarily ancient reptilian brain overlaid by a paleocortex, also known as the limbic system, which is shared by all mammals, and which in turn is overlaid by the neocortex, which is most highly evolved in the human species (MacLean, 1972) (Figure 1-6). Thus the behavioral bisexuality of parthenogenic whiptail lizards may provide a key to understanding the bisexual potential of mammalian species.

It has long been known that the mammalian embryo, in the early stages of its development, is sexually bipotential. The undifferentiated gonads differentiate into either testes or ovaries. Thereafter, the biblical principle that Eve sprang from Adam's rib makes a complete about-face in embryo-

Figure 1-3. 46,XY Androgen-insensitivity syndrome, showing normal female external genitalia, postpubertally. Note the effect of androgen insensitivity in impairing growth of pubic hair.

logical science, for it is beyond all possible doubt that, in the development of the embryo, Eve takes precedence over Adam. Chromosomal sex notwithstanding, the new embryological principle is that, after the early bipotential phase, and after the differentiation of the unformed gonadal tissues into either testicles or ovaries, in the remainder of sexual differentiation, the principle of feminization takes priority over the principle of masculinization. Something must be added to induce masculinization. This is the principle of Eve first, then Adam! It is symbolized in Figure 1-7.

The something that must be added is hormonal—two different types of gonadal hormones, to be specific. In normal embryonic and fetal development, each is normally secreted by the male baby's own testicles. One of these two masculinizing hormones from the fetal testes is actually a defeminizing hormone, müllerian-inhibiting hormone (MIH). It appears early in prenatal development and has a brief life span. What it does is to atrophy the embryonic müllerian ducts and thus prevent them from growing into a uterus with its bilateral fallopian tubes or oviducts, along which eggs are transported from the ovary, in the female.

The other masculinizing hormone acts not by defeminizing, but by actively inducing the growth of masculine sexual organs—first the internal, and then the external sexual organs. It is testosterone, a steroidal sex hormone, or else one of its biochemical derivatives. Together with its derivatives, testosterone promotes the growth of the bilateral wolffian ducts into the male internal accessory sexual organs—the vas deferens, one on each side, to connect the testicle with the urethra, and the seminal vesicles and prostate gland which produce, at maturity, the seminal fluid in which sperms are transported through the penis. The development of the penis itself, and its foreskin and scrotum, is dependent on testosterone.

Differentiation of the internal genitalia is ambitypic. That is to say, at the outset, a set of both the male and female precursors or anlagen is present,

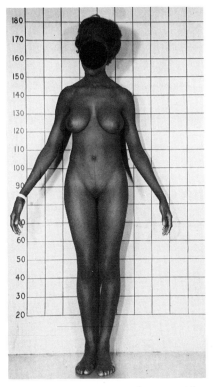

Figure 1-4. 46,XY Androgen-insensitivity syndrome, without treatment, showing spontaneous pubertal feminization.

regardless of whether the genetic sex of the embryo is male and chromosomally 46,XY, or female and 46,XX. Then one set of precursors atrophies and disappears, while the other set grows and develops (Figure 1-8). By contrast, differentiation of the external genitalia is unitypic. That is to say, there is a single set of precursors or anlagen that have two possible destinies, namely, to become either male or female (Figure 1-9). Thus, the clitoris and the penis have the same beginning—are homologues of one another. So also are the clitoral hood and the penile foreskin. The tissues that become the labia minora in the female wrap around the penis in the male and fuse along the midline of the underside to form the tubular urethra. The swellings that otherwise form the divided labia majora of the female fuse in the midline to form the scrotum of the male. Unitypic signifies that the external genitals must be either male or female. They may be incompletely differentiated and unfinished as either male or female, but they cannot be both male and female simultaneously. By contrast, ambitypic signifies that, though it is rare, it is actually possible to have a combination or partial combination of both male and female organs internally.

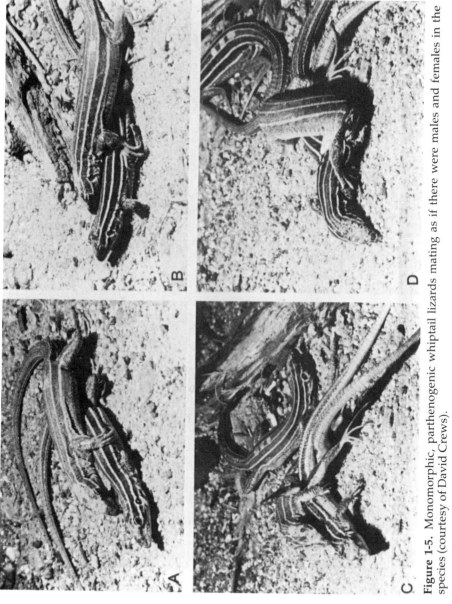

Figure 1-5. Monomorphic, parthenogenic whiptail lizards mating as if there were males and females in the species (courtesy of David Crews).

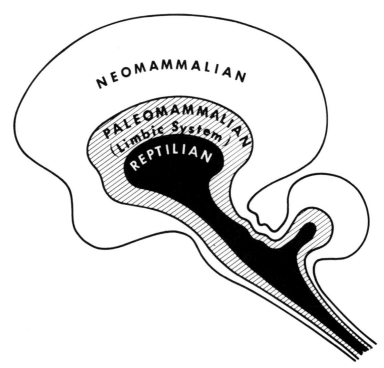

Figure 1-6. MacLean's diagrammatic representation of man's three brains. The innermost brain is shared with lower vertebrates, including reptiles. The paleocortex or limbic system is shared with other mammals. The neocortex, the outermost brain, is poorly developed in lower mammals, and most highly developed in humans (courtesy of Paul McLean).

The modern embryological principle already referred to as the principle of Eve first, then Adam, applies not only to the hormonal control of the differentiation of the genital anatomy as dimorphic, that is as either male or female. So far as can be judged from animal research, the same principle applies also to the differentiation of dimorphism of the brain, or at least to the dimorphic differentiation of the sexual centers and pathways of the brain that have a part to play in the sexual and erotic functioning of the genital organs. According to present evidence, hormone-induced brain dimorphism takes place later than that of the genitalia, and, dependent on species, may extend into the first few days or weeks of postnatal life. The primary masculinizing hormone is testosterone, although it is not necessarily used in all parts of the brain as such. Within brain cells themselves, as within cells of the pelvic genitalia, it may be reduced by enzymatic action to dihydrotestosterone. Paradoxically, it may also exert its masculinizing action only if first aromatized by the body's own chemistries into estradiol, one of the sex steroids that received its name when it was considered to be exclusively an estrogenic, feminizing hormone. In both sexes, estradiol is

Figure 1-7. Eve first, then Adam! A cartoon representation of the embryological principle of sexual differentiation that reverses the biblical principle. Eve differentiates, unaided, whereas Adam is depicted as needing the help of the archangel who appears with an injection needle loaded with testosterone, the masculinizing hormone, shoots up Eve, and lo! Adam comes forth.

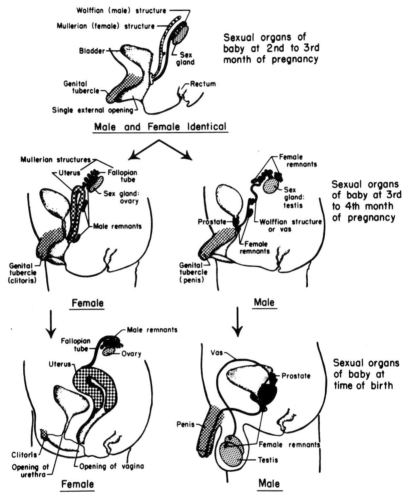

Figure 1-8. Cross-sectional diagrams to illustrate internal, ambitypic genital differentiation in the human fetus.

metabolized within the body from testosterone, which, in turn, is metabolized from progesterone, of which the antecedent is the steroidal substance cholesterol, from which the body derives all of its steroidal hormones.

On the basis of animal experimental studies of the effects of prenatal brain hormonalization on subsequent sexually dimorphic behavior, it is now generally acknowleged that the converse of brain masculinization is not feminization but demasculinization. The converse of feminization is defeminization. Hypothetically, it is possible for brain/behavior masculinization to take place without defeminization, and for feminization to take place without demasculinization (Beach, 1975; Whalen and Edwards, 1967; Ward, 1972, 1984; Ward and Weisz, 1980; Baum, 1979; Baum et al., 1982). That means that, in the laboratory species so far studied, the differentiation

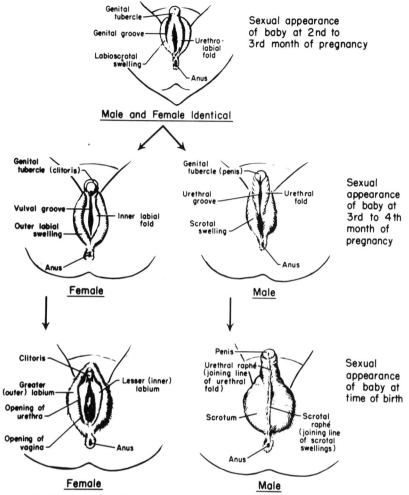

Figure 1-9. Diagrams to illustrate external, unitypic genital differentiation in the human fetus.

of sexual dimorphism in the brain is not unitypic, like that of the external genitalia, but ambitypic, like that of the internal genitalia. Ambitypic differentiation allows for the possible coexistence of both masculine and feminine nuclei and pathways, and the behavior they govern, in some if not all parts of the brain. The two need not necessarily have equality. One may be more dominant than the other. To illustrate, when cows in a herd are in season, the central nervous system (CNS) functions in such a way as to permit cow to mount cow, whereas when a bull is present, the cow is receptive and the bull does the mounting. Mounting is traditionally defined as masculine behavior, but it would be more accurately defined as ambisexual, since it is shared by both sexes. On the criterion of mounting, cows are bisexual insofar as they mount and are mounted. Bulls are less so, insofar as they are seldom mounted.

The first evidence of the hormonal induction of sexual dimorphism in the brain was inferred from its effects on the mating behavior of laboratory animals—the crouching (lordosis) or presenting position of the female, and the mounting and thrusting of the male. The first experiment was done by Eugen Steinach in the early years of the twentieth century, prior to World War I (see Steinach, 1940). He demonstrated that the mating behavior of female guinea pigs would be masculinized if, in fetal life, they had been exposed to male hormone injected into the pregnant mother. The theoretical implications of Steinach's finding were too advanced for their time. Although his experiment was replicated and confirmed by Vera Danchakoff in the late 1930s, its theoretical implications continued to lie dormant until William C. Young did a second replication in the 1950s (Young, Goy, and Phoenix, 1964). Since then there has developed a whole new science of hormone-brain-behavior dimorphism.

By the 1970s it had become evident that hormone-mediated dimorphism of the brain was no longer an inference based on sexually dimorphic behavior, but an actuality that could be neuroanatomically demonstrated directly in brain tissue. In 1969, Doerner and Staudt reported that the nuclear volume of nerve cells in the preoptic area and ventromedial nucleus in the rat hypothalamus was larger in females than males, and that androgen administered in late prenatal and early neonatal life would reduce the volume of these cells in females and castrated males. In 1971, Raisman and Field reported their discovery of sexual dimorphism in the dendritic synapses of the preoptic area of the rat brain (see also Greenough et al., 1977). Thus began a new era of research into neuroanatomical sex differences, and their possible prenatal hormonal determinants, in those regions of the brain that mediate mating behavior in various laboratory animal species (see reviews by Bleier, Byne, and Siggelkow, 1982; Arnold and Gorski, 1984; De Vries et al., 1984; Gorski, 1985a,b,c; De Voogd, 1986).

Confirmatory findings followed in quick succession. In rats, Gorski and his research colleagues found and named the sexually dimorphic nucleus of the preoptic area (SDN-POA) (Gorski et al., 1978). The SDN-POA of male rats is bigger than that of females, and becomes so under the influence of steroid hormone from the testes (testosterone or its metabolite, estradiol), during the critical period of the first few days after birth (Doehler et al., 1982).

In the ferret (Baum, 1986), the SDN of the male remains feminine in size if, prenatally, it is deprived of the steroid hormone that it needs to enlarge and masculinize. In consequence, the male's mounting behavior in the mating of maturity is diminished, despite adequate stimulation with testosterone in adulthood. Neonatal exposure to testosterone is necessary to induce the male ferret's mature response to the female. Otherwise, the male would, like a female, respond to a male (Martin and Baum, 1986).

As a sequel to his discovery of the SDN-POA in rats, Gorski referred to the corresponding sexually dimorphic tissues in the human brain as the interstitial nuclei of the anterior hypothalamus (Allen et al., 1986). Swaab and Fliers (1985) used the original acronym, SDN-POA, and reported that the nucleus was not only larger in men than in women, but also contained slightly more than twice as many cells. They noted that "although no function has yet been established for this nucleus, it is located within an area that is essential for gonadotropin release and sexual behavior in other mammals." Subsequently, Swaab reported in an abstract (Netherlands Institute for Brain Research) that the cell count in the SDN-POA was the same at birth in girls and boys, and that a sex difference did not show up until later in childhood, when the size of the nucleus began to decrease in girls and increase in boys. The latest finding from Swaab's laboratory is still under investigation, namely, that two male-to-female transexuals and one woman with a rare congenital developmental defect (Prader-Willi syndrome) had an unexpectedly large cell count in the suprachiasmatic nucleus of the hypothalamus (Swaab et al., 1987).

Swaab's finding that the SDN-POA cell count at birth does not differ in boys and girls is compatible with the most recent finding of Abramovich and his associates (1987) in research into the sex-differentiating neurochemistries of the prenatal brain during the midtrimester of gestation. They undertook an extensive neurochemical search of tissues from fetal brains, aged fourteen to twenty weeks of gestation, for evidence of receptors that would take up estrogenic, androgenic, or progestinic sex hormones. The evidence was nil. Therefore, they concluded that when the male/female differentiation of the external sex organs is taking place during the midtrimester of pregnancy, there is no corresponding male/female brain differentiation. The stage in development when hormones influence the differentiation of the human brain as dimorphically male or female remains to be discovered. It may be in the third trimester of pregnancy, or it may extend through the first three postnatal months of age when, in boys, there is a transient surge of testosterone released from the testicles to circulate in the bloodstream, which would carry it to the brain.

It is generally assumed that, after the age of three months, the years of childhood are quiescent with regard to sex hormones. However, the evidence is incomplete. For instance, it has twice been observed that the childhood rate of statural growth differed, in the case of identical male twins, if only one of the pair had testicles. In the prepubertal years, the one with testicles grew taller. Whether or not there was a covert hormonal influence on growth, and whether or not there was a corresponding covert hormonal influence on the brain before the visible onset of puberty, remains unknown.

The biology of the onset of puberty remains a scientific mystery. So also does its timing, which, obviously, begins in advance of the initial observable and measurable evidence. One may postulate the existence, in the infancy and early childhood of mammals, of an as yet undiscovered puberty-inhibiting substance (PIS) like the juvenile hormone of insects. When PIS wanes, it releases the onset of puberty. If this hypothesis should prove correct, then it is possible that the diminution and eventual loss of PIS releases also the further development of male/female differences that were set in place in the brain prenatally, but subsequently remained quiescent.

Neuroanatomical sex differences are not restricted to the brain. Breedlove and Arnold (1980) discovered sexual dimorphism in the number of motor neurons innervating the perineal muscles in rats. They discovered also that it is during the critical period of the first few days after birth that the larger number of these motor neurons in males is produced by the presence of steroid hormone from the testes (Breedlove, 1986).

In songbirds, as well as in rats, the presence of testicular hormone during a brief critical period proved to be the determinant of the neuroanatomy in the male brain that governs song (Nottebohm and Arnold, 1976). In the zebra finch, testicular hormone exerts its masculinizing effect once and forever during the early critical period. There is no backtracking. The song pattern of the first spring singing season persists unchanged in subsequent years. In the canary, by contrast, the entire process is reactivated each spring, which allows the male to change his song and learn a new one each year instead of having only the one that he learned in the first year of life. An adult female, provided she is treated with steroid hormone, is able to learn a song for the first time as an adult. Learning the song first as a newly hatched nestling is not imperative. Male songbirds copy the song they hear in the nest, even though they do not sing it until weeks later.

The findings with respect to canary song demonstrate a type of sexual dimorphism in which the ambisexual window is not forever closed after the neonatal critical period, but is reopened annually. Thus a canary of either sex may sing one year but not the next, depending on the degree of steroidal hormonalization of the sexually dimorphic brain in the springtime of each year. As songsters, canaries thus have the possibility of being serially rather than concurrently bisexual.

Concurrent bisexuality would require two coexistent, dimorphic neuroanatomical systems, one subserving masculine and one feminine dimorphism of behavior, for example, mounting versus presenting so as to be mounted, respectively. In rat experiments, Nordeen and Yahr (1982) found such a duality in the form of hemispheric asymmetry in the neighborhood of the SDN-POA of the hypothalamus. They implanted pellets of the steroid hormone estradiol, separately into the left and right sides of the hypothalamus of newborn female rat pups. The subsequent effect of the hormone on the left side was to defeminize, that is to suppress lordosis (presenting); and on the right side to masculinize, that is to facilitate mounting behavior, after the rats became mature.

In the rat, the lateral distribution in the hypothalamus of masculine to the right and feminine to the left raises the hypothetical possibility that the two sides may develop so as to be either concordant or discordant (Table 1-1). Thus masculinization of one side matched by defeminization of the other would signify that masculine prevails. Similarly, feminization matched by demasculinization would signify that feminine prevails. By contrast, masculinization of one side and feminization of the other would signify that neither prevails, but that masculine and feminine both coexist. Demasculinization of one side and defeminization of the other signifies not only that neither prevails, but also that there is an absence of either masculine or feminine, that is a kind of neutral or epicene state.

If any of these purely hypothetical disparities should be proved to occur independently of laboratory experimentation, then their origin could be sought on the basis of the amount of hormone absorbed and utilized on each side; a difference in the timing of the availability of hormone on each side; the synchrony or dissynchrony of the readiness for hormonal programing on each side; and the pulsatility or continuity of the hormonal supply on each side. The point is that there are different hypotheses to be tested in trying to explain, for example, how one side of the hypothalamus might be rendered masculine and able to induce male mounting behavior, whereas the other side might not be defeminized and so would be able to induce female presenting (lordosis) behavior, producing in effect a degree of bisexualism.

Because the experiment of Nordeen and Yahr was done on the right and left hypothalamus of rats, its findings must be considered species specific, until experimentally demonstrated to apply across species. It will be ethically impossible to conduct such an experiment with human beings as subjects. Therefore, the experiment on rats has human relevance only insofar as it suggests an animal model for the experimental demonstration of a bisexual phenomenon. The function of animal models is not to prove anything about the human species, but to lead to conjectures and hypotheses for further consideration. Another word of caution: lateral asymmetry of the hypothalamus with respect to a hormonal effect on male mounting and female presenting tells absolutely nothing about lateral asymmetry in the human cerebral cortex with respect to male/female differences in specific cognitive abilities and mental functioning.

In animals, predisposing the brain to be either bisexual or homosexual may occur not only as a sequel to experimental manipulation, but also adventitiously. These same adventitious predispositions may affect human beings also, for example as an unrecognized side effect of hormone imbalance secondary to nutritional, medicinal, or endocrine changes, including stress-derived changes, in the pregnant mother's bloodstream. Sleeping pills containing barbiturate, for example, may have a demasculinizing effect on the brain of the human fetus, as the drug has been shown to have such an effect on male rat pups (reviewed in Reinisch and Sanders, 1982). Also in rats, maternal stress that alters maternal adrenocortical hormones may exert a prenatal demasculinizing effect on male pups, subsequently evident in their bisexual and homosexual mating behavior (Ward, 1984). Doerner (1976) created a storm of scientific controversy by using Ward's findings to construct his own theory of the cause of homosexuality in human males.

TABLE 1-1 Combinations of Masculinization/Demasculinization and Feminization/
Defeminization: Hypothetical Outcomes

	Masculinization	Demasculinization
Feminization	Ambitypic: androgynous	Monotypic: feminine
Defeminization	Monotypic: masculine	Ambitypic: epicene

In laboratory animals, the dramatic power of the steroid hormones in prenatal life to foreordain sexual orientation and mating behavior to be, in varying degree, homosexual in adult life has been demonstrated in experiments in which fetal females are hormonally masculinized, or males demasculinized. In prenatal development, there is a critical period when hormonal intervention changes first the sex of the external genitalia and then of the brain. After the external genitalia have formed, hormonal intervention changes the brain only, thus providing science with an animal model for the genesis of homosexuality.

There is a remarkable film (Short and Clarke, undated; Clarke, 1977) that shows how the brains and behavior of ewe lambs, independently of their bodies, can be masculinized in utero by injecting the pregnant mother with testosterone at the critical period of gestation, day 50 and thereafter. To use poetic license, the lamb then grows up to be a lesbian ewe. Its brain is so effectively masculinized that its mating behavior, and its urinating behavior also, are completely masculinized. It engages in mating rivalry with other rams in head-on, butting contests. Its proceptive courtship ritual is never like that of a ewe, but exactly like that of a ram, even though while it is courting a ewe in heat, its own ovaries are secreting estrogen, not androgen. Moreover, the normal rams and ewes of the flock respond to the lesbian ewe's masculinized mating behavior as if it were that of a normal ram.

As compared with primates, sheep, cattle, and swine (reviewed by D'Occhio and Ford, 1987) and other four-legged species are, more or less, hormonal robots insofar as a masculine or a feminine mating pattern can be foreordained on the basis of regulating the prenatal hormonalization of the brain. Even among sheep, however, the final outcome will be to some degree influenced by whether the lamb grew up in a normal flock of ewes and rams or in a sex-segregated herd. Primates are even more influenced by the social conditions of growing up, and are less subject to hormonal robotization.

In the now well-known hermaphrodite experiments from the primate research centers in Oregon and Wisconsin, female rhesus monkeys were masculinized prenatally so that they were born with a penis and empty scrotum. Although they engaged in tomboyish play in childhood, unlike the sheep, they did not grow up to mature sexually as lesbians. According to the evidence available, the postpubertal sexological outcome of prenatal hormonalization was modulated, in some degree, by the social condition of their rearing in a coeducational as compared with an all-male or all-female group of age-mates (Goldfoot, 1977; Goldfoot and Neff, 1987; Goldfoot and Wallen, 1978; Goldfoot et al., 1984).

The adult sexological outcome of prenatal hormonalization was influenced by more than social rearing. Other variables needed to be taken into account also, as shown in studies by Phoeniz and Chambers (1982a,b), and Phoenix, Jensen, and Chambers (1983). One of these variables was the age when the monkeys were put through mating tests; another was whether they had been previously castrated or not, and if they had been castrated, whether they had been treated, in preparation for testing, with either estradiol or testosterone as a replacement hormone. The dosage of the hormone was also of significance. So also was the sex of the partner, male or female, with whom the hermaphrodite monkey was paired.

Taking into consideration these different variables, one concludes that, as a sequel to its having been hormonally masculinized, prenatally, a female hermaphrodite monkey may grow up to manifest masculinized mating behavior in adulthood when paired with an estrous female partner. Although there are some individuals that fail to manifest the male pattern of mounting and thrusting, those that manifest it do so regardless of whether they have their own hormonally functioning ovaries, or whether they have been ovariectomized and then given hormonal replacement therapy. Moreover, the masculine mating pattern is manifested regardless of whether the replacement hormone is estradiol, the predominant ovarian hormone, or testosterone, the predominant testicular hormone. On testosterone, the younger the hermaphrodite, the more is it likely to get an erection, but the prevalence of intromission is low, as are the movements of ejaculation (without semen), though they are not zero.

While the hermaphrodites were still young, the effect of their prenatal masculinization was not tested by pairing them with male partners. The hermaphrodites had no external vaginal opening and could not be given one by plastic surgery, as they would mutilate the postsurgical wound. Themselves aggressive, the hermaphrodites were at risk of attacking and of being attacked by a male partner. At a later age, Phoenix and co-workers circumvented this risk by using partners of proven gentleness, namely aged monkey eunuchs treated with testosterone. The hermaphrodites and the control females as well were treated with estradiol, as both groups had a history of having been ovariectomized. In this experiment, the hermaphrodites were sexologically not different from the controls in responding to the males as females. The males mounted them, but were able to achieve intromission and ejaculation only with the control females.

The conclusion from the foregoing is that, in a primate species, prenatal hormonal masculinization, whereas it is compatible with subsequent masculinized mating, does not necessarily ensure it; furthermore, whereas it does not promote feminized mating, it does not necessarily obliterate it. Masculinized and feminized mating responses may coexist in an experimentally manipulated manifestation of monkey bisexuality.

The significance for human sexology of the experimental manipulation of heterosexuality or homosexuality in the mating of monkeys, sheep, and other laboratory animals has provoked adversarial reactions professionally, academically, and amoung the public at large. At one extreme is the school of what is generally classified as biological determinism. It is exemplified by, for example, Diamond (1965, 1977), Doerner (1976, 1987), Goldberg (1973), and Hutt (1972). At the other extreme is the school that repudiates biological determinism and is generally classified as social determinism or social philosophy. It also goes under the names of social constructionism and labeling theory, and is exemplified by, for example, De Cecco (1987), Gagnon and Simon (1973), Hoult (1984), Plummer (1975), Rogers and Walsh (1982), and Reiss (1987).

Animal sexologists themselves mostly stay clear of dispute by publicly warning against anthropomorphism, or the attribution of human significance to the behavior of animals. In private, however, they are quite likely to agree that they are interested in how to bridge the ethical gap between animal experimentation and the study of human beings—the gap between the laboratory and the clinic. It is in clinical practice that one encounters the human counterpart of contrived animal experiments, namely the uncontrived experiments of nature. There, in the clinic, one is able to study nature's own sexual experiments, namely birth defects of the sex organs, sex-hormonal disorders, and other sexual syndromes.

4 HUMAN INTERSEXUALITY: GROUP-COMPARISON AND MATCHED-PAIR STRATEGIES

Although the sequential influence of prenatal hormonal and postnatal rearing effects cannot be studied experimentally by inducing intersexuality in human beings, it can be studied in the so-called experiments of nature, namely, the syndromes of intersexual and other birth defects of the sex organs. These are the syndromes that are known collectively by the term, hermaphroditism, as well as by its synonym, intersexuality. They are augmented by syndromes of agenesis of the sex organs, as in congenital absence of the penis, congenital micropenis, and congenital absence of the vagina, and by syndromes of traumatic or surgical loss of the genitalia.

By definition, intersexuality, and likewise its synonym, hermaphroditism, signifies ambiguity as to whether an individual is male or female. In all mammals, as already said (see Section 3, this chapter), it is not possible to be both male and female, either simultaneously or sequentially. Intersexual ambiguity means, therefore, that the multiple criteria of sex (see page 231) are not consistently either all male or all female, but that there is some degree of inconsistency or incongruity among them.

The criteria of sex are as follows: chromosomal sex, typically though not invariably 46,XX for females, and 46,XY for males; H-Y antigenic sex, microscopically recognized in most instances on the surface of 46,XY but not 46,XX cells; gonadal sex, prevalently ovarian or testicular, very rarely a combination of both in an ovotestis, and also, less rarely, represented by inert streaks of tissue; prenatal hormonal sex, either masculinizing or feminizing, or sometimes failing; internal morphologic sex, and external morphologic sex, both either masculine, feminine, or possibly deficient or ambiguously mixed; and pubertal hormonal sex, either masculine, feminine, or incongruous. These seven criteria apply to mammals in general. In human beings, there is also the sex of assignment and rearing, and the developmental establishment of gender identity and gender role or gender-identity/role (G-I/R) (Money, 1955a; Money, Hampson, and Hampson, 1955; see also Dorland, 1981).

In some instances, intersexuality is concealed: the external genitalia appear to conform to the criterion of being either male or female, but are inconsistent with all or part of the internal reproductive anatomy (Masica, Ehrhardt, and Money, 1971; Money and Daléry, 1976; Lewis and Money, 1983). In other instances, and more prevalently, intersexuality is visible as ambiguity of the external genitals: what might be a penile clitoris might also be a clitoridean penis, and what might be labial fusion might also be a labioscrotum (Money, Schwartz, and Lewis, 1984; Money, Devore, and Norman, 1986; Money and Norman, 1987). Internally, the reproductive structures may be predominantly either male or female.

Discordances among the criteria of sex, as manifest in intersex syndromes, can be explained embryologically in terms of the principle of Eve first, then Adam, as already mentioned (see Section 3, this chapter). Incomplete or partial masculinization of the external genitalia leaves a protuberant penoclitoris (or clitoropenis) with an open gutter on its underside and a urogenital opening or funnel at its base. This ambiguous condition is named hypospadias, if the individual is designated as a male and surgically corrected as a male. Correspondingly, the same condition is named partial urogenital fusion with clitoromegaly, if the individual is designated as a female and surgically corrected as a female. In such cases among the newborn, the final intersexual (or hermaphroditic) diagnosis cannot be established by visually inspecting the "unfinished," birth-defective genitalia. The diagnosis is not necessarily the final criterion of the sex in which the baby would best be assigned, reared, and clinically habilitated. It is on this account, and because, historically, medical opinion has not been unanimous regarding the sex of assignment in cases of birth defect of the sex organs, that science has serendipitously been provided with two or more cases that are concordant for prenatal history and diagnosis, but discordant for postnatal history and treatment. There are two grand strategies for utilizing partially concordant, partially discordant intersexual cases to investigate the genesis of homosexual, bisexual, or heterosexual status: the group-comparison strategy and the matched-pair strategy.

The group-comparison strategy requires a sufficient number of individuals with the same diagnosis to constitute a sample homogeneous for intersexual diagnosis. It is compared with either a matched clinical control group or a matched normal control group, or both. The clinical control group is homogeneous for its own diagnosis, which is specifically selected because of either its similarity to or divergence from the primary research sample. The investigative design allows status (or orientation) in adulthood as homosexual, bisexual, or heterosexual to be the dependent variable. It is compared with the other variables or determinants of sex from conception onward (see above), namely chromosomal sex, H-Y antigenic sex, gonadal sex, prenatal hormonal sex, internal morphologic sex, external morphologic sex, assigned sex and rearing, and, subsequently, pubertal hormonal sex (see page 231).

The matched-pairs strategy matches pairs or sets of pairs of individuals who are intersexually concordant for prenatal etiology and diagnosis, but discordant for sex of assignment and rearing, and compares them with respect to adult homosexual, bisexual, or heterosexual status. The matched-pairs strategy may also be applied to intersexed individuals who are concordant for sex of rearing and for some, though not all, of the other variables of sex; for example, genetic sex and gonadal sex may be male in one case (androgen-insensitivity syndrome) and female in another (Rokitansky syndrome), with the other variables of sex in both cases being female (Lewis and Money, 1983).

In the nineteenth century, the nomenclature of intersexuality was assigned on the criterion of the gonads (Klebs, 1876). When both ovarian and testicular tissues were found, either separately or combined in an ovotestis, the diagnosis was true hermaphroditism. If both gonads were ovarian, the diagnosis was female pseudohermaphroditism; and if both were testicular, male pseudohermaphroditism. Today the prefix, pseudo-, is falling into disuse as it is redundant and also incorrectly implies that the condition is not authentically intersexual. Today it is also known that intersexuality may exist in the presence of vestigial gonads that are neither ovarian nor testicular (Ehrhardt, Greenberg, and Money, 1970). Contemporary classification of intersexuality tends increasingly to reflect advances in etiological knowledge of inborn errors of hormonal synthesis (e.g., 21-hydroxylase deficiency in adrenogenital female hermaphroditism [Money and Daléry, 1976; Money, Schwartz, and Lewis, 1984], and 5α-reductase deficiency in male hermaphroditism) or hormonal metabolism (e.g., intracellular inability to use androgen in the androgen-insensitivity syndrome of male hermaphroditism [Masica, Ehrhardt and Money, 1971; Lewis and Money, 1983]).

A diagnosis on the basis of endocrine etiology is currently more readily established in the case of female than male hermaphroditism, true hermaphroditism, or agonadal hermaphroditism. Especially in the case of male hermaphroditism, the method of establishing an etiological diagnosis today is not a routine procedure, but a research laboratory one. Additionally, there are some cases of male hermaphroditism for which an etiological diagnosis has not yet been established. Thus, for a given etiological diagnosis, the available sample may be small, in which case the matched-pairs strategy takes precedence over the group-comparison strategy. In female hermaphroditism, by contrast, there are fewer limitations on assembling a larger sample group, specifically in the case of the adrenogenital syndrome, the most prevalent form of female hermaphroditism. However, there are also some less common varieties of female hermaphroditism, as in what follows.

5 ANDROGEN-INDUCED HERMAPHRODITISM

The least commonly recorded variety of female hermaphroditism is that in which an embryonically normal female is hormonally masculinized prenatally in fetal life by an excess of androgen that passes through the placenta from the mother's bloodstream. The excess androgen has its most likely source in an androgen-secreting ovarian or adrenocortical tumor that becomes hormonally active in the mother during the course of the pregnancy. In the fetus, embryonic differentiation of fertile ovaries is not affected. Unlike testes, ovaries make no müllerian-inhibiting hormone, so that the müllerian ducts do not vestigiate but differentiate into a uterus and oviducts. Differentiation of the external genitalia, by contrast, is profoundly altered by the excess of androgen. The clitoris becomes hypertrophied so as to become a penile clitoris with incomplete fusion and a urogenital sinus, or, if fusion is complete, a penis with urethra and an empty scrotum.

According to the principle of the statistics of extremes, it would need only one case of this type to break the stranglehold of the traditional dogma that sexual orientation and erotic status in adulthood are innately and genetically preordained by the gonads and their hormonal functioning at puberty. To break the stranglehold, it would be necessary to have a case in which, at birth, the baby was assigned, reared, and clinically habilitated as a boy. The latter would entail surgery to masculinize the external genitalia, if necessary. To prevent hormonal feminization (breasts and menses) at puberty would require either surgical removal of the ovaries or treatment with testosterone to suppress their secretion of female hormones. Testosterone treatment would induce pubertal virilization. It would then be necessary to follow the case to adulthood in order to establish that the erotosexual status and sex life were those of a man.

That was, indeed, the outcome in not only one such case (Money, 1952 and 1967; Money, Hampson, and Hampson, 1955) but three, the other two unpublished. In each case, the individual grew up to be an adult who was universally accepted by his professional peers and friends as a man, by his wife as a husband, and, in the two older cases, by his adopted children as a father, not notably different from other fathers in the kinship or the community. Absolutely no one ever thought of them as being lesbian, or even as bisexual.

Their lives have great value for homosexological theory. With a different postnatal social and clinical history, they could have grown up, as others like them have done, to become women, wives and mothers who carried their own pregnancies. Instead, they grew to adulthood with a heterosexual orientation or status as men. Their masculine orientation may have been facilitated by some degree of prenatal hormonal masculinization of the brain in parallel with the prenatal hormonal masculinization of the external genitals. It may also have been facilitated by the clinical intervention, at the time of the spontaneous onset of ovarian puberty, to arrest breast enlargement and put an end to menstruation through the penis. Hormones and surgery notwithstanding, their adult status as men was certainly not only facilitated by, but developmentally engendered by, the cumulative influences of their having been reared and socialized as boys.

Cases like these two demonstrated that both prenatal hormonal and postnatal social factors contribute to adult erotosexual status; but they do not spell out the details as they might apply to nonintersexed, morphologically normal girls who grow up, in the absence of hormonal masculinization, to be lesbians. No one yet knows what, if any, covert prenatal hormonal influences may predispose to lesbianism in anatomically normal girls. In addition, no one yet knows the social-learning formula, if there is one, that will unfailingly guarantee lesbianism as its outcome in anatomically normal girls, with or without a predisposition. Conjectures and hypotheses that have been put forward have not been confirmed. They exist only as doctrines and dogmas, no better substantiated than is the dogma that lesbianism is an erotic preference, voluntarily chosen as a political protest, and a declaration of emancipation from the domination of men.

6 PROGESTIN-INDUCED HERMAPHRODITISM

There is one form of human intersexuality that resembles an experiment of nature but is actually an experiment of iatrogenic trial and error. The error in this instance occurred when in the 1950s newly synthesized steroid hormones came on the market. Although they eventually proved to share both androgenic and progestinic properties, as well as chemical structure, they were initially prescribed as a progesterone substitute in the belief, false as it turned out, that they would prevent threatened miscarriage. In a small minority of unexplained cases, the external sex organs of a female fetus were masculinized, so that they had an intersexual external genital appearance (Money and Mathews, 1982). With very rare exceptions, the babies were assigned and surgically corrected as girls. They needed no hormonal treatment to develop at puberty as females. During childhood they had a penchant for tomboyism (Ehrhardt and Money, 1967), which suggested the possibility (wrongly as it turned out) of a sufficient degree of brain masculinization that they might, in adolescence, have bisexual imagery, ideation, and experience.

It was possible to get a follow-up on eleven of these individuals in adulthood (Money and Mathews, 1982). The finding at this time was that their earlier tomboyism had not persisted, and that they had only heterosexual imagery, ideation, and practice, with no homosexual inclinations. They were more interested in marriage and motherhood than in a nonmaternal career.

Evidently the synthetic hormone that masculinized their external genitalia did not have a lasting masculinizing effect on that part of the brain that, at puberty and thereafter, governs sexuality. Possibly the prenatal hormonal effect was too weak, or did not persist long enough to have an enduring effect on the brain. Another possibility is that hormonally sensitive brain cells did not recognize and were unable to respond to the synthetic hormone, whereas the cells of the developing external sex organs were able to do so. Whatever the explanation, the heterosexual outcome in the progestin-induced syndrome of female hermaphroditism was not replicated in the adrenocortical-induced syndrome (adrenogenital syndrome) of female hermaphroditism.

7 ADRENOGENITAL SYNDROME

The adrenogenital syndrome is also known as congenital adrenal hyperplasia (CAH) and congenital virilizing adrenal hyperplasia (CVAH). Inclusion of the term virilizing denotes the fact that, if left untreated, the syndrome induces the onset of puberty as early as the age of eighteen months, and that it is invariably masculinizing, in both sexes. During fetal life and continuously thereafter, unless corrected, the masculinizing hormone is secreted instead of cortisol by the affected individual's own adrenocortices in response to a recessively transmitted genetic error of cortisol synthesis. The error takes various forms, of which the most common is the 21-hydroxylase deficiency.

In fetal life, 21-hydroxylase deficiency does not alter the masculine differentiation of the chromosomally (46,XY) and gonadally (testicular) male fetus. By contrast, 21-hydroxylase deficiency has a profound effect in altering the feminizing differentiation of the chromosomally (46,XX) and gonadally (ovarian) female fetus, namely, by inducing masculinization of the external genitalia. The internal genitalia, which differentiate earlier, escape alteration. Masculinization of the external genitalia may be so extreme that the clitoris and its hood and labia minora become a normal penis with foreskin and covered urethra opening at the tip of the glans (Money and Daléry, 1976). The divided labia majora fuse and they do so completely, so as to become an empty scrotum when the formation of the penis is complete, thus producing normal-appearing external genitalia except for the missing testes. In the least extreme degree of masculinization, the sole evidence may be clitoral enlargement. Between the two extremes are various degrees of clitoromegaly plus external urogenital closure, with resultant ambiguity as to the sex of the newborn baby. On the basis of visual inspection alone it cannot be decided whether the surgical correction should be designed to make the ambiguous organs more feminine, or more masculine. At different times and places, and for different reasons, each decision has been made. Here, as in other syndromes, the outcome is of great relevance to the theory of homosexology.

The 21-hydroxylase deficiency in a chromosomally 46,XX, gonadal female born with a penis and empty scrotum is one of the intersexual conditions that holds a key to the very definition of homosexuality. Some such individuals have been assigned and reared as boys, either because they were given a diagnosis of undescended testes, or because, in the era prior to 1950, there was no known treatment to prevent the relentless and precocious progress of pubertal virilization (Money and Daléry, 1977). Such a boy encounters no unusual hazards in growing up to have an adolescent romantic and erotosexual life with a female partner, and in adulthood to become a husband and a father by either donor insemination or adoption. Yet, like his wife, he was born as a genetic female with two ovaries and female reproductive organs internally. Had his case been differently managed endocrinologically and surgically, he could have become pregnant and delivered a live baby by cesarean section. Hence the question: Are he and his wife both lesbians?

The answer is that they are not. This is another of the cases that confirm the proposition that, in general usage, homosexuality is not defined on the basis of the chromosomal sex, nor of any of the internal and concealed variables of sex. Instead, it is defined on the basis of the external sexual anatomy and the sexual characteristics of the body in general. Two people are identified as having a homosexual encounter or relationship provided their external sex organs are anatomically of the same sex, regardless of how different they may be in secondary sexual characteristics. The 46,XX gonadal female with a penis and empty scrotum assigned and reared as a boy would be classified as homosexual if he had an affair with another person with a penis. However, if he were to do something so far unheard of, namely to undergo surgical sex reassignment and then continue the affair with the same lover, then the relationship would be redefined as heterosexual. Hormonal treatment alone, even if it brought about breast growth and menstruation through the penis, would not suffice to change the definition of the relationship from homosexual to heterosexual. Only one partner should have a penis to permit a relationship to be defined as heterosexual, and, vice versa, only one should have a vulva.

Social conformity to the cultural criterion of femininity (or, vice versa, masculinity) does not, per se, override the genital criterion of homosexuality. To illustrate, in the case of a morphologically normal male who is a female impersonator: no matter how ladylike the appearance, or how hormonally feminized the body, the impersonator who is a lady with a penis is still regarded morally and legally as a homosexual (or perhaps as a preoperative transexual) if she has a sexual partner who also has a penis. Her syndrome is gynemimesis—the miming of a female by a person who has a penis (Money and Lamacz, 1984).

The syndrome of gynemimesis, otherwise known as syndrome of the lady with a penis, has not yet been known to have occurred in association with a diagnosis of 46,XX, CVAH with a penis. Quite to the contrary, congenital virilizing adrenal hyperplasia seems to blockade, utterly, the possibility of gynemimesis (Money and Lewis, 1982). The responsible blocking factor is, presumably, the high degree of prenatal androgenization, which, by inference, masculinizes, or supramasculinizes the sexual brain as well as the external genitalia. The effect of prenatal supramasculinization may completely override the effect of pubertal feminization, according to the evidence of a unique case of the 46,XX adrenogenital syndrome (Money, 1974).

In this case the baby was one of those born with a fully formed penis and empty scrotum. The diagnosis was not changed from male with undescended testes until age ten, when it was established as congenital virilizing adrenal hyperplasia in a genetic and gonadal female hermaphrodite. On the basis of an erroneous belief that hormones would feminize the mind as well as the body, and without his own consent, the boy's local physician gave him hormonal treatment with cortisol, thus releasing his ovaries to secrete their own feminizing hormones of puberty. His breasts developed and heralded the approach of first menstruation, through the penis. He was mortified.

Behaviorally he was very much a macho boy. His parents said he was the very antithesis of his sister. His mother discovered a love letter that he had written to his girlfriend. She and his father agreed that to convert him to a girl (despite the fact that he had two ovaries and no testes) would be the equivalent of forcing him to be a lesbian, with a girlfriend as a lover. They saw no point in forcing him to have his penis amputated as the first step in surgical feminization; nor in forcing him to undergo further hormonal treatments that would enlarge his breasts and induce menstruation, but would not demasculinize his voice or body hair. They decided, instead, to seek a second opinion regarding surgical and hormonal masculinizing treatment. They were, of course, correct. They had a son, not a daughter, irrespective of his clinical diagnosis as a female hermaphrodite with two ovaries and 46,XX chromosomes. He had the sexual orientation of a heterosexual boy. It was too late to change it by edict or by any known method of intervention.

This particular boy had missed being diagnosed neonatally because his life was not threatened by the salt-losing symptom associated with one variant of congenital virilizing adrenal hyperplasia. Babies who are salt-losers are diagnosed; otherwise they die. Some of them have had a penis and empty scrotum, and some an enlarged clitoris, variable in size, with incomplete labioscrotal fusion. In either case, today's standard pediatric recommendation is to assign the child as a girl or, in some instances to make a reassignment, if the child had initially been announced as a boy. Assignment as a girl entails surgical feminization of the genitalia. It entails also antimasculinzing hormonal treatment with a substitute for the missing glucocorticoid, cortisol, throughout life. This treatment, which arrests the continuation of masculinization, postnatally, and permits puberty to be feminizing, was discovered only in 1950. Thus the first generation of babies to be treated with cortisol now constitutes the first generation of young adults whose prenatal history of masculinization was not followed by a postnatal history of progressively more masculinization. Thus, with respect to homosexology, they provide an opportunity to investigate the role of prenatal hormonal masculinization relative to sexual orientation as homosexual, bisexual, or heterosexual.

On the basis of longitudinal follow-up findings (Money, Schwartz, and Lewis, 1984), it does appear that prenatal hormonal masculinization may have the same long-term sexological effect on 46,XX, adrenogenital syndrome babies who are clinically habilitated as girls as it does on those who are clinically habilitated as boys. That is to say, both are able to grow up to be romantically and sexually attracted to girls. In the case of those who grow up as boys, this predisposition is unhindered. It is incorporated into the postnatal effects of clinical and social masculinization, so that the ultimate outcome is socially approved heterosexuality as a male.

By contrast, in the case of those who grow up as girls, the predisposition set by prenatal hormonal masculinization is at odds with the postnatal effects of clinical and social feminization. In adulthood, the ultimate outcome is heterogeneously distributed between heterosexuality, bisexuality, or homosexuality as a female. In a sample of 30 follow-up cases, the actual percentages were heterosexual, 40 percent ($N = 12$); bisexual 20 percent ($N = 6$); homosexual, 17 percent ($N = 5$); and noncommittal, 23 percent ($N = 7$)—all grossly different from the control group (chi-square = 18.5; $p < 0.001$). If the noncommittal group is omitted and the percentages recalculated, then 48 percent ($N = 11$) classified themselves as bisexual on the basis of imagery or activity, of whom 5 classified themselves as predominantly or exclusively lesbian as adults. This proportion, 48 percent, is similar to that obtained in an earlier study (Ehrhardt, Evers, and Money, 1968) of twenty-three women who grew up in the pre-1950, precortisol era and who were therefore highly masculinized in physique. Evidently the high degree of masculinization that these 23 women underwent postnatally did not augment the predisposition set by prenatal masculinization. In the CVAH syndrome, prenatal brain masculinization alone is sufficient to predispose to a bisexual or lesbian orientation.

One young woman in this CVAH follow-up study who did develop a lesbian orientation said, after having had two different boyfriends with whom she attempted in vain to relate in sexual intercourse, that she had to admit that she could fall in love only "with a chick, not a guy." She became lovesick over a girlfriend who, though her close companion, was unable to fall in love homosexually, only heterosexually. Driven to the despair of love unrequited, which was worsened by adversarial parents, the CVAH girl drove her car into isolated swamp country, and was found there, two weeks later, dead of self-inflicted gunshot wounds.

In the human species, the site where hormonally responsive brain cells are prenatally masculinized so as to induce a predisposition toward subsequent bisexuality or homosexuality has not yet been demonstrated. One must infer, on the basis of studies of laboratory animals, that the site of masculinization is not in the neocortex of the brain, but in the old brain, the paleocortex, also known as the limbic system, which is intimately connected with the hypothalamus (see Section 3, this chapter). In the adrenogenital syndrome, there is as yet no way of identifying either a timing or a dose-response effect that would distinguish those who eventually become bisexual from those who become monosexual as either homosexual or heterosexual. The difference might not prove to be prenatal exclusively, but postnatal also. Postnatally there would be an overlay of developmental events and experiences to augment a prenatally established disposition that by itself alone would be too weak to preordain the status of adult sexual orientation.

8 ADOLESCENT GYNECOMASTIA

The adrenogenital syndrome occurs in 46,XY gonadal males, as well as in 46,XX gonadal females. Since 1950, the year when treatment became available, CVAH boys have been hormonally regulated with cortisol so that they do not undergo a precociously virilizing puberty which, in older texts, was termed the infant Hercules syndrome. Before birth, however, their own bodies made a flood of male hormone of adrenocortical origin, which exposed the brain to a supramasculinizing level of the hormone (see Section 7, this chapter).

Youths with a history of the treated adrenogenital syndrome ($N = 8$) were selected in late teenage or early adulthood as suitable for a contrast group of controls for youths ($N = 10$) who at puberty developed breast enlargement like that of a girl (Money and Lewis, 1982). The latter condition, idiopathic adolescent gynecomastia, is of unknown etiology. One possibility is that the glandular tissue below the nipple is unduly sensitive to estrogen in the amount normally secreted by the male's testicles. An alternative possibility is that the same tissue is unduly resistant to the effect of testosterone in overriding the effect of estrogen. Before puberty, there are no signs of unusual body development. No retrospective evidence has as yet been obtained that would point to unusual hormonal functioning in prenatal life; and no cases have turned up in prospective studies. Thus there is no evidence, one way or the other, of the possibility of deficient brain masculinization, or of a demasculinizing process, prenatally. Similarly, since there is no evidence either for or against prenatal brain feminization, there is no evidence for or against brain ambisexualization.

The ten boys with adolescent gynecomastia constituted an unbiased and geographically available sample from a larger clinic list. Three of them proved to have a homosexual status, about which they talked openly. Long before puberty they had been stigmatized as sissy by their peers, and recognized as atypical by adults. Their boyhood lives had been marked by family adversity. Some of the CVAH boys also experienced family adversity. Nonetheless, there was no evidence of either a homosexual or bisexual status in any CVAH boy.

Thus, one may assume that, with a history of hormonal supramasculinization prenatally, the CVAH boys had no leeway to develop other than heterosexually, no matter what. By contrast, one may assume that the boys who were destined to develop breasts were destined also to have leeway to veer toward homosexuality, provided other circumstances so conspired. It is possible that in prenatal life their brains were insufficiently responsive to androgen, or in some other way were suboptimally masculinized hormonally. It will require a new and advanced research technology before this issue can be addressed.

It may be argued that the sample size in this study, being small, may have produced a fortuitous finding that will fail to be replicated. That argument is refuted by the data from the full list of patients from which the study sample was drawn. Among the full list of thirty-three CVAH males, there was only one known instance of a homosexual status. That patient had a rare, asymptomatic case of CVAH, and would not have been ascertained, except that he was a cousin of two CVAH brothers, and participated in a pedigree study. Among the forty-one adolescent gynecomastia males, there were eight who had homosexual (or bisexual) imagery and ideation. One of them was explicit in disclosing details of actual homosexual participation. One youth, struggling to resolve his dilemma, declared that if he could not become heterosexual, he would become either a priest with an abstinent sex life or a male-to-female transexual. Instead, he became reconciled to being a practicing gay.

9 ANDROGEN-INSENSITIVITY SYNDROME

Whereas the adrenogenital syndrome is characterized by prenatal supramasculinization, the reverse applies to the androgen-insensitivity syndrome (AIS), formerly known as the testicular-feminizing syndrome. Inframasculinization characterizes partial androgen insensitivity, whereas a more complete degree of demasculinization characterizes complete androgen insensitivity (Masica, Ehrhardt, and Money, 1971). It is for this reason that patients with the complete syndrome of androgen insensitivity were selected to constitute the clinical contrast group of controls for the women with the 46,XX adrenogenital syndrome, aforementioned.

The complete androgen-insensitivity syndrome occurs in girls and women who, paradoxically, are chromosomally 46,XY, and whose gonads are histologically testicular, though without spermatogenesis, and without the capacity to do the work of testes. Their incapacitation stems from a genetically transmitted, X-linked recessive error that blocks, in all cells of the body, either the uptake or the utilization of the hormone testosterone, secreted by the testes. Unable to use testosterone in both prenatal and postnatal life, the body fails to masculinize. Confronted with that failure, embryogenesis reverts to its primal template, namely, to construct Eve first, then Adam. In fetal life, this reversion takes place after the gonads have formed and secreted their antimüllerian hormone, which blocks the growth of the müllerian ducts into a uterus and fallopian tubes (see Section 3, this chapter). Thereafter, no further masculinization occurs, so that the baby is born as Eve, but without Eve's internal reproductive organs. The vagina is present, but lacks depth until dilated. The vulva appears externally normal except that, in adulthood, pubic hair is sparce or absent. Pubic and axillary hair follicles, if unable to utilize androgen, are unable to grow hair. At puberty, the breasts develop and the body feminizes in contour, under the influence of the androgenically unopposed amount of testicular estrogen that normally circulates in the bloodstream of all males.

Two characteristics of the syndrome most commonly responsible for bringing the individual to medical attention are the shallow or atresic vagina and failure to menstruate. These same two characteristics, vaginal atresia and amenorrhea, are found also in women who are chromosomally 46,XX and gonadally female with a diagnosis of Rokitansky syndrome [or Mayer-Rokitansky-Kuester (MRK) syndrome; Lewis and Money, 1983]. MRK women do not menstruate because, like AIS women, they are born without a uterus and also without fallopian tubes. The uterus and tubes are represented only by a cordlike structure. MRK women femininize at puberty under the influence of hormones secreted by their own ovaries. The occurrence of the MRK syndrome is sporadic. In this respect it is not like AIS syndrome, which is transmitted in the maternal line as a genetically X-linked recessive trait and therefore may occur in successive generations of the family tree.

The two syndromes, AIS and MRK, are admirably suited to be clinical contrast or control groups for one another, since they are similar on all counts except chromosomal sex, gonadal sex, and hormonal cyclicity. A comparative study of an unbiased sample of eighteen women (Lewis and Money, 1983; Money and Lewis, 1983), nine in each diagnostic group, showed the two groups to be identical on a range of erotosexual variables.

All 18 were exclusively heterosexual as women in their sex lives, not only in their erotosexual practices, but also in the erotosexual imagery and ideation of their dreams, fantasies, thoughts, conceptions, and beliefs. The significance of this finding for homosexology is that it rules out three of the criteria of female sex (namely, chromosomal status, gonadal status, and hormonal cyclicity) as essential to the development of a feminine sexual orientation, for the two groups were antithetical on these three variables. The variables that they shared in common as heterosexual women were female external genital anatomy and body build, spontaneous hormonal feminization of the body at puberty, and a history of having been assigned and reared as girls.

The androgen-insensitivity syndrome is another of the syndromes that points to the definition of homosexuality as sexual and erotic expression between two people who have the same external genital anatomy and body morphology. No one would ever consider a married androgen-insensitive mother with two adopted children to be a male homosexual simply because her husband has the same chromosomal sex as she has, and the same gonadal sex as she had preoperatively. Common sense demands that she be accorded the same heterosexual status as her MRK woman counterpart.

The similarity between the two syndromes proved to be so perfect that it was, in fact, quite in order to combine the two diagnoses in order to get a sufficiently large control group for the aforementioned study of 30 adreno-genital women (see Section 7, this chapter).

10 MALE HERMAPHRODITISM

In male hermaphroditism, the chromosomal sex is 46,XY and the gonads are testicular, though with a greatly reduced probability of fertility and an increased long-term risk of carcinoma. In prenatal life, masculine differentiation of the sex organs fails to reach completion, either because the tissues are partially androgen insensitive and therefore unable to utilize fully all of the available male hormone, or because the fetal testicles fail to make available a sufficient quantity of the hormone. Whether from hormonal insensitivity or insufficiency, the baby is born with a birth defect of the external sex organs, so that the genital appearance is ambiguously hermaphroditic or intersexed. Some such babies have been assigned and reared as boys, and some as girls. At puberty, irrespective of their sex of rearing, some have undergone spontaneous hormonal feminization and developed breasts. They do not menstruate, as they lack a uterus. The puberty of those who do not feminize is likely to be partially masculinizing or eunuchoid, rather than complete.

In androgen-insensitivity cases, when the individual's own hormonal puberty is inadequate, hormonal treatment to bring about feminization is successful, whereas treatment to bring about masculinization is unsatisfactory. The consequences are dire if the partially androgen-insensitive individual has been assigned and reared to live as a boy, for he forever fails to gain the physical appearance of masculine maturity. If he has grown up to the age of puberty self-identified as a boy, and if his imagery and ideation are heterosexually masculine, then it is impossible for him to espouse the rational logic of becoming hormonally and surgically reassigned to live as a woman, even if, untreated, he has already developed breasts and a feminine body morphology. To impose feminizing surgery on his birth-defective genitalia would be totally incompatible with the history of the multiple operations to which his penis had already been subjected in order to affirm genital masculinity and to permit urination as a male.

In the annals of male hermaphroditism, instances of sex reassignment from male to female are rare, even in cases of impaired masculine body maturation on the basis of partial androgen insensitivity (Money and Norman, 1987), whereas sex reassignment from female to male is not so rare (Money, Devore, and Norman, 1986). The parallel phenomenon occurs in female hermaphroditism insofar as a sex reassignment from female to male is virtually unheard of, no matter how extensive the degree of masculinization (Money, 1968a). However, there is no corresponding parallel in female hermaphroditism with respect to the prevalence of reassignment from male to female, the explanation being that only a very few female hermaphrodites are assigned and reared as boys. Even if they are announced as boys neonatally, a reannouncement is likely to follow very soon thereafter. The explanation lies in the fact that female hermaphroditism is almost always associated with the adrenogenital syndrome, which produces a sufficiency of complicating symptoms, especially severe salt loss that is lethal if not neonatally detected and treated, to lead to the diagnosis of gonadal sex (ovarian) and chromosomal sex (46,XX).

There is absolutely no doubt that in the traditional wisdom of most parents and their religious advisors, as well as of many doctors, primacy is attributed to chromosomal and gonadal sex, and to the prospect of fertility as the criteria on which to decide the sex of assignment. Surgically, it is technically more feasible to demasculinize and feminize the external genitalia than it is to defeminize and masculinize them. Thus, the greater simplicity of corrective feminizing surgery also is a criterion in announcing the sex of a female hermaphrodite as female. This criterion is quite often disregarded in announcing or reannouncing the sex of a chromosomally and gonadally diagnosed male hermaphrodite as a boy. In consequence he may be nosocomially traumatized—that is, traumatized by clinical and hospital procedures and experiences. He may undergo multiple surgical admissions in childhood, only to have, in adulthood, a small and deformed penis inadequate for copulation (Money and Lamacz, 1986), and possibly for urination as well.

The primacy accorded the chromosomal sex, and more especially the gonadal sex, as the ultimate criteria by which to decide the sex of an hermaphroditic baby influences the destiny of the male hermaphrodite at any age. For the baby assigned and reared as a girl and not diagnosed as gonadally and chromosomally male until later in life, the diagnosis may lead to an imposed sex reassignment. Or, if in childhood or adolescence, the male hermaphrodite living as a girl is ambivalent about her status as a girl or rejects it, the covert if not the overt influence of the primacy of the chromosomal and gonadal criteria tips the scales of professionals in favor of permitting a sex reassignment that otherwise they would veto. They would veto sex reassignment in the corresponding case of a male hermaphrodite living as a boy and ambivalent about or rejecting his status as a boy. Similarly, sex reassignment from girl to boy would be vetoed for a female hermaphrodite (Money, 1968a; Jones, 1979).

Sex is a binary system: male and female. A hermaphroditic child who grows up ambivalent about his/her status in the sex of assignment has effectively only one alternative, namely, to change to the other sex. If this alternative is congruous with the criteria of the agents of society, including parents and professionals, who set the rules as to who may change, then sex reassignment is more likely to be permitted or endorsed.

A hermaphroditic individual's nonconformity with respect to his or her status in the sex of assignment and rearing manifests itself in nonconformity regarding social and legal stereotypes with respect to the male/female division of labor, play, education, dress, adornment, wealth, and so forth, but more specifically with respect to the imagery, ideation, and practices of falling in love and sex life. In love and sex life, nonconformity may be manifested as bisexuality, or as homosexuality defined on the criterion of assigned sex, or as a change of sexual status through sex reassignment.

With respect to the theory of homosexology and heterosexology, it is of major significance not that some male hermaphrodites, assigned and clinically habilitated as girls, grow up to be bisexual, homosexual, or sex-reassigned, but that others grow up with a heterosexual status as women who have men as romantic partners and husbands. Unless informed of the clinical history and intersex diagnosis of these women, other people do not suspect anything amiss, nor do they have reason to do so. Socially and in physical appearance, as well as romantically and in sex life, the male hermaphrodite successfully habilitated as a woman is not conspicuous and not identifiable as odd among other women. The same applies also to the related birth defect of micropenis (Money, 1984a). Each type of case further substantiates the principle, exemplified several times already, that homosexuality is defined in terms of the genital and body morphology of the two partners, not in terms of the chromosomal sex, or of the sex of the gonads.

Correspondingly, of course, heterosexuality is also defined on the criterion that the two partners have not the same, but different genital and overall body conformation. Thus, the woman with a history of having been treated for either male hermaphroditism or micropenis is defined as heterosexual, regardless of her chromosomal or gonadal status, provided her habilitation has been to develop physically and mentally from girlhood to womanhood, with a romantic and erotic life shared with at least one boyfriend or husband. By contrast, this same woman, with her history of having been reared and clinically habilitated as a girl, would be defined as homosexual and a lesbian if she had grown up to be attracted erotically only to another woman and to be repelled by the advances of a would-be boyfriend whose attraction to her she would personally equate, in reference to herself, with the homosexuality of two men being together. She might resolve her dilemma by changing to live as a man with a woman lover, or she might continue to live as a woman with a woman lover and be known as bisexual. Each outcome would qualify as a manifestation of some degree of gender transposition away from the ideological norm of femininity toward the ideological norm of masculinity. The criterion standard is the ideological, not the statistical norm. The extreme degree of transposition is sex reassignment. Living as a lesbian is a lesser degree of transposition, and as a bisexual lesser still.

The prevalence of gender transposition was the object of the study (Money, Devore, and Norman, 1986) of adult patients ($N = 32$) with a history of having been diagnosed as male hermaphrodites, assigned as girls, reared as girls, and clinically habilitated to live as girls and women. In this study, sex reassignment from female to male was classified as a gender transposition phenomenon, as were imagery and ideation or actual experience of attraction to a female either exclusively, as a lesbian, or bisexually.

The high proportion of patients ($N = 15$) who were classified as manifesting a transposition phenomenon is in part an artifact of sampling, since one reason for a patient's psychohormonal referral to Johns Hopkins was the presence of a transposition dilemma. Thus the ratio of 15:17 exaggerates the prevalence of transposition in the syndromes of male hermaphroditism at large. That proved to be an advantage for present purposes, insofar as it provided a nice balance of cases among which to search for correlates or determinants of the phenomenon of transposition.

In this study, the only variable that proved to be significantly correlated (chi-square = 10.98; $p < 0.001$) with transposition phenomena was a history of stigmatization during the childhood years. Stigmatization at home took the form of never mentioning the unspeakable birth defect, never explaining frequent clinic checkups or anything else connected with the defect, and never allowing the genitalia to be exposed except medically. Among peers it took the form of being teased as a sexual freak on the basis of a leakage of information about either the genital condition, or the neonatal history of indeterminacy regarding the sex of announcement or reannouncement.

The stigmatization effect proved to be prepubertal in origin, and not related to the incongruity of undergoing a masculinizing or eunuchoidal puberty instead of a feminizing one. Those children who would masculinize at puberty are presumed to have been more likely than the pubertal feminizers to have undergone stronger hormonal brain masculinization, prenatally. However, childhood stigmatization did not happen exclusively to the future pubertal masculinizers. This finding seems to rule out the possibility that prenatal brain masculinization might somehow or other have preordained an early behavioral manifestation of a gender transposition, such as uncompromising tomboyism of behavior, that would provoke teasing and stigmatization during childhood. Moreover, if a girl is tomboyish in behavior and a winner in athletics, her success builds self-esteem and inures her against the otherwise deleterious effects of teasing and stigmatization.

A male hermaphrodite with a history of having been assigned as a girl, and of subsequently having subjectively sensed the prospect or realization of a sexual relationship with a man as homosexual, is cited as a triumph of nature over nurture by those who label themselves as biological determinists. To maintain the triumph, however, they neglect or discard the converse evidence of cases in which nurture may be said to triumph over nature.

The example most quoted by the naturists is that of a pedigree of male hermaphrodites in an inbred population inhabiting three isolated mountain villages in the Dominican Republic (Imperato-McGinley and Peterson, 1976; Imperato-McGinley et al., 1974, 1979). In this pedigree, the biochemical error responsible for the intersexed condition is 5α-reductase deficiency. At birth the defective sex organs closely resemble those of a female rather than those of a male.

In the first Dominican generation of intersexed births, affected babies were assigned as girls. When they reached the age of puberty they failed to feminize, but developed in a eunuchoid, masculine way instead. The clitoridic organ enlarged and protruded sufficiently so as to qualify in some instances as a small, hypospadiac penis that would require surgical intervention to release it for copulatory use. In the absence of local hospital facilities, there was no available corrective surgery for the deformed sex organs and no available hormonal treatment either to feminize or to masculinize the body better.

Since all the first generation of intersexed children had the same condition, they all developed in the same nonfeminine way. In the next two generations, therefore, newborn intersex babies were assigned as boys. Their predecessors who had already grown up and failed to feminize had been more readily tolerated in the village if they had changed to live and earn a living as men, and perhaps try to have the sex life of a man.

Imperato-McGinley and her coauthors proposed the hypothesis that the testosterone of puberty had a masculinizing effect not only in the body, including the sex organs, but also on the mind, including the sex drive. Hence the changing of sex in the hermaphrodites of the first generation.

There is a flaw in the biological reductionism of this hypothesis: it ignores the nonhormonal variables that affected the intersexed children's lives. Though assigned to live as girls, they had been stigmatized as freaks by being known pejoratively as *guevodoces,* translated literally as eggs at twelve, for which the idiomatic English is balls (testicles) at twelve. They were also known as *machi hembra,* which translates as macho miss, with a strong implication of half-girl, half-boy freakishness, as well as of being tomboyish. There was no possibility in a traditional Hispanic village culture for such a person to be a wife and mother, and there was no other role for her as a woman except to be an economic liability as an unmarriageable freak supported by her family. The alternative was to adapt as well as possible to being a man.

A consideration of the sociological variables in these cases of 5α-reductase deficiency does not exclude the possibility that they were superimposed on a substrate somehow made compliantly masculine by reason of the 5α-reductase deficiency. The ideal test, in the best of all possible experimental designs, would be to have as a control group another pedigree, in another location, where all cases would be clinically and socially habilitated as girls from birth onward, beginning with surgical feminization of the genitalia in early infancy. The onset of puberty would be clinically regulated and would be exclusively feminine. Vaginoplasty, if required, would be available on an elective basis as soon as the body was adolescently mature. There are individual cases of 5α-reductase deficiency that have been treated in this way. The outcome is not as in the Dominican pedigree. The girl becomes a woman and has a heterosexual status as a woman, even though it is contradictory of her chromosomal and gonadal sexual status.

The Dominican Republic pedigree does not stand up to the claim of being unique in demonstrating the triumph of nature over nurture. On the contrary, it demonstrates, as do all other examples of intersexuality, that the status of sexual orientation in adulthood cannot be attributed to any one variable that is either exclusively nature or exclusively nurture. By itself alone, testosterone at puberty cannot be held responsible for male heterosexuality in 5α-reductase-deficient hermaphroditism. That would be tantamount to claiming that testosterone is responsible for all male heterosexuality. If that were so, then the vast majority of homosexual men would be heterosexual, for they have a normal level of testosterone. Similarly, the vast majority of male-to-female transexuals would be heterosexually normal men, for they also have a normal level of testosterone prior to reassignment.

It is a basic requirement of any theory that it cannot be used to explain one set of data if that explanation is inconsistent with, or is totally contradicted by a related set of data. Imperato-McGinley's theory fails to satisfy this requirement. It fails to take into account gender transpositions not associated with the 5α-reductase syndrome. It is, for example, challenged by the hormonal facts of male-to-female transexualism, in the face of which it is embarrassingly mute.

11 KLINEFELTER'S (47,XXY) SYNDROME

The supernumerary X chromosome that is the defining characteristic of Klinefelter's (47,XXY) syndrome has been known to occur in association with the hermaphroditic birth defect of the genitalia, though with extreme infrequency. The chromosomal status itself is what makes the syndrome of interest to hermaphroditic theory, and to homosexological theory also, insofar as it may be construed as a supernumerary Y added to the standard 46,XX of the female; or a supernumerary X added to the 46,XY of the male. Hence, by stretching the meaning of hermaphroditism, Klinefelter's syndrome might be characterized as chromosomal hermaphroditism. So characterized, it is a syndrome that should show whether or not chromosomal hermaphroditism has a direct effect as a determinant of mixed masculinity/femininity or androgyny in the specific sexuoerotic sense. The evidence of the clinic is that it does not. There is no dominant trend for 47,XXY boys and men to be sexuoerotically androgynous or bisexual. The trend that is dominant is for 47,XXY men to be hyposexual (Schiavi et al., 1987).

Hyposexuality in the 47,XXY syndrome is consistent with other symptoms characteristic of the syndrome, namely degeneration of the testicular tubules and consequent sterility and testicular shrinkage after the onset of puberty, enlargement of the breasts in about one-third of cases, and eunuchoid body build. The level of pituitary gonadotropin (luteinizing hormone, LH, and follicle-stimulating hormone, FSH) is high, as the testes do not respond to it well enough to active the feedback mechanism that reduces its secretion from the pituitary gland. The circulating level of testosterone in the bloodstream may be either low or within the normal range. The response of target cells to testosterone is typically weak. If supplemental exogenous testosterone is given, the dosage needed for a satisfactory sexuoerotic response is greater than used for hormonal replacement in a castrate.

It may well be that the presence of a supernumerary X chromosome in target cells that take up testosterone interferes in some way with the intracellular metabolism of the hormone. If this hypothesis is correct, then it may be assumed to apply also to brain cells that take up testosterone and govern sexuoerotic responsiveness.

The supernumerary X chromosome in all cells of the brain and peripheral nervous system may be implicated in the prevalence and diversity of symptoms and syndromes of psychopathology found in the 47,XXY syndrome. It qualifies as being a living atlas of virtually every degree and variety of neuropsychiatric and psychiatric disorder or defect. Some individuals are profoundly disabled, whereas others escape, and there is, as yet, no reasonable explanation for either extreme, nor for the spectrum between.

Disorders classified in the psychiatric nosology as psychosexual are among those that coexist with Klinefelter's (47,XXY) syndrome (Money and Pollitt, 1964; Money et al., 1974). There are no systematic epidemiological statistics, to permit an incontrovertible statement about prevalence of these disorders in the 47,XXY population as compared with the 46,XY population. Thus there is no basis on which to make a comparative statement regarding the prevalence of homosexuality in the two populations. The same applies to the various forms of eonism (Money and Pollitt, 1964) now known as gender crosscoding or gender transposition (see Chapter 3, Table 3-1). Eonism includes transexualism, which formerly was subsumed under transvestism.

Considering that the incidence of the 47,XXY syndrome in neonatal surveys is 1:500 male-declared births, and that the incidence of male-to-female transexualism, though unknown, is estimated to be far more rare, cases of dual diagnosis do seem to turn up in the literature and the clinic more often than one would expect by chance alone. If there is more than a chance association between the two syndromes, then it is probably related to the supernumerary X chromosome on the same basis as other psychiatrically classified disorders in 47,XXY people. There are no indicators pointing to 47,XXY chromosomal hermaphroditism as a cause specifically of eonism or psychic hermaphroditism, otherwise known as transexualism, occurring in Klinefelter's syndrome. There are also no indicators of hormonal causes of transexualism in Klinefelter's syndrome, or in general.

12 47,XYY SYNDROME

In the 1960s, when the 47,XYY syndrome had only recently been discovered, the supernumerary Y chromosome was naively sensationalized as a double dose of masculinity. There is no sensational double masculinity in the sexuoerotic lives of 47,XYY men, however, just as there is no sexuoerotic androgyny in the sex lives of 47,XXY men. Quite to the contrary, 47,XYY men have a sex life that either is similar to that of 46,XY men, or else is predominantly bisexual or homosexual, with or without paraphilia (see Chapter 4, Section 6).

In an early literature survey of sixteen case references to 47,XYY sexuality (Money, Gaskin, and Hull, 1970), the breakdown was as follows: seven bisexual, seven homosexual, two heterosexual. In these sixteen cases, the following nine types of paraphilia were also mentioned: bisexual child incest (1), pedophilia (2), voyeurism (1), exhibitionism (3), indecent assault (1), transvestic sadomasochism and lust murder (1).

These sixteen cases tell something about the range of sexual variation that may be found in the 47,XYY syndrome. Because the sample is sexologically biased, they tell nothing about the prevalence of sexual variation in the XYY population at large.

Another study (Money et al., 1974) demonstrated that XYY men ($N = 12$) are sexologically different from a matched comparison or control group of XXY men ($N = 12$). The comparative breakdown, for XYY and XXY, respectively, was as follows: heterosexual $0:6$, bisexual $10:2$, autosexual exclusively $1:3$, and noninformative $1:1$ ($p < 0.10$, comparing bisexual versus all other in a chi-square test of two independent samples). In addition, the XYY:XXY ratio for paraphilia was $6:2$ (p < 0.10).

If the supernumerary Y chromosome is in some way responsible for the sexological diversity of XYY men, then the range of diversity indicates not a direct cause but an indirect one, mediated through at least one intervening variable. That intervening variable is not precocious onset of puberty; nor is it hyperspermia (a large proportion of XYY men are sterile) or hypersecretion of testosterone. The level of circulating testosterone in XYY men is distributed more or less on a normal curve, from low-average to high above average.

The most likely intervening variable responsible for the diversity of XYY sexuality is the same one that is responsible for the diversity of XYY antisocial behavioral pathology, namely ungovernable impulsiveness, which, in turn, is undoubtedly the product of other as yet unascertained variables. Corresponding to the supernumerary X chromosome in Klinefelter's syndrome, the supernumerary Y chromosome in the XYY syndrome is in every cell in the brain and the peripheral nervous system. Thus, it is into the neurochemistry and neurobiology of the cells of the sexual nuclei and pathways of the brain that research will need to be directed in order to ascertain how the extra Y chromosome generates an affinity for bisexualism and paraphilia in the 47,XYY syndrome.

13 TURNER'S (45,X) SYNDROME

Turner's syndrome, like the 47,XXY and 47,XYY syndromes, has its origin in a chromosomal error—not an extra X or Y, but a missing one. The typical pattern is 45,X (45,Y is embryologically nonviable) but there are diverse mosaic variations, such as 45,X/46,XX.

The prenatal hormonal history of the 45,X fetus, like that of the 47,XXY or 47,XYY fetus, has not been studied, as the likelihood of identifying a case prenatally is fortuitous, except for mass screening, which is nowadays condemned as ethically suspect. However, it is known that the 45,X fetus does not secrete gonadal steroid hormones, because one of the defining characteristics of the syndrome is that the gonads fail to differentiate. They are represented only by fibrous streaks. Thus, Turner's syndrome has significance for sexological theory insofar as it demonstrates that the principle of Eve first, then Adam applies to the differentiation of sexual dimorphism even when the fetus is devoid of gonads and of gonadal hormones (except those that might cross the placenta from the mother).

In accordance with the Eve-first principle, the Turner baby is born with external genitalia that replicate those of a girl. She is assigned and reared as a girl, and may grow up diagnostically unrecognized until, at the expected age, there is no onset of puberty. Replacement treatment with estrogen may be delayed while, in an attempt to correct the syndrome-typical deficiency in height, growth hormone treatment is prolonged. Eventually, however, pubertal maturation is achieved, and menstrual cyclicity is established by means of cyclic administration of estrogen and progestin. There have been no cases yet recorded of pregnancy by in vitro fertilization and implantation of a donor's egg, but sooner or later there will be.

Women with Turner's syndrome have a history of a high level of parental interest and involvement dating from the doll-play of childhood. Typically, they do not have tomboyish interests and activities. Occupationally, many of them gravitate toward work with children. In teenage, they are responded to socially as juveniles, and are hindered in implementing their romantic interests, until after hormonal maturation has been effected. Thereafter, short stature continues to be a hindrance, and so does self-knowledge of infertility (Money and Mittenthal, 1970). In addition, there may well be a factor, difficult to pin down, of diffidence and insufficient self-confidence in giving and taking cues to initiate and establish a friendship of a romantic, sexual, and erotic nature. In the vernacular, it would be said that Turner women are not very sexy or horny, and there is some evidence that the same applies to having sexual intercourse with a partner or husband (McCauley, Sybert, and Ehrhardt, 1986). Coital difficulty may, however, be secondary to insufficient data regarding the ideal replacement dosage and blend of estrogen, progestin, and in minor amount, androgen, with respect to erotic arousal, coitus, and orgasm.

An excess of erotic diffidence and erotic inertia is interpreted socially as an excess of conformity to a stereotype of feminine deference and passivity.

It is not a lack or repudiation of femininity. In this respect, Turner's syndrome demonstrates the continuity of the Eve-first principle into the social development of the romantic and sex life of adulthood from its beginnings in the sexual differentiation of the embryo and fetus.

The incidence of bisexuality or lesbianism in Turner's syndrome is so rarely reported that it may be considered, to all intents and purposes, nonexistent. The complete absence of fetal gonads and fetal gonadal hormones signifies, by implication, a complete lack of any hormone-mediated masculinization or defeminization of the brain, in prenatal life. Thus there is no prenatal residual either to interfere with or to enhance postnatal differentiation of femininity and a heterosexual status, variations in the social environment notwithstanding.

14 EPILOGUE AND SYNOPSIS

In the culture of the West, we characterize homosexuality as sporadic and pathological in occurrence. Elsewhere, as among the Sambia of New Guinea, homosexuality is characterized as a phase of universalized sequential bisexuality, the absence of which is sporadic and pathological in occurrence. A theory of homosexuality must encompass both manifestations.

Human sexological syndromes in the clinic represent experiments of nature that are the counterpart of animal sexological syndromes induced experimentally in the laboratory. Despite species differences and variations, data from these two sources are mutually compatible. They indicate that, in all species, the differentiation of sexual orientation or status as either bisexual or monosexual (i.e., exclusively heterosexual or homosexual) is a sequential process. The prenatal stage of this process, with a possible brief neonatal extension, takes place under the aegis of brain hormonalization. It continues postnatally under the aegis of the senses and social communication and learning.

Dimorphic hormonalization of the brain prenatally takes place under the influence of a steroidal hormone. Normally, the hormone is testosterone, secreted by the fetal testes. Some target cells receive testosterone and change it into one of its metabolites, notably either estradiol or dihydrotestosterone. Steroidal hormone masculinizes and defeminizes. Its lack or insufficiency demasculinizes and feminizes. It is possible for masculinization and feminization both to coexist to some degree, with consequent ambisexual or bisexual rather than monosexual manifestations in behavior, and in mental life.

Whereas brain dimorphism formerly was inferred from its effects in producing male/female dimorphism of behavior, in recent years it has been directly demonstrated in neuroanatomical structures that differ in the brains of males and females, especially in the region of the hypothalamus.

In nonprimate species, prenatal hormonal differentiation of the brain preordains subsequent mating behavior as male or female more inexorably than is the case in primate species, especially the human species. Even in subprimates, however, the final outcome is not immune to postnatal modulation by variations in the circumstances of infant care and social contact. In primates, as compared with subprimates, the influence of prenatal and neonatal hormonalization is more susceptible to subsequent superimposed variations in social communication and learning. In particular, juvenile sexual rehearsal play is prerequisite to both masculinized and feminized proficiency in adult mating skill (see Chapter 2, Section 9).

In the human species there are only a few infrequently occurring clinical syndromes in which it is possible to reconstruct the prenatal and neonatal hormonal history and relate it to subsequent orientation as heterosexual, bisexual, or homosexual. In other homosexual and bisexual people, one may conjecture the possibility of unsuspected nutritional, medicinal, or hormonal changes, including stress-derived changes in the chemistries of the pregnant mother's bloodstream—changes that may induce a masculinizing or demasculinizing, feminizing or defeminizing effect on sexual differentiation of the baby's brain. Prenatal maternal stress, for example, is known to have a demasculinizing effect on rat pups; and, likewise, barbiturates ingested by the mother are demasculinizing.

With respect to orientation as homosexual or bisexual in the human species, there is no evidence that prenatal hormonalization alone, independently of postnatal history, inexorably preordains either orientation. Rather, neonatal antecedents may facilitate the subsequent differentiation of a homosexual or bisexual orientation, provided the postnatal determinants in the social and communicational history are also facilitative.

Logically, there is a possibility that the postnatal determinants may need no facilitation from prenatal ones. Defense of this proposition precipitates, yet once again, the obsolete nature/nurture debate, with no resolution. On the issue of the determinants of sexual orientation as homosexual, bisexual, or heterosexual, the only scholarly position is to allow that prenatal and postnatal determinants are not mutually exclusive. When nature and nurture interact at critical developmental periods, the residual products may persist immutably. It will require new methodology and new increments of empirical data before the full catalogue of these residuals can be specified.

Meanwhile, it is counterproductive to characterize prenatal determinants of sexual orientation as biological, and postnatal determinants as not biological. The postnatal determinants that enter the brain through the senses by way of social communication and learning also are biological, for there is a biology of learning and remembering. That which is not biological is occult, mystical, or, to coin a term, spookological. Homosexology, the science of orientation or status as homosexual or bisexual rather than heterosexual, is not a science of spooks. Nor is the science of heterosexology.

CHAPTER

TWO

Gender Coding

1 DIECIOUS AND MONECIOUS

A diecious species is one in which the male and female reproductive organs are housed in two separate and distinct individual beings; derived from Greek, diecious means, literally, two houses. A monecious species is one that has the male and female organs housed in one individual being. Parthenogenic creatures, like the whiptail lizards (see Chapter 1, Section 3), are a special instance of a monecious species, for their brains have two separate and distinct patterns of breeding behavior, although every member of the species has the same genital morphology and produces eggs exclusively. These eggs do not need to capture and join with a sperm in order to be fertile and produce young ones. Reproductively, the species is monomorphic; that is, it has only one form. There are no sperm-bearing males. Since the species exists without the dimorphism of male and female, each with its own form, there are, strictly speaking, therefore, no females. Nonetheless, the dimorphism of language is so powerful that it is all but inevitable to refer to a lizard that lays eggs as a female. It is equally inevitable that when this same lizard, during an anovulatory phase, mounts another ovulatory lizard, the mounting behavior will be referred to as masculine. The criterion of masculine in this instance is that it simulates the behavior of males in those whiptail species that, having two forms, one for sperm-bearing males, and one for egg-bearing females, are diecious.

In this example, one confronts the issue of the ultimate criterion of what is masculine, what is feminine, and what is bisexual. The workaday criterion is that if, in a diecious species, males do it, it is masculine, whereas if females do it, it is feminine. If both do it, it is sex-shared, or ambisexual, or bisexual. This workaday criterion would be acceptable if it were applied with strict mathematical obedience to the statistical norm of what is manifested by males only, by females only, or by both. The statistical norm, however, insidiously yields to the ideological norm, which is not the norm of what males and females actually do, but of what they ought to do. Ideologically, what is masculine is what males ought to do, and what is feminine is what females ought to do, according to criteria that are assumed to be eternal verities, but are actually culture-bound dogmas of history, authority, and the cultural heritage. Ideologically there is practically no place for what is sex-shared or ambisexual. The very term, ambisexual, is seldom used, being replaced by bisexual. Bisexual does not imply that something is shared in common by both males and females, but is used with pejorative overtones to indicate that something appropriate to one sex is incongruously manifested by a deviant member of the other sex. We are heirs to a long history of a cultural fixation on sex divergency rather than sex sharing.

This fixation has insidiously infected sexual science so as to ensure that its focus is on explaining sex difference, not sex similarity. The naming of the sex hormones when they were isolated in the 1920s and subsequently synthesized is an example. Androgen (from Greek, *andros*, man) became the name for a male hormone, especially testosterone, secreted by testes. The female hormones were named estrogen (from Greek, *oistrous*, gadfly; Latin, *oestrus*, the period of sexual heat) and progesterone (from Latin, *pro + gestatio*, gestation + *sterol*, as in cholesterol + -one). The progesterone level is higher during pregnancy than in the nonpregnant state. Simply by being characterized as masculinizing and feminizing, the names of the gonadal hormones have insidiously supported the idea of sex difference, whereas in fact all three hormones are sex-shared. Their ratio differs in males and females, but not their occurrence. Moreover, the body synthesizes all three from cholesterol, the progression being in both sexes from cholesterol to progesterone to testosterone to estradiol.

2 SEX AND GENDER

Although they are carelessly used synonymously, sex and gender are not synonymous. They are also not antonyms, although they are frequently used almost as if they were. In one such usage, sex is defined as what you are born with, as male or female, and gender is what you acquire as a social role, from a social script. This usage lends support to a second one in which gender is sex without the dirty and carnal part that belongs to the genitalia and reproduction. This is the Barbie-doll usage in which human beings are cast in the role of Barbie and Ken. Though blantantly sexy in shape and clothing these dolls are molded with nothing between their legs, except that some Kens may have a nipple of a penis—but there were no nipples on the chest, nor on Barbie's!

It is the Barbie-doll definition of gender that made possible the political term, gender gap, for which sex gap would be an unacceptable synonym, because of its double meaning. In the politics of the women's movement, the separation of gender from sex was a godsend, because it allowed sex differences in procreation to be set aside in the fight for gender equality in earning power and legal status.

Used strictly and correctly, gender is conceptually more inclusive than sex. It is an umbrella under which are sheltered all the different components of sex difference, including the sex-genital, sex-erotic, and sex-procreative components. The need to find an umbrella term became for me an imperative in the early 1950s when I was writing about the manliness or womanliness of people with a history of having been born with indeterminate genital sex. They were hermaphrodites and their genital sex was ambiguous. In some instances, they would grow up to live as women, but would not have a woman's sex organs. In others, they would live as men without a man's sex organs. In the case of the man, by way of illustration, it made no sense to say that such a person had a male sex role when, in fact, he had no male external genitalia, could not urinate as a male, and would not ever be able to copulate as a male. No matter how manly he might otherwise be, his genital sex role was not that of a man. There was no noun that could be adjectivally qualified to characterize him as manly or masculine, despite the deficit of the very organs that are the criterion of being a male. That is why I turned to philology and linguistics and borrowed the term, gender (Money, 1955b). Then it became possible to say that the person had the gender role, and also the gender identity of a man, but a deficient or partially deficient male sex role with respect to the usage of the birth-defective sex organs. The new term made it also possible to formulate such statements as, for example, a male gender role despite a female (46,XX) genetic sex. Without the term gender, one would get bogged down in statements such as this: a male sex role, except that his sex role with the sex organs was not male, and his genetic sex was female.

In popular and in scientific usage, gender role and gender identity have become separated, whereas they are really two sides of the same coin. Other people infer your private and personal gender identity from the public evidence of your gender role. You alone have maximum intimate access to your own gender identity. The acronym, G-I/R (gender-identity/role), unifies identity and role into a singular noun.

There is no finite limit to the number of adjectives that may be used to qualify a G-I/R. One classification is into homosexual, bisexual, or heterosexual G-I/R. A homosexual G-I/R itself ranges widely from that of a full-time drag queen or gynemimetic (one who mimes women) to that of a stereotypically macho football hero or Marine Corps sergeant who has a masculine G-I/R, except for the sex of the partner to whom he becomes erotically attracted and male-bonded in a love affair. Some people would say that the macho homosexual has a masculine G-I/R, except for a homosexual partner preference or object-choice. The correct statement should be that he has a masculine G-I/R except for the erotosexual and falling-in-love component.

3 REDUCTIONISM

Reductionistic thinking as applied to gender coding is based on the split between sex and gender, according to which sex belongs to biology, nature, and lust, and gender to social science, nurture, and romance. For reductionists, biological means genetic, neuroanatomical, endocrinological, or in some other way physiological. Reductionist theory fails to recognize that there is a biology of learning and remembering, the effects of which may become permanently programed into the brain. Reductionism adopts the common, though erroneous, assumption that what the brain assimilates it may always discard—that learning may always be undone by unlearning, or that memory may always be undone by forgetting.

Reductionist theory is popular on both sides of the false fence that erroneously claims to separate biology from social learning. It allows its proponents on either side to earn a living by ignoring each other's specialty knowledge, training, and certification. The bureaucracy of scholars is not well suited to interdisciplinary knowledge, nor to the concept of multivariate, sequential determinants that cross the boundaries of scientific specialties. Gender coding is both multivariate and sequential, and it is neither exclusively biological nor exclusively social, but a product of both.

In the years of childhood, the gender-coded development of boys and girls invariably mirrors the masculine and feminine stereotypes of their social heritage. In the human species, there is no way in which to ascertain what culture-free masculinity and femininity would be like, for they are always packaged in culture, just as linguistic ability is always packaged in a native language. Primordial masculinity and femininity are unascertainable in their entirety. It is possible, however, to gender-code male/female differences into those that are classified as sex irreducible, sex derivative, sex adjunctive, and sex adventitious.

4 SEX-IRREDUCIBLE GENDER CODING

Despite the multiplicity of sex differences, those that are immutable and irreducible are few. They are specific to reproduction: men impregnate, and women menstruate, gestate, and lactate. Ovulation is omitted insofar as gestation does not take place without it. Lactation might be omitted, insofar as modern nutritional technology has made it possible, though not desirable, for maternal neonatal breast-feeding to be replaced by a formula-milk substitute.

The procreative sex difference exists independently of orientation as heterosexual, bisexual, or homosexual. In all three categories there are some men and some women who are sterile, but there is no evidence that sterility is either more common or less common in heterosexuals than in homosexuals or bisexuals. Other things being equal, homosexuals are as capable of procreation as are bisexuals and heterosexuals.

Immutability of the procreative sex difference will undoubtedly remain as if absolute for most men and women forever. However, in the light of contemporary experimental obstetrics, being pregnant is no longer an absolutely immutable sex difference. Cecil Jacobsen, geneticist, and the late Roy Hertz, endocrine oncologist, got male baboons abdominally pregnant 20 years ago by using the technique of embryo transplantation. The fertilized egg was implanted in the omentum, an internal apron of fatty tissue, well supplied with blood vessels, in the lower abdomen below the navel. In one case, six and one half months later, they delivered a live baby baboon by caesarean section, two weeks premature. The experiment had been designed to find out if pregnant women whose ovaries had to be removed because of ovarian cancer would be able to keep the pregnancy. Male baboons were used because males have no ovaries, and they demonstrated that a pregnancy can exist without ovarian hormones from the mother. "There is no question in my mind," Dr. Jacobsen recently stated, "that the hormones and stimuli required for normal fetal development are intrinsic and within the early embryo. Most developmental biologists are now coming round to that view. But back in the '60s it was heresy" (Barsky, 1986).

The foregoing information came to light as a sequel to scientific (unpublished) and media discussions on male pregnancy (Teresi and McAuliffe, 1985) prompted by a unique case of ectopic pregnancy in Auckland, New Zealand, seven years ago (Jackson et al., 1980). This case is unique, not because the pregnancy was ectopic; there have been other cases of pregnancy outside the womb (Niebyl, 1974), such as one recently reported from Sweden in which the baby grew with the placenta attached to the outside of the dome of the uterus (Norén and Lindblom, 1986). What is unique about the case in Auckland is that the mother had no womb: gestation began after she had had a hysterectomy. According to the coital history, the only chance for an egg to have become fertilized was on the third night prior to the operation. This fertilized egg survived the surgery. It escaped into the abdominal cavity and implanted itself into the exterior wall of the small intestine. There it grew its own placenta and proceeded to develop as does a normal pregnancy. Remarkably, the condition was correctly diagnosed, and the baby was delivered surgically, by laparotomy, after 36 weeks of gestation. She has grown as a healthy girl.

In July 1986, in the series, "Where There's Life," Yorkshire Television in Great Britain broadcast a program on male pregnancy, featuring the seven-year-old girl from New Zealand, her parents, and me. That broadcast evoked among some men an interest in the possibility of male pregnancy for themselves. Most people in the studio audience had perhaps expected that heterosexual men would be totally without interest. They were wrong, and visibly a bit dumbfounded, as they heard husbands volunteer to take their wives' places, if only they could become parents, after all other attempts had failed.

Afterward, one man who had watched the broadcast wrote:

My wife and I have been trying for children for some four years without success. You can therefore see the interest that another road of opportunity presented. Could my wife's eggs be used? Can the process achieve real end results? I am quietly confident that this can be done as long as all known factors are made aware to all, and that a proper mental attitude is taken to the process. We are not rich people by any means, but even so have chosen to pursue the matter to its logical conclusion. We would therefore be forever in your debt if you could supply further information about the possibilities of such a move and whether this could be done alongside my wife's treatment? As you may also have gathered, I am solidly for trying this treatment, even as an experiment, as long as the chances are good. I am not someone that has to have everything tied down, and I also realise the risks involved. All I would like is the OK to proceed and the criteria involved. We await with interest any information you can provide and in the shortest time.

Another letter was written by a male-to-female transexual:

I saw you on YTV the other night. You were talking about no womb pregnancies. I am seeking your advice and help. I'm thirty years old, successful, happy, divorced (through my childlessness), and transexual. Do not judge me or my request upon the last. In five years time I hope to be ready to take a break from my career, marry again, and have children, God willing. The programme you did gave me hope. The dangers involved would not trouble me too much. For me this will be the only hope of having a child. Anything you can tell me will be gratefully received.

The second letter is written from the special vantage point of a male-to-female transexual whom society had once classified as a male. The first was from a husband like the male-pregnancy candidate in the live audience whom society would unhesitatingly classify as heterosexual. There was one young gay man in the audience who considered it would be more moral to carry a pregnancy himself than to exploit a woman as a womb object. The response of heterosexual husbands was the sleeper, however. It shows that pregnancy, one of the most absolute sex differences, can be gender-recoded as acceptable not only to men who already have some degree of feminine orientation, but also to those who do not. They are men for whom the idea of male pregnancy is compatible with being masculine.

5 SEX-DERIVATIVE GENDER CODING

Male/female differences that are classified as sex derivative are derived from the irreducible difference between male and female in procreation. Their derivation is by way of the sex hormones of the testicles and the ovaries, respectively. The differences for which the sex hormones are responsible are not absolute, however, but capable of overlap.

Some differences that might at first glance appear to be irreducible appear, upon closer analysis, to be derivative. Thus, to be bearded is predominantly a male characteristic, but some females are facially hirsute. The growth of hair on the face is under the control of androgen. Androgen insufficiency in a prepubertally castrated male suppresses the maturation of facial hair follicles at puberty or thereafter (and conversely prevents baldness). By contrast, too much androgen in a female encourages the growth of facial hair (and also balding of the head). After the hormonal changes of the menopause, facial hair becomes a more prevalent problem than at a younger age.

Insufficient hirsutism in men, and too much of it in women, may occur idiopathically in a family pedigree, without an underlying pathological etiology. When there is an underlying pathology, the extremes of either insufficiency or excess become exaggerated. For example, a woman with an androgen-producing tumor may become covered in body hair, like a hair-coated man. If androgen excess predates pubertal feminization, then a girl's pubertal maturation will be virilizing, and her body will develop to resemble that of a man in bone structure, shape, and overall appearance. The voice will also be deepened.

Breast growth or gynecomastia in the male is a counterpart of hirsutism in the female. A small and transient nubbin of glandular breast tissue below the nipple occurs idiopathically in as many as one in four pubertal boys. The underlying pathology that induces extreme gynecomastia in some cases defies an etiological diagnosis, whereas in others it may be an estrogen-producing tumor that is responsible. If breast tissue in a male is stimulated by an excess of the hormone prolactin, from the pituitary, it is capable of secreting milk, though not in large volume. Prolactin is normally secreted from the pituitary in males and females, though in differing quantities. It is at its highest level after parturition and for the duration of breast-feeding in mothers. In men, a very high level of prolactin, possibly in association with an underlying error in the release of the neurotransmitter dopamine, is known to interfere with the mechanism of penile erection, inducing impotence.

A dramatic example of the effect of transposing the blood hormone levels of males and females is seen in transexuals undergoing hormonal sex reassignment. Female-to-male transexuals treated with testosterone grow body and facial hair, and eventually may undergo balding if there are other males in the family pedigree who do also. The Adam's apple enlarges, thus lenthening the vocal cords and deepening the voice. Subcutaneous body fat lessens, and muscle mass increases (which is why athletes take testosterone and related anabolic steroids). Bone structure, once having matured beyond puberty into adulthood, does not alter (although it also may be masculinized prepubertally). Breast tissue does not disappear, although the breasts may shrink a little. The ovaries become dormant and menstruation ceases, but returns if the blood level of testosterone becomes too low, for which reason hysterectomy with ovariectomy is usually performed. The clitoris enlarges to its maximal potential, which is individually variable. The orgasm remains, and may be intensified in feeling. Whether or not fluid escapes through the urethra at the time of orgasm (from a presumed enlargement of the paraurethral glands, also known as the G-spot, or Grafenberg spot) remains unknown.

Male-to-female transexuals treated with estrogen grow breasts. As in normal females, their full size is determined not by hormone alone, but by the individually variable amount of undeveloped glandular tissue available to be hormonally stimulated into development. Muscle mass decreases, and subcutaneous body fat increases. Bone structure can be feminized only before puberty, not after the skeleton has undergone full postpubertal maturation. The growth of facial and body hair may be retarded, but not stopped. The hair fibers over a period of years may become more silken, but not eradicated, except by electrolysis. The voice, having once deepened, does not become high-pitched again, as in prepuberty. Under the influence of estrogen therapy, the testicles shrink and become dormant, and remain so for as long as the hormone is taken. The penis also shrinks, and loses some, if not all, of its erectile capability. The prostate and seminal vesicles shrink and become dormant so that there is no ejaculate. The feeling of orgasm is not necessarily lost, but becomes more a climax of body glow than a set of spasmodic contractions in the genital tract. All of these genital changes are reversible if estrogen therapy is discontinued.

Transexuals undergo hormonal reassignment so that their body-sex will be more congruous with their self-perceived mental sex. Mentally, masculine has already metamorphosed into feminine (or vice versa) before the taking of hormone. Thus the transexual condition does not provide information on the effect of sex hormones, if any, on bringing about the metamorphosis. The information recorded in Chapter 1, Section 3, indicates that the time for such a hormonal metamorphosis, if ever, is during prenatal life, with a possible short extension into neonatal life.

6 SEX-SHARED, THRESHOLD-DIMORPHIC GENDER CODING

Insofar as it might exist, sex-derivative, hormone-dependent gender coding of behavior does indeed appear to be a long-term aftereffect of prenatal and neonatal hormonal coding of the brain, according to such data (both animal experimental and human clinical) as are available today. This early hormonal coding does not, however, generate irreducible and immutable sex differences, but rather it changes the threshold for responses that are sex-shared but have different thresholds for their manifestation in males and females.

Parentalism is an example, for there are many species from rats to monkeys in which males, as compared with females, are inordinately slow to respond to the pleas of the young. In the rhesus monkey, for example, if a lonely baby bombards a father-aged male with signals, cajoling him to pay attention and be cuddling and protective, he sits, sublimely unresponsive, until at last the signals surmount the threshold barrier. Then he begins to cuddle and groom the young one exactly as the mother would do. The mother, by contrast, would have required not many minutes but only split-second timing to do the same. Juvenile females would also have done the same, though somewhat less rapidly than the mother. Juvenile males would have been more indifferent, like the adult male. Once the adult male responds, however, his body language is identical with that of the mother, whether in affectionate grooming or in gaping a bare-toothed threat at a potential intruder (Figure 2-1).

In addition to parenting, there are other sex-derivative, gender-coded ways of doing things in the agenda of existence that are sex-shared but threshold dimorphic. The one-word name for a way of doing things is praxon, from the Greek word, *praxis*, meaning custom or practice. A sex-shared, threshold-dimorphic praxon passes the test of the following criteria: it is widely distributed across species, especially primate species; in subhuman species its threshold dimorphism can be experimentally altered under the influence of sex hormones administered at a critical period of development, which is usually prenatal or neonatal; and in the human species there is some clinical evidence, consistent with the animal experimental evidence, that its dimorphic threshold is hormonally coded early in development and subsequently reinforced socially. The list of sex-shared, threshold-dimorphic praxons so far identified is subject to revision as more data are accumulated. At present it comprises nine items, as follows.

1. *Kinesis or overall muscular energy expenditure.* Especially in vigorous outdoor activities, it is more prevalent in boys than girls from infancy onward, not only after boys go through puberty and develop, on the average, a more muscular, taller, and heavier build than girls do. According to faulty popular stereotypes, boys who will become gay are more delicate and weak in body build than are those who will not, and vice versa for girls who will become lesbians. There are no statistics to back up these stereotypes, which are patently wrong in the case of gay football heros and lesbian fashion models, to take but two examples. As stereotypes, they may have originated in an erroneous conjecture derived from the fact that a boy is nicknamed a sissy if he is femininely self-identified and follows the sedentary pursuits traditionally ascribed to girls. There is no exact antonym of sissy to apply to girls. Tomboy does not carry the same pejorative connotation as sissy, and a tomboy is not socially stereotyped as a future lesbian, no matter how vigorous her kinetic energy expenditure.

2. *Roaming.* This is more prevalent in boys than girls. At all ages, roaming leads more boys than girls to their deaths. Phylogenetically, roaming is probably related to becoming acquainted with the boundary of the home

Figure 2-1. Father monkeys develop strong attachments to adopted infants (top left) and protect them (top right) much as natal mothers protect their own infants (bottom).

range. In subprimate species, boundary markers are odors or pheromones secreted by marking glands that are under the control of androgen. In primates, odor gives way to vision, and boundary markers are visual. Whether or not visual boundary marking is, like pheromonal marking, androgen related is purely speculative. So also is the hypothesis that the relationship to androgen is not only in maturity but prenatal also, when it androgenizes more boys than girls and eventually has an expanded effect not only on establishing the dimensions of the territory but on dimensions in general. Dimensionality is related to mathematical and praxic reasoning rather than verbal reasoning. In society today, there are more boys than girls among high achievers in mathematical and praxic reasoning. However, the tests of praxic reasoning are designed to be biased in favor of activities that are stereotypically prestigious for males—mechanical constructions, for instance, rather than fine arts or domestic arts and crafts.

The alternative to the prenatal androgenization hypothesis as applied to mathematical and praxic reasoning is that both are gender-coded not prenatally and hormonally but postnatally and socially, exclusively. The relationship of each hypothesis, separately or together, to stereotypes and the attribution of various occupations and achievements more prevalently to homosexuals than heterosexuals is conjectural only. To advance beyond conjecture, what is needed, as a first step, is a statistically controlled survey of the ratio of homosexual to heterosexual and bisexual men and women in different occupational categories. For informants, the risk of self-incrimination would put a formidable constraint on such a survey, as it does on all sexological research.

3. *Competitive rivalry, assertiveness, and jockeying for position in the dominance hierarchy of one's peer group.* It is more readily apparent in boys than girls, insofar as boys challenge one another and fight to obtain or maintain dominance by displaying aggressive superiority. Failure to meet a challenge to engage in dominance-rivalry fighting is sufficient for a boy to be labeled a sissy by his peers. It is often said, though not systematically and statistically confirmed, that prehomosexual boys are dubbed as sissies by their age-mates because they avoid fighting, and retreat when attacked. In adulthood, it is not universal but also not uncommon for gay men to recall that they had been labeled in this way (Bell, Weinberg, and Hammersmith, 1981), and that their place in the dominance hierarchy of boyhood was at the bottom. Other adult male homosexuals recall a history of a very macho boyhood, however. Extremely effeminate boys have a higher than average probability of growing up to be homosexual (Money and Russo, 1979; Green, 1986). Thus, a juvenile deficit in dominance aggression may be of predictive significance in the genesis of some, though not all, instances of homosexuality in males (see Section 9, this chapter). If so, then one may conjecture the hypothesis of a specific deficit in prenatal hormonalization of the brain. The converse conjectural hypothesis as applied to lesbianism would not presently be justified, as there is a paucity of evidence regarding an excess of dominance aggression in girls who become lesbians.

4. *Intruder aggression in fighting off marauders and predators.* In primate species, defense of the troop and its territory is typically more readily elicited in males than in females. Male defenders are more expendable than females without threat to species survival, since many females can breed with one male. The data are insufficient to allow speculation on whether or

not the levels of intruder aggression and dominance aggression are linked in either homosexuality or heterosexuality, male or female.

5. *Parental aggression in defense of the young.* In both popular and scientific mythology, women are characterized as passive because they have no Y chromosome and no male hormone. In actuality women are as deadly as men in jealous aggression, especially in love rivalry. They either are equal to or can surpass men in parental aggression in defense of the young. Lesbian or bisexual mothers are not known to be less or more aggressive than other mothers in defense of their children. Gay or bisexual fathers are neither more nor less aggressive than other fathers in defense of their children.

6. *Nestling the young, and providing a sheltered place not only for their birth but also their subsequent suckling and nurturance.* Nestling is bisexually coded in many species of birds, whereas it is female preponderant in mammals. In the human species it enters more into the play of girls than boys. When boys build shelters, they are in the category of treehouses, clubhouses, and forts, not nurseries for babies. It is possible that nestling goes together with domestic neatness in girls more than boys. There is a segment of the gay male population characterized by neat homemaking and aesthetic decoration, and of the lesbian population that lives in bachelor disarray. In each instance, there is no way of ascertaining whether homemaking or its lack is gender-coded on the basis of postnatal social example alone or with the assistance of prenatal hormonal coding for nestling.

7. *Parentalism.* This has already been mentioned (see above, this section). The animal experimental and human clinical evidence together indicate that the male/female difference in the threshold for parenting has a prenatal hormonal precursor determinant, but that there is a postnatal social overlay as well, especially in human beings. Men are capable of high-quality parentalism, as evident in those who become single parents. By contrast, women are capable of extreme cruelty and neglect as criminal child abusers. They do not have a generalized defect in parenting, for only one child becomes the sacrificial victim (Money, Annecillo, and Hutchinson, 1985). There are no adequate data from which to conclude whether or not there may be a prenatal hormonal coding positive for parentalism in gay men (or the converse in lesbian women). There is evidence, however, that a proportion of the gay male population is highly gifted in the service professions that require personalized attention, care, and nurturance—service that has traditionally been classified as women's work. The converse among some lesbian women is giftedness at men's traditional work. In both instances, the possibility of exclusively postnatal gender-coding on the basis of social learning cannot be ruled out.

8. *Positioning in sexual rehearsal play.* In the human species, there is a dearth of information concerning juvenile sexual rehearsal play in child-

hood development. To record sexual rehearsal play is to run the risk of being charged with the crime of sexual abuse of children. Possession of a nude picture of anyone under the age of eighteen is unconditionally a federal crime as soon as someone else sees it. The statutory age of childhood was increased from sixteen to eighteen by federal legislation in 1984, so as to enable prosecutors to enlarge the number of prosecutions for child molestation and abuse. In view of the prevailing ethos and judicial climate of the United States, it is impossible to get funding for research into the nature and outcome of sexual rehearsal play, even in those ethnic societies where the prevailing ethos does not forbid it. Although some information was recorded from those societies in an earlier, more auspicious era (Figure 2-2), for the most part anthropologists were obedient to the taboo under which they were reared and educated and did not record the sexuality of childhood in the same detail as primatologists record the sexuality of monkeys and apes (de Waal, 1987).

The lesson from primatology, learned especially from the rhesus monkey, is that young infants begin sexual rehearsal play at the age of three months, which is three years (more or less) before puberty (see Chapter 1, Section 3) (Figure 2.3). Initially they tumble and climb onto one another from front, rear, or either side, in twos and threes or more, without distinguishing boys from girls. After six months they have become proficient. Females stand on all fours in the presenting position. Males mount from behind with a footclasp mount. That is, they support themselves entirely on the female, clasping her ankles with their own feet and grasping her lower back with their hands. Monkeys reared in isolation never achieve this positioning and do not reproduce their species. One-third of isolation-reared monkeys achieve the footclasp mount if they are allowed half an hour a day to play with their age-mates, but with a delay until age eighteen to twenty-four months. Subsequently they produce fewer pregnancies than normal monkeys. Those that are raised in sex-segregated groups of all girls or all boys do their rehearsal play homosexually (Goldfoot et al., 1984). In adulthood they are bisexually capable, but are more at ease in homosexual than heterosexual partnerships. In both sexes, they change from mounting to presenting positions, and males mounting males achieve intromission.

Sexual rehearsal play emerges spontaneously in the repertoire of baby monkeys deprived of the opportunity to observe the example of copulation in older animals. Thus, it is not exclusively a product of postnatal social learning, although it is shaped by the opportunities available in the social environment, which can be manipulated to induce a degree of bisexuality. Among human beings, it is quite possible that there is a parallel effect of the interventions of the social environment on spontaneous sexual rehearsal play. It remains for another generation of homosexologists to find out whether children who will become homosexual have a different history of juvenile sexual rehearsal play than do children who will become heterosexual.

One hypothesis, awaiting confirmation, is that homosexual development

Figure 2-2. Normal juvenile sexual rehearsal play in children 5 or 6 years of age. Sequence reads from left to right down (telephoto lens, photographer anonymous, 1960).

Figure 2-3. Normal juvenile sexual rehearsal play in rhesus monkeys as manifested between 3 months and a year of age. Sequence reads from left to right and down (courtesy of David Goldfoot).

is facilitated by too great a deprivation, delay, or thwarting of heterosexual rehearsal play, or by traumatic humiliation and punishment for being caught engaging in it. Another hypothesis, also awaiting confirmation, is that homosexual development is facilitated by too much exposure to homosexual rehearsal play, or, possibly, by a too intense or too traumatizing exposure to homosexual rehearsal play, precociously or wrongly timed, or with a partner wrongly matched for age. A major source of trauma is the "catch-22" of doing something tabooed and prohibited, namely of being damned for disclosing it and damned for not disclosing it. All children are potentially victimized by this "catch-22" dilemma as it applies to their sexuoerotic development.

Facilitation does not mean causation. Orientation as homosexual, bisexual, or heterosexual cannot be attributed to the variable of sexual rehearsal play alone. It is determined multivariately.

9. *Visual sexuoerotic arousal.* There is no doubt that this is a sex-shared strategy that promotes mating, but the degree to which it is threshold dimorphic is more tentative. To be more precise, the degree to which threshold dimorphism is prenatally and hormonally, versus postnatally and socially determined, is tentative. The working hypothesis is that men are more dependent than women on the eyes for sexuoerotic arousal and initiative, and have a lower threshold barrier for sexuoerotic response to visual imagery and ideation. Women, by contrast, are more dependent than men on the skin senses for sexuoerotic arousal and initiative, and have a lower threshold for sexuoerotic response to tactual or haptic imagery and ideation. Evidence in support of prenatal hormonal coding of this visual/tactile threshold dimorphism is the prevalence among boys at puberty of wet dreams, while asleep, in which the visual imagery and ideation of their sexuoerotic turn-on presents itself, whereas among girls at puberty there is a lesser prevalence of sexuoerotic dreaming to orgasm while asleep. The extent to which this male/female difference will hold up under further scrutiny, and in cross-cultural comparisons, remains to be ascertained.

It is through the content of his wet dreams that a boy might get, if not a first intimation, then confirmation of his sexuoerotic future as homosexual, bisexual, or heterosexual. The dream will probably also give an additional premonition of whether his future will be homosexually or heterosexually normophilic or paraphilic. The imagery and ideation of the dream will reappear also in the context of a masturbation fantasy, from which it may be translated into homemade pornography. Eventually the designer of homemade pornography may discover that its theme is widely enough shared so that it has been mass-produced as commercial pornography. The corresponding pornography for girls is commercially produced as romantic narratives in which visual depiction is subsidiary to that of the skin senses, as in hugging, kissing, cuddling, fondling, as well as in "going all the way."

Homosexual and heterosexual men do not differ in being turned on by the eyes, but by what the eyes see, either in direct perception or in mental replay and imagination. Similarly with homosexual and heterosexual women and the skin senses: the difference is not in being aroused tactually, but in the sex of the partner with whom one is aroused. The depiction of homosexual imagery and ideation is not a turn-on for heterosexual people, and homosexual people are not turned on by heterosexual ideation and imagery. Those who turn on to both are bisexual.

7 SEX-ADJUNCTIVE GENDER CODING

In the conceptual line of descent, sex-derivative coding is descended from sex-irreducible coding by way of prenatal sex-hormonal coding. Sex-adjunctive coding is descended from sex-derivative coding by way of social coding that is an extension or adjunct of prenatal hormonal coding applied to the sex-divergent division of labor.

In evolutionary history, sex-divergent division of labor long antedates recorded history. Its basis is the diminished mobility of the female, as compared with the male, not only under the handicap of being pregnant, but even more so of suckling the dependent infant. Confined to home base, the work of the female extended from feeding the infant to feeding those of all ages, and doing also much else domestically in providing food, shelter, and clothing. Men's labor, by contrast, was compatible with mobility and compatible with long distances and long absences for war, work, or adventure, punctuated by intermittent breeding duties, and regular contributions to family sustenance. Men's mobility on foot eventually gave way to traveling in boats, on the backs of domesticated animals, or on wheels hauled by animals. When in recent history, horse-drawn vehicles gave way to automotive engines, driving the engines became work that was sex-coded for men. Building, maintenance, and repair of engines, the automobile included, is still sex-coded as men's more than women's work, although the code has been broken to some extent. Driving an automobile, which is not sex-coded in most contemporary jurisdictions around the world, is forbidden to women, even foreign visitors, in conservative Saudi Arabia. In that country, as elsewhere in Moslem culture, there is an ancient presupposition that an unescorted woman will be construed by male onlookers as potentially an adulteress or a whore. Thus it would be improper for her to be alone at the wheel of an automobile (Wikan, 1977), and so driving licenses are issued only to men.

Despite inconsistencies and contradictions across cultures, gender-coded division of labor is worldwide. It is transferred to the young as a gender-coded division of curriculum in extramural socialization as well as in academic education. It is incorporated into the doctrines and rituals of religion and so gains the prestige and authority of eternal verity, ordained by God and attributed to natural law.

In recent times, the gender-coded division of labor has been swept by a tidal change of history brought about by changes in the demographics of life expectancy and population crowding, by the invention of effective birth control and planning of family size, and by the irrelevancy of gender coding to automated and computerized labor-saving technology. The occupational roles of men and women have become interchangeable. Change threatens. Conservative segments of the population are threatened by gender uncoding of the division of labor, and they resist it, vehemently. For them it is against God and natural law. It is the equivalent of the forfeiture of masculinity and femininity in entirety—like a change of sex.

The resistant conservatives are wrong, of course. Unisex gender coding of occupational roles does not spill over into sexuoerotic roles, and does not change the sex of the partner with whom one falls in love. It does not change heterosexuality into homosexuality or bisexuality. If there is a social illusion to the contrary, then it stems from the error of reversing cause and effect when trying to account for the presence of homosexual men and women in occupations formerly coded, respectively, for females and males only. The phenomenon of men in women's occupations and women in men's occupations has an ancient history and a wide distribution across cultures. The explanation is that those who gravitate to a gender-transposed occupation in a society that has strict occupational gender coding do so on the basis of having grown up with a predisposition toward a gender-transposed career, insofar as they are sufficiently gender-transposed within themselves. Occupational gender crossing is something they assimilate and identify with from early childhood. In childhood the antecedents of occupational gender crossing in adulthood may be manifested in play that rehearses the occupations of adulthood. Thus, some gender-transposed boys will delight in designing clothing or interiors for women, or in styling their hair. Correspondingly, some gender-transposed girls will delight in being a stablehand or guerrilla terrorist, and so on.

Occupational rehearsal play is a prominent feature of childhood recreation. In addition, some of the gender-coded play of childhood becomes professionalized into gender-coded careers of adulthood—for example, professional fighting and professional big league sports that are symbolic battles. Childhood playacting itself and other expressions of the arts also may be developmental preparations for careers in adulthood that are gender-coded. Theatrical tradition that excludes women from the stage must cast men to act female roles, which creates the paradox that a man's career is to impersonate a woman. Female impersonation is an ideal vocation for those—effeminate male homosexuals, for example—who have a proclivity for role-taking, particularly if their proclivity is to take the role of a woman.

Occupational and recreational gender coding carry with them not only the force of custom and the weight of religion, but also the power of the law. The law distributes power between the sexes inequitably, and it penalizes those who do not conform to its edicts of gender coding, particularly with respect to the use of the sex organs. The power of the law is the link between sex-adjunctive and sex-adventitious gender coding.

8 SEX-ADVENTITIOUS GENDER CODING

Sex-adventitious gender coding, fourth in the line of descent, is descended from sex-adjunctive coding by way of an extension of social coding to the sex-divergent distribution of power. It is called adventitious gender coding because the gender-coded praxons or ways of doing things appear to be not intrinsic to sex but extrinsic, and to be arbitrarily distributed between males and females as signals of their sex. A second look, however, discloses that most, if not all, of these sex-adventitious praxons bear also a hidden agenda, namely the distribution of power unequally between the sexes. Throughout history and across cultures, males have generally been allocated more power over females than vice versa—in private and in public, in the bedroom and in the boardroom, academically and vocationally, economically and politically, morally and legally. In consequence, insofar as women have had power over men, it has of necessity been achieved deviously by stratagems of obduracy and neglect, conspiracy, seduction, and subterfuge—the sources of the proverbial power behind the throne. The antithesis of the tyrannized wife is the hen-pecked husband.

The assertion of power may appear innocuous enough when it is manifested in ornamentation, clothing style, grooming, cosmetics, and etiquette. However, the gender-coded way of doing things in these contexts may all add up to signify that women are showpieces of men's wealth and power and are dependent on them. They wear elongated, manicured fingernails as evidence of not being dependent on manual labor to earn a living. They teeter on spike-heeled shoes as evidence of not requiring a peasant stance in order to work, and as evidence also of a mincing walk that requires support on slick or rugged surfaces. Had they been born as recently as half a century ago in China, girls at age six might have had their feet bound and crippled so that their fathers could use their incapacity to walk as evidence of family wealth sufficient to support them, unemployed, until a wealthy husband is found.

Mutilation of the genitalia as a demonstration of authority and power is widely diffused across cultures and includes circumcision of both males and females. In northern and eastern Africa above the equator, girls at around the age of seven have their genital organs cut upon—the clitoris, labia minora, and labia majora completely extirpated, in the extreme form of pharaonic circumcision, and the wound left to heal with only a pinpoint opening (Lightfoot-Klein, 1987). When they marry, sexual intercourse is a form of tyranny, for the husband is obliged to tear or cut the opening larger.

Mutilating, stretching, piercing, scarifying, tattooing, and painting various parts and organs of the body serves in many cultures as a form of visible gender coding. The style of haircut does the same. So also, if the body is covered, does clothing style, which often accommodates to the urinary posture.

Gender coding of the appearance of the body goes along with gender coding of language usage and vocalization, and of body language and gesture, all of which vary culturally. In some cultures there is also gender coding of edible flora and fauna, some for men only and some for women only; and also gender coding of where and when to eat, and with whom to share the meal.

The human species in many of its cultures has been very inventive in the application of sex-adventitious gender coding to declare the sex of an individual on the basis of extrinsic evidence independently of exposing the intrinsic evidence, namely the genitalia. Of course, it is assumed that the extrinsic and intrinsic evidence are concordant. However, developing youth do not invariably arrive at this assumption. Instead they may dissociate the extrinsic from the intrinsic evidence, as when romantic love is gender-coded as extrinsic and extragenital, whereas carnal lust is coded as intrinsic and belonging to the genitals. The discordance between the two may never be reconciled. If, in addition, the extrinsic and the intrinsic evidence are discordantly gender-coded, one as male and one as female, respectively, then one has a person with female external genitalia and a position somewhere between the bisexual midpoint and the exclusive female homosexual extreme point of the gender-divergent continuum. Vice versa, the same principle applies when the external genitalia are male, bisexualism is the midpoint, and exclusive male homosexuality the extreme point.

Exclusive male homosexuality in adulthood, including long-term pair-bondedness with a lover, was the outcome of a split between extrinsic and intrinsic gender coding in one longitudinally followed case. The split had had its onset very early in life, before the boy was seven. It was at this age that his pediatrician had referred him and his parents by adoption for evaluation of incongruous gender role. He did, indeed, manifest a high degree of incongruence between the intrinsic sex of his male genitalia and the extrinsic sex of gender coding, which was predominantly female. With the covert and ambivalent collusion of his parents, he had reached the stage of reducing the gender chaos generated at home by adopting the proposition that he would change to be a girl. Having been taught that God has the power to answer prayer, he dealt with the contradictory evidence of his penis by praying to be changed into a girl. He had formulated his own theory that God had two ways of creating a girl. One was to have her born as a girl. The other was to have her born with a penis that would eventually drop off. In his highly intelligent mind, his theory was as logical as that a navel showed where an umbilical cord had dried up and dropped off, or that nipples showed where breasts would enlarge.

9 IDENTIFICATION AND COMPLEMENTATION

In development that is destined to end up heterosexually, identification is the process of applying to oneself the example and precepts of those who are accorded the same sex as oneself—the same gender-dimorphic nouns and pronouns, the same extrinsic evidence of sex over and beyond language, and the same intrinsic and primary evidence, namely the sex of the external genitalia. Concurrently, complementation is the process of diverging oneself from the example and precepts of those who are accorded the sex other than oneself, and of having their gender-coded identification reciprocate one's own.

Gender identification and complementation are coded not only as templates in the mind. Each is coded also as a template or schema in the brain. Mind and brain constitute one unity. Typically the identification schema is coded also as mine, instructing me about myself, and the complementation schema is thine, instructing me about you and what to expect from you. In most people, regardless of their orientation as heterosexual, bisexual, or homosexual, the two schemas are coded in conformity with the male and female sex of the genitalia and have boundaries that keep them fairly separate and discrete, even though there may be a zone of androgynous overlap.

Developmentally, identification and complementation in gender coding are analogous to listening and speaking in language acquisition. For example, children who are developmentally bilingual do better in acquiring each language if the people who speak each language not only speak that language exclusively, but also listen in it exclusively. To get attended to and listened to, and to obtain a response, the child has no alternative but to speak the listener's language and not to mix it up with the second language.

The same principle of listening and talking was also made evident to me in the case of two children, siblings, referred for severe linguistic disability in the early years of grade school. They were the only two children of parents with a history of congenital total deafness whose communications with others, including their children, was exclusively in sign language. Until they went to school, the children had lived in seclusion, ostensibly to be protected from the jeers and persecutions of their age-mates because of their peculiar speech. Almost their sole contact with spoken English was on television, which they watched regularly. But they did not speak with the syntax of television English. Instead they used what could only be described as the spoken dialect of sign language, with its own idiom and syntax. Evidently, the language that got for them the attention and response of their parents took priority, in their linguistic brains, over television language. They were permanently handicapped as far as the world of school was concerned.

Some languages more than others differentiate forms of speech on the criteria of the sex of the speaker and the sex of the person addressed. Thus the dimorphism of sex plays a role in language acquisition that reinforces other postnatal, social gender coding during the developmental years of childhood. Gender coding is by definition dualistic. One-half of the code is for female, the other for male. A child must assimilate both halves of the code, identifying with one and complementating the other.

I first recognized the importance of the principle of complementation as the missing half of the long-familiar principle of identification in the case of a family whose second child at birth had the genital appearance of a girl and was declared a girl (Chapter 7 in Money and Ehrhardt, 1972b). At nine days of age, biopsy samples from the two small masses in the labioscrotal folds showed them to be imperfectly testicular, and the sex chromatin test was found to be negative, that is, chromosomally male. On the basis of these findings, the child was reannounced as a boy. This decision was reversed at the age of seventeen months, in view of the extreme demasculinization of the genitalia and their failure to show a masculinizing response to an ointment containing male hormone (testosterone). After seventeen months of rearing their child as a boy, the parents and their other child, a boy aged four, had to get used to having a daughter and sister.

In the month after her third birthday, the father told a story about his response to his daughter's dancing. "During the week," he said, "when I come home, the four of us go upstairs and put a record on and dance. For a while, she watched her brother do jitterbug-type dancing and wanting to copy him. But I would pick her up and put her cheek to cheek. Now she wants to do that all the time." Thus the family tradition became established that the girl dances with her father, who *complementates* her role in which she identifies with her mother. The mother dances with her son, complementating her role to his, in which he identifies with his father.

The two principles, identification and complementation, fit hand-in-glove. Both are essential to understanding the acquisition of sex coding. Contrary to standard psychodynamic doctrine, they apply not only between child and parents, but also between child and other people of significance who, typically, are present in person, although they may be characters on television or in print.

The people with whom boys and girls identify and complementate are not only adults, but may be also those of their own age or only a few years older whom they admire, idolize, or hero-worship. The power of the peer group in identification and complementation during childhood is both positive and negative. It sets fashions and standards of conformity, imposes sanctions, and stigmatizes nonconformists. For example, boys who fail to respond to attack by fighting back, and who do not meet challenges for position in the dominance hierarchy of childhood, are stigmatized as sissy. Conversely, girls who challenge the dominance of boys are stigmatized as unladylike.

In the case of children with a diagnostic history of male hermaphroditism (Money, Devore, and Norman, 1986; Money and Norman, 1987), gender stigmatization derives from their having birth-defective genitalia that may disqualify them from being either properly a boy, or properly a girl. In such cases, a childhood history of stigmatization correlates with the development of a gender transposition manifested as bisexuality, or as homosexuality within the sex of rearing, or as reassignment from the sex of rearing to the other sex.

In the case of children born with anatomically normal genitalia, gender stigmatization derives from nonconformity to the gender stereotype of behavior, no matter what the basis or origin of their nonconformity. In the case of boys who are stigmatized as sissy for not fighting, the origin of their lack of aggressiveness has not yet been ascertained. It might, conceivably, be a sequel to prenatal insufficiency of hormonal masculinization (see Section 6, this chapter). By itself alone, however, nonaggressiveness does not lead to sissiness, but to being stigmatized as a sissy. Stigmatization itself thereupon becomes not an effect, but a determinant of future development toward gender transposition. Thus may be explained the failure to have engaged in rivalry and fighting for a position of power in the dominance hierarchy of childhood, which is prevalent, although not universal in the juvenile histories, retrospectively recalled, of adult homosexual males. The same phenomenon is recorded in the prospective study of boys who become adult homosexuals (Money and Russo, 1979).

Identification and complementation pertain not only to gender coding that is sex adjunctive and sex arbitrary, but also to gender coding that is sex derivative. Sex-derivative praxons, the ways of doing things that are sex-shared but threshold dimorphic, include the copulatory positionings of presenting and mounting. In primates, procreative success requires juvenile sexual rehearsal play in order to guarantee the success of both sexes in copulatory positioning in maturity (see Section 6, this chapter). In the human species, some societies are positive and some negative with respect to sexual rehearsal play in children.

In our own society, children are consistently deprived of access to explicit examples of copulation. Except surreptitiously, they have no exposure to copulatory identification and complementation exemplars or models whom they might emulate for gender-dimorphic copulatory success. Their own copulatory-play improvisations are vituperatively abused and traumatically penalized. Unless they are fortunate enough to have unorthodox parents or guardians who approve of the premonitory signs of their copulatory heterosexuality, they are extravagantly punished and humiliated for showing explicit signs of being heterosexual with their sex organs. At the same time as they are victims of punishment and humiliation for being heterosexual, the evidence of their senses is that there is less supervision and policing of occasions and opportunities for boy–boy or girl–girl sexual rehearsal play.

In an attenuated form, there is something of the culture of the Sambia (see Chapter 1, Section 1) present in our own. Clandestinely and unspoken, one of the presuppositions of our society is that, before and apart from marriage, homosexual encounters are preferable to heterosexual, because they are sterile. Hence the contradictory logic of punishing homosexual men and women by imprisoning them with their own sex, while failing to recognize the paradox and irrationality of what we do—even though, in the present era, sex-segregated prisons become breeding grounds for HIV–I, the AIDS virus, and the spread of the epidemic, since official recognition of devices for safer sex is construed as an offense against sexual morality. Similarly, we fail to recognize in full the illogicity of sex-segregated educational, recreational, religious, military, and other institutions for pubertal and adolescent boys and girls, although admittedly the prevalence and influence of such institutions has waned as compared with a century ago.

The organs of gender identification and gender complementation are the eyes, the ears, the skin senses, and probably to a lesser degree the organs of smell and taste. The gender identification/complementation program or schema that is socially coded into the brain via the senses is no less potent than is that part of the program or schema that precedes it and is coded into the brain prenatally by hormones carried in the fetal bloodstream.

In postnatal life, gender coding of the brain via the senses may become immutable, as is the case with native language. A native language can fall into disuse, but it can be eradicated only by brain damage from a cerebrovascular accident (stroke) or by the action of a neurosurgeon's knife. It cannot be eradicated by being unlearned or behaviorally modified into nonexistence. So also with the coding of gender-identity/role (G-I/R) and, in particular, its sexuoerotic component as homosexual or heterosexual. It may become as immutable as is native language, no matter how many additional languages are superimposed.

There are no data from which to evaluate individual difference in adeptness at identification and complementation. It is highly likely, however, that some children are more adept than others—in the way that great actors are adept at becoming identified with the character whose role they enact and, in doing so, complementate it to the roles of other members of the cast on stage.

Children do, in fact, have to assimilate a multiplicity of identifications and complementations that apply not only to the male/female disparity. There are age disparities also. The identification and complementation schemas that apply among peers differ from those that apply to parent-aged adults, which in turn differ from those that apply to grandparent-aged adults. In addition to sex and age disparities, there are disparities that pertain to troopbonding, and separate "us" from "them." The criteria for these disparities and the identification and complementation schemas that they entail are language, race, skin color, religion, wealth, authority, and so on.

Developmentally, identification/complementation schemas may adhere together and form a more-or-less cohesive whole. Or they may become decentralized, with one or more of them taking on a quasi-autonomous existence, as manifested in dual- or multiple-personality phenomena. I recall, for example, a boy who was being evaluated at age seven for gender-crosscoded development. He was one of a cohort of boys with incongruous gender development referred by pediatricians on my request for a study to complement the study on gender development in hermaphroditic children. (Richard Green, who at that time was a Johns Hopkins medical student, assisted in the study.) Upon request, this boy was able separately to demonstrate being a girl and being a boy, using for each the appropriate body language and manner of talking.

It was around this same time, more than twenty-five years ago, in the course of the long-term follow-up of the boys in this gender incongruity study, that it dawned on me that several of the twenty boys had a prepotent and persistent interest in dramatics. This interest was documented in the clinical histories of nine of the twenty boys, in one case as early as age three, and in the others between the ages of six and ten when they were first seen. The three year-old was lost to follow-up. The others, at the time of follow-up in mid-teenage, still pursued drama as either an avocation or a future career (Green and Money, 1966).

The boyhood playacting in these cases had provided the boys with a legitimate opportunity to dress up as a girl or woman and play a female role. It raises the chicken-and-egg controversy of whether they took up playacting so as to express their feminine crosscodedness, or whether they became femininely crosscoded as a sequel to a special talent or adeptness, on stage and off, for taking on a changed role and with it a changed identity. If the latter, then gender crosscoding requires only a quite simple switch: the identification and complementation schemas change places, reversing their gender plus-and-minus signs, so to speak. Both are coded in toto in the brain, ready for use. For a typical boy, identification is coded as male and mine; and complementation as female and thine. Crosscoded, the complementation schema becomes female and mine; and identification as male and thine.

Later in development, versatility in making the male-to-female switch may be either retained or lost. It begins to be lost early in development in those boys destined to become male-to-female transexuals—and likewise in female-to-male transexuals. In its more restricted, sexuoerotic application, it becomes lost also in those boys and girls who grow up to become exclusively homosexual, able to be sexuoerotically attracted toward and to fall in love with only a person of their own sex. It is retained, at least in part, in those who become bisexual. It is retained with a flamboyant dramatic flare in those boys who become travestophiles with two names, two wardrobes, and two personalities (Money, 1976). They may also have two occupations and two sex lives, one as a male and one as a female. With advancing age, the episodic alternation of male and female personalities in some transvestophilic men metamorphoses into full-time living as a woman, and as a preoperative male-to-female transexual bent on hormonal and surgical sex reassignment.

Such a metamorphosis from episodic transvestophile to full-time male-to-female transexual does not necessarily preclude the possibility that, even after sex reassignment surgery, the male-coded personality may return. In one such case (Money and Wolff, 1973), the patient first appeared dressed in the unisex garb of Sandy, the eunuchoid personality who was neither Lloyd, the preoperative male, nor Lusanne, the postoperative, sex-reassigned female, but a compromise who had actually predated the autonomous existence of Lusanne. Sandy was in a suicidal crisis. In an early interview, she requested in her soft-spoken, feminine, falsetto voice that I look away while she went to the far side of the room. There the booming, baritone voice of Lloyd made itself heard, declaring Lloyd's intention to return and displace Sandy, and Lusanne with her. Lloyd did return, and the suicidal crisis dissipated.

In another, somewhat similar case of male-to-female sex reassignment, the return of the male-coded personality was transient. It occurred when Bertha, a very elegant middle-aged blonde in a red convertible, was sexually harassed by a gas station attendant. Out of the blue, Bertram, the retired military officer, took over, raged at the attendant, upturned him into an empty 44-gallon oil drum, shoved a ten-dollar bill into his back pocket to pay for the gas, and then drove off, triumphantly, as Bertha again.

10 EPILOGUE AND SYNOPSIS

In the theology of natural law, there is decreed an absolute standard of what is normal in sex, and that standard is procreation. If we were a species in which all the sexual acts of all males were exact replications of one another, and the same for females, then there would be an absolute standard by which to measure masculinity and femininity. That being not the case, we as a species must live with two standards of normality, the statistical and the ideological. The statistical norm tells us what the majority of people do most of the time. The ideological norm tells us what everybody ought to do all of the time in conformity to an ideological standard set up by a moral, religious, or legal authority.

There are neither divine nor scientific revelations as to what is absolutely pure masculinity or absolutely pure femininity, for the same reason that there are no such revelations as to what is absolutely pure language. There is no measurement of language until it is already being used. Similarly, there is no measurement of masculinity or of femininity until they are already being manifested. No one ever argues that one's own native language is innate, for it self-evidently is learned. By contrast, there are many who argue that masculinity or femininity is innate or instinctive. Yet, the very existence of differing ideological norms is evidence enough that masculinity/femininity is not innate, at least not in its entirety. Like language, the masculinity or femininity of gender-identity/role (G-I/R) needs a healthy human brain in which to take root. Metaphorically, the developing limbs and buds of the G-I/R are shaped by the environment in which it grows and from which it assimilates its mental nourishment through the sense organs into the brain. Whether innate or assimilated, once the masculinity, ambisexuality, or femininity of G-I/R gets into the brain, it becomes rooted there, in perpetuity, irrespective of its conformity to either the statistical norm or the ideological norm. Since there are many different ideological norms, there are many different ways of being masculine, feminine, or mixed.

With respect to your own G-I/R as a whole, the masculinity and/or femininity of your gender role is like the outside of a revolving globe that everyone can observe and read the meaning of. Inside the globe are the private workings of your gender identity. Even if the interior is lighted, it does not give outside observers the same degree of intimate internal access that you yourself possess. There is only one person who has maximum direct access to your gender identity. That person is yourself. Yet even you may not have total, unrestricted, and direct access to every detail of its past and future differentiation and development.

There are not many different ways in which the procreative component of a G-I/R can express itself, although there are some alternatives in this present era. There is donor insemination, for example, and in vitro fertilization—and, yes, even the possibility for a male to carry a pregnancy. Nonetheless, if there is any sex difference that can be said to be absolute and irreducible, it is that men impregnate, and women menstruate, gestate, and lactate.

All other sex differences are not authentically sexual in the genitosexual sense of G-I/R, unless they involve the function or use of the organs of procreation. Rather, they are differences between people who are classified as different on the basis of having different sex organs, male or female. Of course, people could be classified not as different, but as similar, on the criterion that we all have similar heads, arms, and feet. However, it is not the similarity but the difference between the sexes that has fascinated human beings for millennia. Because sex differences are not only genitally sexual, although they may be secondarily derived from the procreative organs, I found a need some thirty years ago for a word under which to classify them. That word, which has now become accepted into the language, is gender. Everyone has a G-I/R, one part of which is one's genital or genitosexual G-I/R.

Most G-I/R differences are not absolute or irreducible, although there is a male/female difference in how easily they make their appearance. In other words, they are sex-shared, but threshold dimorphic. For example, mother animals are attuned to respond immediately to an infant's cry of distress. If the father is around, he is much slower at first, but eventually he does respond, and his response is the same as the mother's. Both have the response pattern microchipped into their brains, but one has a fast turn-on threshold, and the other a slow one.

There are three grades of G-I/R difference. The grade closest to the irreducible sex difference is the sex-derivative grade. It is closest because of its association with the hormones secreted by the gonads, the ovaries and testicles. Male and female differences in feats of strength are an illustration. They are different because of the different effects of male and female hormones on the growth of bone, muscle, and fat padding.

One grade further down the scale are the sex-adjunctive differences, that are not directly associated with hormones, but with their sex-derived effects. For example, until the recent invention of labor-saving devices and baby food, women when pregnant and breast-feeding were obliged to be more sedentary than men. In the division of labor, they became responsible for homebound labor, whereas men roamed farther afield. Eventually roaming on foot changed to riding on domesticated animals and then in wheeled vehicles. Even today auto mechanics are men more often than they are women.

Still further down the scale, and related to the distribution of power, are sex-arbitrary differences, for example, in the use of cosmetics, body adornment, speech patterns, and body language. Arbitrary differences in clothing style partly reflect differences in urinary posture. Differences in adornment also reflect the woman's dependence on the man, as she wears his wealth to exhibit his power and prestige, and his authority over her.

Homosexual men and women do not differ, respectively, from heterosexual men and women with respect to the irreducible sex difference of procreative fertilty. They, too, can, and in many cases do, become parents (which, to be literal and exact, means that they have a bisexual history). The differences between homosexuals and heterosexuals are primarily at the sex-arbitrary grade, to a somewhat lesser degree at the sex-adjunctive level, and to a still lesser extent at the sex-derivative level. There are many different permutations and combinations. To illustrate: two male homosexuals may have in common only their erotic attraction toward the male as an erotic partner. One may be femininely oriented at each grade of sex-shared, threshold-dimorphic difference, and the other masculinely oriented. The former is a female-impersonating drag queen, and the latter a macho military hero, perhaps. Both are capable of fertility as males.

Identification with exemplars of one sex, and complementation to exemplars of the other sex are the two great sexological principles by which G-I/R is established in the course of growing up. Nature and nurture combine in the working of both principles, and they do so at critical periods of development, at the conclusion of which they leave a permanent residual or imprint. One important critical period is the extended one of juvenile sexual rehearsal play. Mismanagement of this period is a major feature of the childrearing customs that are our social heritage. When not mismanaged, juvenile sexual rehearsal play progressively evolves typically into heterosexual rehearsal play. The history of juvenile sexual rehearsal play in those who become homosexual males or females in adulthood still has not been systematically ascertained. It may or may not play a causative role, or it may be an early effect of a homosexual G-I/R in the making. Either way, the history of sexual rehearsal play and its vicissitudes should have predictive significance. It is a priority for future research.

CHAPTER

THREE

Gender Crosscoding

1 RELATIVITY OF MASCULINITY AND FEMININITY

In a sexophobic society, of which our own is an example, extrinsic, nongenital evidence of gender coding is extensively separated or dissociated from the intrinsic evidence of the external genitalia. From one generation to the next, continuity of this dissociation is maintained by the indoctrination of children from infancy onward. Dissociation is also institutionalized as a principle of fashion, morality, and religion, and in the law it is institutionalized under the Fifth Amendment, which grants an informant the right of silence so as to avoid self-incrimination.

By the laws of logic, that which is extrinsic and that which is intrinsic may be either congruous or incongruous. Thus for a child growing up in a culture that institutionalizes separation and dissociation of the extrinsic from the intrinsic manifestations of gender coding, there is a certain arbitrariness as to whether the two will be, in that child, personally coded as concordant or discordant. If concordant, the two will be either both masculine or both feminine. If discordant, they will be crosscoded. That is to say, the intrinsic evidence of the genitalia (intrinsic coding) will be discordant with the extrinsic evidence of gender dimorphism (extrinsic coding). When discordance exists in a child with male genitalia, he will appear to be effeminate; and a child with female genitalia will appear to be masculinate.

There is a covert assumption in the foregoing, namely, that there are absolute criteria against which to define both the extrinsic and intrinsic evidence of gender (see Chapter 2, Section 1). But there are no absolute standards, only approximations. Having a penis does not inevitably guarantee even that the other parts of the pelvic procreative anatomy will be male, not to mention the sexual neuroanatomy of the brain. Nor does having a vulva guarantee complete female reproductive anatomy in either the pelvis or the brain (see Chapter 1, Section 3). In addition, ethnocultural relativity in gender coding is so great that what one society endorses, another repudiates—as in the coding of homosexuality as an imperative of masculinity among the tribal Sambia of New Guinea, and as a repudiation of masculinity in our own society (Chapter 1, Section 1).

One way out of the dilemma of relativity is to tolerate it. Thus in genetics, one tolerates the stipulation that the genetic male is chromosomally XY and the female XX, despite the undisputed evidence that some males are XX, XXY, and XYY, not to mention a multiplicity of chromosomal mosaics (e.g., 46,XY/47,XXY); and females are likewise XY, XO, XXX, and mosaic (e.g., 45,X/46,XY). In traditional biology, one tolerates the stipulation that male is sperm-bearing and female is egg-bearing, despite their relativity in hermaphroditic species in which the same individual bears both eggs and sperms. In comparative sexology, one tolerates the stipulation that having a penis is the criterion of being male and having a vulva is the criterion of being female, despite their relativity in the intersexual or hermaphroditic syndromes. Rigid coding of the XY/XX, the sperm/egg, and the penis/vulva criteria as, respectively, male/female imposes a too rigid antithesis on the coding of what is male and what female in mating behavior, by excluding the relativity of behavior that may be to some degree sex-shared.

In human sexology, one tolerates the penis/vulva criterion as a good enough approximation for stipulating that masculine is what males do and feminine is what females do. As an approximation, however, it is far from perfect, because of the high degree of cultural relativity in the social stipulation of gender coding. The hazard of cultural relativity is that it is conducive to cultural chauvinism. The danger of cultural chauvinism for a science of sexology is that the stipulations of one culture (usually one's own, of course) will be universalized, and the cultural lessons of human gender diversity, worldwide, will be lost.

Extrinsic gender coding is inextricably culture bound. Like native language, it cannot be tested until it has already been culturally acquired. There is no escape from a culture-bound to a culture-free stipulation of the criteria of masculine and feminine in extrinsic gender coding. There is no alternative to a culture-bound definition that contains, explicitly, an admission that it is a culturally relative approximation to a universal definition of extrinsic gender coding as masculine and feminine. Such a culture-bound definition is a good enough approximation, but only for study of gender coding or crosscoding in the culture to which it is bound. It will require modification for application to other geographical and historical cultures.

2 PRENATAL PROCLIVITY AND POSTNATAL DEFLECTION

In both boys and girls, gender cross-identification and cross-complementation are not inevitably predestined in prenatal life by gender-crossed hormonalization of the brain. Rather, the gender crossing of identification/complementation is facilitated if there is a proclivity stemming from prenatal brain hormonalization that bisexually combines masculinization with feminization, either equally, in a 50 : 50 ratio, or unequally, in a disproportionate ratio, such as 60 : 40 or 20 : 80, and so on.

Prenatal brain bisexuality and postnatal bisexuality of identification/ complementation may be exactly matched in their masculine/feminine proportions. However, in our society, growing children recognize the polarization of masculine and feminine. The gravitational pull, socially, is away from ambisexual or bisexual toward monosexual. A developing child encounters few models or exemplars of a bisexual mode of existence. The masculine and the feminine monosexual models, even though idealized and stereotyped, are ubiquitous. Sex is a binary system. If masculine doesn't fit, the alternative is feminine, not androgyny. Correspondingly, the alternative to feminine is masculine.

The magnet of monosexuality notwithstanding, external gender coding may be deflected toward bisexuality provided a prenatal proclivity toward bisexuality, in which masculinity and femininity are equitably proportioned, is matched by postnatal forces of deflection that also are equitably proportioned, in the midrange between masculine and feminine.

The more likely probability is one that would produce a disproportional bisexuality with either heterosexuality or homosexuality predominating. Disproportional bisexuality might be expected to eventuate when two strong forces meet. Thus, if a strong prenatal heterosexual proclivity is met by a strong postnatal deflection toward homosexuality, a bisexual potential that is predominantly heterosexual and subdominantly homosexual is likely to ensue. Conversely, a strong prenatal homosexual proclivity matched by a strong postnatal deflection toward heterosexuality is likely to produce a predominantly homosexual and subdominantly heterosexual potential.

The odds would be in favor of a heterosexual outcome if a strong prenatal heterosexual proclivity is strongly reinforced postnatally, with or without a weak deflection toward homosexuality.

The converse applies to a homosexual outcome. The odds would be in its favor if a strong prenatal homosexual proclivity is strongly reinforced postnatally, with or without a weak deflection toward heterosexuality.

Postnatal homosexual reinforcement of a prenatal homosexual proclivity does not mean participation in actual homosexual genital practices from an early age. Some adolescent and adult homosexuals do report such a history, but the majority do not. In the prospective longitudinal study of boys who become homosexual in adulthood (Money and Russo, 1979), there were none who had early homosexual genital contact. For them, reinforcement of what matured into homosexual eroticism began rather as an endorsement of gender crosscoding, possibly related to sensuous closeness and affectionate closeness with a male, in some instances a father. By contrast, boys who in late childhood establish an explicitly sexual and genital relationship with an older, pedophilic male lover are not inevitably foreordained to have a homosexual status in adolescence and adulthood (Money and Weinrich, 1983).

Contrary to established doctrine, the fathers of boys who exhibit gender crosscoding do not repudiate their sons' masculine insufficiency and conformity to girlish criteria of development. They are more or less acquiescent and regard it as something that will be grown out of. The following excerpt (Money, 1984b) illustrates.

For years, I did not know what to make of this paternal blandness and indifference. I had no hypothesis until a few years ago when a psychiatrist consulted me about his own son, aged five, the younger of two children, both boys. He and his wife excluded the boy from a family appointment, ostensibly to spare him from stigmatizing himself as abnormal. In my office, they distanced themselves from one another, spatially and verbally. Their matrimonial relationship was that of wedded adversaries practicing insidiously clever strategies of mutual sabotage. For example, even though he was a professed agnostic, the husband criticized his wife for being religiously too laissez faire. She reacted by becoming an orthodox conservative. Family religious observances became a source of unending dispute.

The rift thus created was additionally widened in disputation regarding acoustic sensitivity. For her, loud music was noxious, so he was obliged to pursue his interest in live rock performances without her. In fantasy, he anticipated that his younger son would become his companion in music. The older son, by contrast, already at age eight coerced his reluctant father to share his all-boy interest in fishing and the outdoors.

Professionally trained to be self-analytic, this father was also self-revealing. After soliciting my prognosis of his son's cross dressing and girlish inclinations, and hearing that it was not necessary to be pessimistic about change in a boy so young as age five, he asked why he was feeling so angry with me—and angry because of what I had said. My reply was to the effect that perhaps he didn't wholly want his son to stop cross dressing, and did not want to be robbed of the one member of the family whom he might consider his special escort.

Subsequently, I dictated a note "to put on record a new hypothesis or formula regarding the role of the father in the genesis of feminism in a son's G-I/R (gender-identity/role). This is the formula: the father covertly courts his son's allegiance, in place of what he finds missing in his wife, and casts him in the role of a wife substitute, if not for the present, then for the future." The son, for his part, may solicit his father's allegiance as a formula for keeping him in the household, and for preventing a parental separation. If the father has already gone, or even if he had died, the son's gender transposition may serve to solicit his dad's miraculous return. His life becomes a living fable of the boy who will become daddy's bride, for the evidence is plentiful that a daddy can be counted on to return to the home that his wife keeps ready for him.

The significance of this note is twofold. First, it recognizes the importance of the postnatal psychodynamics of a child's early life, superimposed on the hormodynamics of his prenatal life, in contributing to the differentiation of his G-I/R as masculine or feminine. Second, with respect to psychogenic theory regarding the etiology of homosexuality, it upends Freudian oedipal orthodoxy by replacing seduction of the mother with seduction of the father. In addition, it upends Stoller's neo-Freudianism, object-relations theory that symbiotic unity in infancy between a mother and her son destines him to become a male-to-female transexual (Stoller, 1968). However, there is, as yet, no psychodynamic theory of the etiology of homosexuality, transexualism, or any other manifestation of gender transposition that is, by itself alone, scientifically satisfactory.

Within a family, the allocation or reallocation of roles is not necessarily covert. It is more or less inherent in the idea of naming or nicknaming a baby after an ancestor, parent, or other relative, and also in the wisdom of the kin regarding a particular relative whom the child takes after. Parents have favorite children—mommy's boy, daddy's girl—just as children may favor one parent over the other, or one relative over another.

The young son who becomes self-allocated to the role of daughter, and thereby becomes a bonding agent who keeps the family intact, is likely to keep that role of bonding agent in perpetuity. He reaches adulthood with a gender status that is homosexual or maybe, in a rare minority of cases, transexual or transvestophile.

There is now new preliminary evidence, unpublished, that the gender-crosscoded course of events may be changed if the child can be relieved of the self-imposed responsibility of keeping his feuding parents together. In one case, that of a three-year-old, the gravity of the boy's responsibility for keeping the parents together could be measured against the intensity of the father's response when he was confronted with the possibility of losing a custody battle in the event of divorce. That was absolutely out of the question so far as he was concerned, he said, and he hinted darkly at homicide rather than permit it to happen.

The son's change away from girl-imitative behavior ensued with unexpected rapidity in the immediate aftermath of the family's first visit—a marathon five hours of individual evaluations and joint discussions. The change in the boy was concomitant with a change in the parents, insofar as they achieved more focus on their homemaking compatibility as parents, and less on their total sexual and erotic incompatibility.

They were strongly compatible in their professional and domestic lives, and equally incompatible in their sex lives. In six years of follow-up, their sexual and erotic incompatibility has remained stubbornly intractable to change. Nonetheless, there was only one brief occasion when it threatened to bring an end to their other compatibilities. It was then that a resurgence of effeminacy threatened in the boy. It was transient. It did not, as had been the case in the original diagnostic toy-play sessions, generate dramas of desperation in which members of a toy family became victims of catastrophe, abusive violence, destruction, and murder.

This boy's play enactments of violence and destruction had not included any dramas of explicit erotic or sexual content. Nor was there a history of overtly initiated erotic or sexual conduct other than age-typical masturbation in private, which the parents did not condemn. On the contrary, rather than appear repressive, the father tolerated and perhaps covertly condoned his son's masturbation when he read stories to him at bedtime. If the boy experienced homosexual erotosexual imagery, its existence and content in his dreams and fantasies have remained private and undisclosed. That does not necessarily mean there has been none. Explicit erotosexual fantasies with the father as partner have been retrospectively dated to boyhood by some young adult homosexual men (Silverstein, 1981).

In a young child's development, male-to-female, or female-to-male gender transposition is a rudimentary and inchoate response to diffusely mixed covert and overt signals that seem to indicate that, by being a girl with a penis or a boy with a vulva, a child will somehow be more satisfactory to each parent. So transformed, the child keeps the two parents together, their continued allegiance to one another is mutually ensured, and the intactness of the family is ensured. This formulation sounds outrageous and absurd only if it is elevated to the status of being a sufficient instead of only a necessary condition in the genesis of developmental gender crosscoding.

3 GENDER CROSSCODIFICATION CLASSIFIED

Homosexuality has in the past been biomedically classified, as it still is in the law, as perversion and deviancy. It has also been classified biomedically as a paraphilia. Its classification as a paraphilia is scientifically untenable, insofar as all of the forty-odd paraphilias may occur in association with homosexual, heterosexual, or bisexual mating. Thus it is necessary to have a conceptual term other than paraphilia for the name of whatever it is that makes homosexual different from heterosexual.

In earlier writings, I have used the term *gender transposition* to signify that, instead of complete concordance of all the components of either masculine or feminine, one or more is transposed so as to be, respectively, feminine or masculine. Gender transposition applies not only to homosexuality but to a range of phenomena that differ on the basis of the number of components involved, and of the persistence of their transposition (Table 3-1). In transexualism, for example, all the components of extrinsic gender coding are transposed (or crosscoded) relative to the criterion of the external genitalia; and the transposition is long-lasting—usually permanent. The gender transposition of transexuals, prior to sex reassignment, is said to be subjectively experienced as gender dysphoria.

The term gender transposition carries no connotations as to the causality,

TABLE 3-1 Gender Crosscoding (Transposition)

	Continuous or Constant	Episodic or Alternating
Total	Transexualism	Transvestophilia (fetishistic transvestism)
Partial unlimited	Mimesis: (gynemimesis and andromimesis)	Transvestism (nonfetishistic transvestism)
Partial limited	Male homophilia; female homophilia	Homo/heterophilia (bisexualism)

immutability, or penetrance of transposition, all three of which must be specified on the basis of empirical data. However, the term has proved to be a stumbling block for those gay activists who have a strong political antipathy to homosexual science, insofar as they believe that to classify homosexuality as a transposition is to stigmatize it as being abnormal. Their alternative is to classify homosexuality as a moral choice or voluntary preference for a same-sexed partner which, in the vocabulary of psychoanalysis, is a same-sexed object choice.

Many social science writers and sex therapists differentiate object choice, gender identity, and gender role. This enables them to say, for example, that a man is masculine in his gender identity and gender role, but homosexual in orientation and object choice. The alternative is to say he has a masculine G-I/R except for the sexuoerotic imagery and ideation of his romantic life, love life, and sex life in dreams and fantasies, and in their translation into actual practices (and vice versa for a lesbian). This alternative formulation circumvents the scientific fallacy inherent in the term object choice, namely that heterosexuality and homosexuality have their origin in voluntary choice and are therefore already fully explained by fiat, without the superfluous addition of more research—which constitutes the fallacy of scientific nihilism.

Terminologically, gender transposition and gender crosscoding are synonymous. However, crosscoding carries more the connotation of extrinsic and arbitrary social coding and less the connotation of genetic, hormonal, or any other type of coding of intrinsic origin. It is possible, therefore, that gender crosscoding, the term that predominates in this present writing, will prove less of a stumbling block than has been the case with gender transposition. Gender crosscoding should not be construed as being exclusively socially programed, however. It may be prenatally programed as well—for example by hormonal crosscoding—at least in part, if not in toto.

One way of classifying gender crosscoding is the simple seven-point (zero to six) scale devised by Kinsey, and now commonly referred to as the Kinsey scale (McWhirter, Sanders, and Reinisch, 1988). It is a scale constructed on the assumption that exclusive heterosexuality (rated zero) and exclusive homosexuality (rated six) are polar extremes on the same continuum. It is a ratio scale, insofar as bisexual is rated as the ratio of heterosexual to homosexual, with the 50 : 50 ratio given a rating of three on the scale. As on all ratio scales, the absolute scores of prevalence or intensity are forfeited. For example, a person who has had bisexual experience with more than 5000 different partners by age fifty, half male and half female, with never fewer than two partners daily, and with frequent participation in bisexual group-sex parties, may get the same bisexual rating as another person who has by age fifty had only two partners, one male and one female, and with a participation frequency no higher than twice a week.

Kinsey ratings are allocated on the basis of self-reported data on erotosexual imagery and ideation in fantasies and dreams, as well as on actual erotosexual experiences. The Kinsey-scale criterion of homosexuality or heterosexuality is participation in a sexual act, actually and/or in ideation and imagery, without taking into account whether or not it is compatible with falling in love, homosexually, heterosexually, or both.

Because the Kinsey scale is a unidimensional ratio scale, a Kinsey rating does not take into account qualitative differences among the different categories, types, and syndromes of gender crosscoding. For example, a Kinsey rating does not disclose whether the person rated six is an exclusively homosexual drill sergeant (with or without a transexual fantasy), a full-time gynemimetic impersonator in the entertainment industry, a gay transvestophile, or a preoperative male-to-female transexual whose sexual partners are exclusively male. It is possible, of course, to allocate a Kinsey rating to people who represent any one of the various qualitatively different manifestations of gender crosscoding. If the rating is to have any scientific value, however, they must first be ascertained and classified as belonging to one subgroup or another.

To be empirically useful and scientific, a classification must be based on the principle that the criteria of classification are stable, all-inclusively exhaustive, and mutually exclusive. That is, they must be able to accommodate all known cases or examples (and ideally all those remaining to be ascertained), and without overlap or ambiguity. Table 3-1 satisfies these conditions by classifying gender crosscoding according to the dual criteria of time (duration or persistence) and degree (penetrance or pervasiveness).

Like any classification, the classified gender crosscodification of Table 3-1 may need revision as more data are accumulated—for example about age of onset, developmental genesis, and underlying causality. To avoid the pitfall of prematurely allocating causality, the classification of Table 3-1 expressly avoids any reference to psychogenic versus organogenic origin or etiology. Etiology in sexology can be established only by painstaking and laborious empirical research, not by doctrinal revelation, and not on the basis of diagnosis by exclusion, the trashcan method by which psychogenesis is all too often attributed. It is better to admit ignorance than to be pilloried for the folly of pretentious psychogenetic error. It is difficult to relinquish dogma. All present-day explanations of gender crosscoding as being either social (nurture) or biological (nature) in origin are dogmas, unless they are presented with the proviso that they are incompletely substantiated.

There is no evidence that gender crosscoding is either all nature or all nurture in its origins. The forces of nature meet the forces of nurture in the course of development from embryonic life onward. When they meet at a so-called critical or sensitive period of some aspect of development, together they program what the outcome of that development will be. In fetal life, for example, thalidomide in the intrauterine environment falsely nurtures what nature is growing from buds to limbs, with the result that the limbs become permanently unformed or deformed. A corresponding example in postnatal life is Konrad Lorenz's now famous demonstration of how newly hatched ducklings became imprinted (nature) not to a mother duck but to him (nurture), provided they had no duck mother, and that he squatted and waddled as their mother substitute during the critical post-hatching period (Lorenz, 1952). Subsequently, they followed him, and forever failed to follow a duck, as mother.

The old paradigm was nature/nurture. The new paradigm is nature/critical period/nurture (Money, 1984c, 1987b). The programing that takes place when nature and nurture interact at a critical period, whether in prenatal or postnatal life, may be irreversible and immutable.

Immutability is a key concept here. It is particularly relevant to gender crosscoding in the ideology of law, legislation, religion, and society, where the issue is not, as it is frequently assumed to be, innate versus acquired, that is, nature versus nurture, but immutability versus mutability.

As in the case of left-handedness, which is immutable (even though the left-handed person practices using the right hand also), the immutability of homosexuality and other manifestations of gender crosscoding is not synonymous with whether their origins are ostensibly biological or not. The origins of left-handedness, ambidextrousness, and right-handedness still remain unascertained. In an earlier era, left-handedness was regarded as an anomaly to be cured at school by tying the left hand behind the back, along with other punishments. The outcome was not right-handedness, but poor writing, dyslexia, and delinquency in response to academic abuse. For society, it has been more expeditious not to punish but to tolerate left-handedness, and to manufacture tools and artifacts to accommodate people with this status.

The lesson of left-handedness can be applied to gender crosscoding. It is more expedient and much less expensive for society to tolerate what it cannot change, rather than to engage in trying to force a cure on what, irrespective of its origin as biological or otherwise, has already become immutably unable to be changed. The false hope of curing left-handedness was based on the appearance of success in cases in which there was, initially, some degree of ambidexterity on which to capitalize. The counterpart in gender crosscoding is bisexuality, which is usually wrongly classified as homosexuality. Most if not all the claimed cures of homosexuality prove, on more detailed investigation, to have been cases in which there was, initially, some degree of bisexuality on which to capitalize. It is in just such a case that the individual may experience a sense of the self divided and in conflict, for the resolution of which he or she seeks treatment to be monosexually one or the other, but not bisexually both together.

4 TRANSEXUALISM

Etymologically, transexual derives from Latin, *trans*, across, over; and from Latin, *sexus*, sex. Thus it means crossing over from one sex to the other. The term was coined by D.O. Cauldwell and used in print, presumably for the first time, in his 1949 article titled "Psychopathia Transexualis," in Volume 16 of the now-defunct periodical, *Sexology*. The new term did not become part of the vernacular until after Harry Benjamin (1885–1986), using a second "s" in the spelling, published in 1966 *The Transsexual Phenomenon*, the first textbook to deal with the syndrome.

In contemporary usage, the term transexualism is used as a name for the sex-reassignment method of rehabilitation, as well as for the syndrome treated by means of sex reassignment. The syndrome of transexualism is known also as gender dysphoria according to a system of nomenclature that is based on concepts of patients' inner feelings and convictions, as an alternative to more empirical and objective evidence. The empirical and objective evidence of transexualism is provided if the patient passes the two-year, real-life test of becoming socially, economically, and hormonally rehabilitated in the role of the sex of reassignment, prior to the final and irrevocable step of surgery. Gender dysphoria and transexualism are not perfect synonyms, for there are many gender-dysphoric patients who are not transexuals, and are not applicants for sex-reassignment surgery.

In vernacular speech, a transexual has the mind of a woman trapped in a man's body or, conversely, the mind of a man trapped in a woman's body. This idiom dates back to 1869, when Karl Heinrich Ulrichs' book, *Argonauticus*, was published in Leipzig. Borrowing from Plato, who in the *Symposium* had represented Urania as a daughter of Uranus, begotten without a mother, Ulrichs coined the term *urning* and applied it to the person who is, "like a woman, sexually repelled by women and attracted to men," because he has the mind of a woman within the body of a man [*anima muliebris virili corpore inclusa*] (Bloch, 1933). This concept of sexual discordance between body and mind represents gender crosscoding which, when it is comprehensively pervasive in degree, and long-lasting or chronic in duration, is characteristic of transexualism, regardless of its origin and etiology.

The transexual applicant has two dogmatic fixations. One is to forfeit those parts and functions of the body that are the somatic insignia of the sex of birth. The other is to simulate the other sex and to pass as a member of that sex, naked and clothed.

Forfeiture of the insignia of the sex of birth is the defining characteristic of transexualism as compared with other manifestations of gender crosscoding. For female-to-male transexuals, it means having a man's haircut, flattening or amputation of the breasts, having no menstrual periods, having nothing insertable into the vagina, and modulating the pitch and intonation of the voice to be more baritone and mannish. For male-to-female transexuals, forfeiture means becoming a eunuch with no testicles, penis, or scrotum, losing facial or body hair, not cutting the head hair, and modulating the pitch and intonation of the voice to a feminine-sounding husky falsetto.

Dogmatic fixation on becoming a eunuch is not unique to male-to-female transexualism. It was an article of faith among Skoptsi, members of the Skoptic Christian sect founded in Russia in the second half of the eighteenth century. A century later there were an estimated 5000 members, including 1000 women. Persecuted and made illegal, the sect had become extinct by the midtwentieth century. Skoptic men forfeited either the testes or the entire external genitalia, and Skoptic women, the nipples. The "Skoptic syndrome" (Money, 1988) occurs sporadically as a clinical entity. Some men with this syndrome castrate themselves (Money and DePriest, 1976; Kalin, 1979). Others have applied to transexual clinics for castration without feminization or, having undergone sex reassignment, revert to living as eunuchs, more contented with their sexuality reduced than they had been previously.

Eunuchizing surgery in conjunction with gender crosscoding and living as a woman has an ancient history among the hijras of India (Figure 3-1a and b) (Nanda, 1984, 1985; Money and Lamacz, 1984). Partly a caste and partly a cult with their own presiding deity, the goddess Bahuchara Mata, the hijras are a community of people who, in the medical terminology of the West, would be called male-to-female transexuals. The surgical technique for removal of penis, testicles, and scrotum is taught by senior gurus to their successors. Only very recently have some hijras had access to female hormonal treatment so as to grow breasts. Traditionally they have dressed like women and lived as if women. Though recognized as hijras, they are more or less tolerated in society, as well as being somewhat scorned.

In Western medicine, surgeons of the twentieth century have made surgical sex reassignment, with supplementary hormonal reassignment, an issue in medical morals. Professional opinion is still divided, sometimes acrimoniously. Nonetheless, sex reassignment has become accepted as a method of rehabilitation. To qualify, a candidate for transexual surgery should pass the 2-year, real-life test (Money and Ambinder, 1978) of becoming rehabilitated socially, economically, and hormonally in the sex of reassignment before the irrevocable step of genital surgery is taken. The two-year, real-life test constitutes a process of self-discovery. It gives the person a chance to discover whether he will do better in life by retaining his sex organs as a gynemimetic homosexual, or as an unreassigned episodic transvestophile.

Hormonal feminization with estrogen, or estrogen combined with progestin, induces breast enlargement, reduces muscle mass, and increases subcutaneous fat padding. These hormonal effects regress upon discontinuation

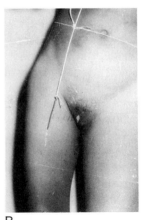

A   B

Figure 3-1a. Hijra on left in social group (courtesy of Serena Nanda).
Figure 3-1b. Hijra after surgery to become a complete eunuch (courtesy of Yogesh Shingala).

of treatment, except that complete flattening of the breasts requires plastic surgery (mastectomy). Hormonal feminization retards the growth of facial and body hair but does not eradicate it. Eradication requires electrolysis, the effect of which is irreversible. Hormonal feminization also does not lower the voice; nor does it change the shape of the Adam's apple or the bone structure of the slim, masculine pelvis and hips.

Surgical feminization of the genitalia is accomplished by preserving all of the skin of the empty penis with its blood supply and nerve fibers intact and inserting it, like the inverted finger of a glove, as a lining for the newly opened cavity of the vagina. With a sufficient length of penile skin, it may be possible to preserve the glans penis at its tip and place it in the position of a cervix. If the length of the penile skin is insufficient, the lining of the far end of the vaginal cavity may be extended with a split-thickness skin graft from the thigh. Part of the scrotal skin is used to construct labia majora. Despite the absence of a clitoris and labia minora, the visible effect may be so satisfactory that a patient may be able to undergo a physical examination, as has occasionally been reported, without being recognized as a male-to-female transexual—this according to follow-up reports from patients in my own psychohormonal research unit. These patients are among those for whom the first transexual surgical sex-reassignment program was inaugurated in 1966. Surgically, it was under the direction of the gynecologist, Howard W. Jones, Jr., now famous as the first "test-tube baby" doctor in the United States, and the plastic surgeon, Milton T. Edgerton.

Postsurgically, the orgasmic feeling of building to a climax is not eliminated in male-to-female transexuals, although what is left is dependent in part on how much of the erotic innervation of the penile skin has been left intact. It is also dependent in part on the effect of estrogen replacement therapy, insofar as estrogen acts as an antiandrogen in the intact male. The composite conclusion inferred from patients' own words is that the new orgasm is a progressively increasing body glow that reaches a peak of satisfaction. It is, in part, the satisfaction of being in the woman's role, serving the male partner, and having his climax contingent on her being there. The new orgasm is not compared with the former one, for the comparison would require an evocation of one's existence as a male that is neither possible nor desired.

The musculature of the perineum constricts and may eventually seal the vagina from penetration with anything unless it is kept open by regular coitus or by use of a dilator, which can be inserted nightly. The severity of constriction varies according to the surgical technique employed, and is least when the inverted skin of the penis (the Burou technique) has been used, with its own blood and nerve supply intact. Regrettably, through paucity of research funding, there are no large-scale, comprehensive follow-up data that relate surgical procedure to coital and orgasmic outcome. However, there are follow-up data to indicate that a successful surgical outcome is positively correlated with a successful life outcome (Satterfield, 1981; Lindemalm, Koerlin, and Uddenberg, 1986).

The two-year, real-life test applies also to female-to-male transexual candidates. They must run the risk, if they revert to female living after having been hormonally masculinized by treatment with testosterone, of having a permanently lowered voice and an increase in facial and body hair that cannot be eradicated except by electrolysis, which is expensive and time-consuming. Testosterone-induced increased muscle mass and reduced subcutaneous fat gradually regress if treatment is discontinued. Testosterone after puberty does not change the bone structure of broad female pelvis and hips.

Surgical breast flattening can be reversed with surgical implants. Hysterectomy and ovariectomy cannot be reversed, but they can be long postponed, provided menstruation is suppressed under the influence of testosterone treatment, without breakthrough bleeding. Genital reconstruction, if it is undertaken, does not require ablation of the clitoris, but only of the vaginal cavity and vulva, so that some degree of backtracking is possible. However, the likelihood of backtracking is reduced because, whereas male-to-female genital surgery is a rapid one-stage or two-stage procedure, female-to-male genital surgery is a prolonged multistaged procedure. Many patients forego the attempt, not only because of the time and expense involved but because, irrespective of variations in surgical technique, the outcome is far from satisfactory with respect to both urination and copulation. Although new techniques of microsurgery promise future improvements, standard surgery produces a skin-grafted penis that is numb, and without tactual, painful, or erotic sensory feeling. It is also flabby. It is not possible to construct an erectile penis surgically because the erectile spongy tissue of the normal penis is found only in the penis. There is no other site in the body from which a graft of spongy tissue can be transplanted.

Because the clitoris is preserved intact in its normal position and implanted into the skin of the newly grafted penis where it attaches to the body, the climax of orgasm is not impaired. On the contrary, under the influence of hormonal replacement therapy with testosterone, the clitoris may have enlarged somewhat and the feeling of orgasm may have intensified. It is stimulated by pressure and rubbing against the partner during copulation, or by oral or digital play.

Because the postsurgical outcome of phalloplasty is always less than adequate, there is no adequate criterion for a comparison to be made between the success of surgical outcome and life outcome. However, there is a general consensus among professionals in transexualism that female-to-male transexualism is not an exact homologue of male-to-female transexualism. Whereas the feminine gender coding of the male-to-female transexual is prevalently that of the attention-attracting vamp, not the devoted madonna, the masculine gender coding of the female-to-male transexual is prevalently that of the reliable provider, not the profligate playboy. Throughout Europe, America, and the English-speaking world, clinicians of transexualism agree that a successfully unobtrusive sex-reassigned life is more prevalent in female-to-male than male-to-female reassignment, even though the success of female-to-male sex-reassignment surgery of the genitalia leaves something to be desired, namely an erectile penis.

Most sex-reassigned transexuals settle into their sex-reassigned lives as heterosexuals, that is with a partner of the natal sex in which they themselves no longer live. There are exceptions, although their numbers are not known. Some who have undergone male-to-female reassignment characterize themselves as bisexuals or, if they have females exclusively as their sexual partners, as lesbians. In a few instances, among those who have been married, male-to-female transexuals stay with their former wives in a relationship that they define as being like sisters or sisters-in-law (Chapter 4, Section 11). There are also those who live as spinsters, devoid of any romantic or erotic relationship.

Some men, attracted to a preoperative or postoperative male-to-female transexual, as for example at a party or a bar, react as to an impostor if they discover the truth about the genitalia. Betrayed by the evidence of their own senses, they may be panicked by the threat of becoming homosexual, or enraged at having been duped. By contrast, there are some male partners of preoperative male-to-female transexuals who are strongly attracted to a lady with a penis as a sexuoerotic partner. Postsurgically, their attraction wanes, and the partnership dissolves. There are still others who, as partners, are so strongly attracted toward the femininity of the preoperative male-to-female transexual that they neglect the incongruity of the genitalia and support the transexual's bid for emotional and financial assistance. Postsurgically, they stay together as a heterosexual couple for years, passing as such in the community, but not hiding the true history from family and friends. Some such partnerships begin not preoperatively, but postoperatively. Either way, they may be legalized in marriage. The husband, like the male partner of an American Indian berdache (Williams, 1986), considers himself heterosexual. His heterosexual status is endorsed in the community and among his work mates, even in the most macho trades and professions. He may or may not have an extramarital affair, or he may have various casual relationships with other women, but not with men, nor with male-to-female transexuals. He and his sex-reassigned wife may have a family by adoption. The children relate to their mother and father in the same way as do other children to their parents.

If some reassigned female-to-male transexuals live as bachelors, as gay or bisexual men, or as if a brother or brother-in-law of the former spouse, then they are a seldom heard from minority. Occasionally, however, there is a relationship established between a reassigned female-to-male transexual and a reassigned male-to-female transexual. The most prevalent type of sexuoerotic relationship that a female-to-male transexual enters into is with a woman who is by history heterosexual. She may or may not have been previously married, and may or may not be a mother. The female-to-male partner typically fulfills the traditional male role of being the breadwinner and the one who can be relied on. Even if he might sometimes have a roving eye, he is jealously possessive of his partner. With or without formal marriage, the couple are accepted in the community, even though the prior history may be known. If the children know the prior history, as the older ones may do, they react to their parents as mother and father, nonetheless. The same applies to children too young to know the father's prior history, and to those who might be born of the mother by donor insemination. Because the surgical technology for reconstruction of the genitalia for the female-to-male transexual is cosmetically imperfect, it may impose special constraints on being seen nude by other members of the household in the normal course of bathing and dressing.

These diversities in the sex lives of reassigned transexuals illustrate well that when gender crosscoding takes place, there is indeed a cleavage between what is anatomically coded in the genitals and what is coded in the nongenital identification/complementation schema. For a minority, reassigning the sex in which one lives is of paramount importance, even though the genital sex of the partner with whom one lives stigmatizes the relationship as homosexual, unless the relationship is one of abstinence. For the majority of transexuals, however, the paramount importance of reassigning the sex in which one lives is that it becomes possible to live in a respected and heterosexual relationship with a partner of the genital sex in which one is no longer obligated to be assigned oneself.

The sex-reassignment imperative is of such paramount importance in the lives of some transexuals that, for reasons concealed in their own privacy, or because they are unable to obtain surgery professionally, they castrate or otherwise mutilate themselves (Chapter 4, Section 11). They live in literal obedience to the biblical injunction: "if thine eye offend thee, pluck it out," except that the offending organ is not the eye, but the genital. Some fail and commit suicide instead.

5 TRANSVESTOPHILIA

Until the publication in 1966 of Harry Benjamin's *The Transsexual Phenomenon*, transexualism had not been distinguished from transvestism in the professional literature. The word transvestism means, according to its Latin derivation, cross dressing (*trans*, across + *vestire*, to clothe). Generically, the term applies to any act of cross dressing, whether as a party gag, an entertainment act, an undercover espionage or entrapment stratagem, or an expression of a sexological syndrome.

In addition to its generic application as the name of any act of cross dressing, the term transvestism has also a specific application as the name of a syndrome. Until this syndrome of transvestism was recognized and named as a separate entity in the writings of the sexologist, Magnus Hirschfeld (1868–1935), it was classified as a form of what was variously named as contrary sexual feeling, antipathic sexual instinct, sexual inversion, and homosexuality. Havelock Ellis (1859–1939) classified transvestism under the eponymous term *eonism* (see Section 7, this chapter). Richard von Krafft-Ebing (1840–1902) classified transvestism sexologically as a form of fetishism, garments being the fetish objects, without which sexual arousal and orgasm are not possible.

Fetishistic dependence on cross dressing for erotic arousal and the attainment of orgasm has been officially recognized in the now published draft of DSM-III-R (*Diagnostic and Statistical Manual*, 3rd edition, revised) of the American Psychiatric Association, insofar as the term transvestism has been replaced by transvestic fetishism, and the syndrome classified as a paraphilia. Syntactically and logically, the single word transvestophilia is to be preferred over transvestic fetishism (Table 3-1). Etymologically, the term is formed from transvestism by addition of the suffix from Greek, *-philia*, affection, love.

As judged on the basis of current ascertainment methods, fetishism is like other paraphilias in having a greater affinity for men than for women. In the case of transvestophilia, this affinity for men is apparently exclusive, for there are no recorded cases of women who are garment addicts, consistently and obligatively dependent on wearing men's garments as a prerequisite to achieving sexuoerotic arousal and orgasm. The converse of paraphilic cross dressing, namely having to wear garments of one's own sex as a prerequisite to achieving sexuoerotic arousal and orgasm, is not known to exist as a syndrome in either men or women. The explanation may well relate to the fact that wearing the garments of one's own sex is not erotically illicit or forbidden.

In male transvestophilia, the fantasy or mental replay of wearing women's garments, most commonly lingerie, may replace the actual wearing of them, as a temporary expediency, in order to maintain an erection and achieve orgasm. Wearing women's garments is, however, in all likelihood only a partial manifestation of a more extensive gender crosscoding from male to female that includes also the body image. If he is a heterosexual transvestophile, a cross-dressed man copulating with his wife or woman partner would be recorded on a video camera as having the body of a man. By contrast, in his own mental camera he would perceive himself as having the body of a woman and his partner that of a man. If he is a homosexual transvestophile with a male as a partner, then the mental image of the partner's body would not need to be changed.

In one case (Money and DePriest, 1976; see also Chapter 4, Section 11), that of a husband and father who eventually fulfilled his lifetime's fantasy of self-castration, the great advantage of having no testicles was that his penis did not erect. While he was performing cunnilingus on his wife, his flaccid penis did not intrude on his fantasy of himself as a woman engaging in oral sex. To have this experience was vastly more erotically gratifying to him than penovaginal penetration, even though he regretted having to deprive his wife of that additional satisfaction.

The male transvestophile's cross dressing is not restricted to wearing lacy and frilly lingerie in the boudoir. As aforementioned (Chapter 2, Section 9), he has two names and two personalities, as well as two wardrobes, and the wardrobe that belongs with his female personality is as extensive as his wealth and opportunity to cross dress permit. Metamorphosed into his personality as a lady, he changes and becomes she. Then, as a lady, until the proverbial stroke of midnight, she seeks the adulation of her public. She may have dozens, if not hundreds of photographs of herself in many different poses and outfits, to suit each occasion, including pregnancy, that is construed as womanly in her idealized conception of womanhood. Each transvestophile has his own idealized conception of womanhood and womanly activities, ranging from the disciplined servant girl or the hardworking farm wife, to the exotic dancer and the glamorous beauty queen.

There is no permit for androgyny in either the male or the female personality of the male transvestophile. Each is an exaggerated stereotype of masculine and feminine, respectively. For example, if the male is ruthless, exploitative, daring, and defiant, the female is demure, devious, entertaining, and vulnerable. Exaggerated stereotypes of masculine and feminine are sufficiently varied and prevalent in the general population that it does not make transvestophilic stereotypes uniquely conspicuous. As female, the episodic transvestophile's transformation may be as convincingly effective as is the permanent transformation of the male-to-female transexual. That is why transexualism and transvestophilia are both classified (Table 3-1) as total crossgender transformations, but differently classified temporally—transexualism as continuous or constant, and transvestophilia as episodic or alternating.

There have been no systematic, prospective studies of the long-term outcome of transvestophilia in later life. If there are instances of spontaneous remission, the likelihood that the case will become lost to follow-up is high. Those cases that are seen in later life are those in whom the syndrome has persisted; and, in perhaps a few rare instances, those of late onset. There are also cases that first come to attention in midlife or later because the episodic alternation of the two personalities has come to a halt, and only the female personality exists without interruption, full-time. When this state of affairs persists, the syndrome may be said to have metamorphosed from episodic transvestophilia to constant gynemimesis (see Section 6, this chapter).

Gynemimesis itself may persist for a further period of time, or it may be only a signal of the continuing metamorphosis of transvestophilia into transexualism (see Chapter 2, Section 9). The timing of this metamorphosis may be simply a function of aging, or it may happen concurrently with, or in response to a major life crisis. In one case, the crisis was the disruption of married life after the husband's chronically schizophrenic mother was taken into the household to die of cancer. From youth onward, he had failed to find a *modus vivendi* with this temperamentally difficult lady. After she moved away, his obsessive fixation on sex reassignment subsided.

In another case, the crisis was precipitated by the death of the transvestophile's wife from cancer, two years after the birth of their seventh child and her seventh cesarean section—a pregnancy that they had been medically advised to avoid, though religiously prohibited from doing so. He became suicidally depressed. He no longer found much relief in episodic cross dressing, which formerly he had kept a secret, except from his wife. Defiantly obsessed, he secretly and unrelentingly pursued his rebirth into a new life, despite more than a year of psychoanalytic psychotherapy, until at last he became surgically transformed, full-time, into his alter ego, a woman. Psychodynamic psychotherapy is ineffectual if attempted as a cure for the syndrome of transexualism.

In the third case, the crisis was precipitated by abdominal cancer in the fifth decade of the life of a former episodic transvestophile who had lived for some years full-time at home as a financially very successful woman entrepreneur and investor, while his wife pursued her very successful professional career extramurally. The children were of college age. After recovering from cancer surgery, he unrelentingly pursued the mystique of a reprieve from death by starting life over again as a new person— metamorphosed into the woman whose existence could no longer be satisfied by cross dressing alone. Against almost impossible odds, *he* did become rehabilitated as *she*. She skillfully engineered the bureaucracy into granting sex-reassignment surgery, and stayed alive to savor for years the satisfaction of being a dowager.

Transvestophilia that does not metamorphose into transexualism, but continues its episodic course, does not respond to treatment aimed at its eradication. Like all the paraphilias, it shares the quality of addiction (see Chapter 4, Section 7), in this case addiction to women's clothes. For the paraphile himself, addiction to women's clothes constitutes a legal problem only if he becomes conspicuous or flamboyant, acting and dressed as a woman in public in a jurisdiction where cross dressing is against the law. It may constitute a financial problem also, dependent on his wealth and compulsive clothing-store spending sprees.

The most common problem, however, is that cross dressing disrupts the sexuoerotic bond with the partner (either female or male), who is far more likely to be turned off by the very cross dressing that is essential to the paraphile's own turn-on. As a sequel, the two become progressively habituated to living together in a companionate relationship, not as lovers and sexual partners. Otherwise they may separate. There are self-help networks across the country for transvestophiles and their spouses, one of the services of which is to provide contacts with professionals whose counseling and psychotherapy is without intolerance of cross dressing, and is directed toward helping the couple.

A policy of tolerance is not feasible if cross dressing occurs as a component of another paraphilia that is lethal, for example, self-strangulation (asphyxiophilia) while dressed in women's clothes; or stage-managing one's own masochistic punishment and injury while dressed as a maid servant or a little girl, which may culminate ultimately in stage-managing one's own murder (autassasinophilia). Syndromes of these types qualify for hormonal therapy with Depo-Provera (medroxyprogesterone acetate, MPA) or other antiandrogen, combined with sexological counseling (see Chapter 4, Section 13; Appendix; Money, 1987d).

There is no contraindication to using MPA in a trial period of treatment of uncomplicated transvestophilia, provided the patient contracts for it with signed informed consent. MPA is a progestinic hormone that reduces the level of testicular testosterone to that of prepuberty. In some cases, a transvestophile experiences this change not as an unfavorable loss, but as a favorable change from masculinity toward greater femininity. Thus it may reinforce the transvestophile's feminine personality, rather than weaken the addiction to women's clothes. In what is probably a minority of cases, it may reduce the clothing addiction and thus, indirectly, contribute to reinforcement of the masculine personality.

6 GYNEMIMESIS/ANDROMIMESIS

In the early years of its usage, the term transvestite was applied not only to transvestophiles and transexuals as cross dressers, but also to those for whom there was no name other than the vernacular slang term, *drag queen.* Drag queen applies to any homosexual male who cross dresses and impersonates a female, either full-time, part-time, or sporadically. In the King's Cross section of Sydney, Australian preoperative male-to-female transexuals as well as other cross dressers who ply the streets call themselves drag queens. On the American scene, the term is more likely to refer to those who cross dress for a masquerade occasion.

Even if it were not slangy, drag queen would lack the precision needed to name the variety of gender crosscoding for which the term gynemimesis (Money and Lamacz, 1984) was coined, along with its counterpart, andromimesis (Table 3-1).

A gynemimetic (from Greek, *gyne,* woman + *mimesis,* imitation) resembles a male-to-female transexual insofar as the change from he to she is comprehensive and continuous, and includes hormonal feminization if female hormone is obtainable. The resemblance stops short of genital surgery, in which respect the gynemimetic resembles the transvestophile. Unlike the transvestophile, the gynemimetic lives not episodically, but fulltime as a lady with a penis.

An andromimetic (from Greek, *andros,* man + *mimesis,* imitation) is the counterpart of a gynemimetic. He lives full-time as a man. If he has access to male hormone and undergoes hormonal masculinization, it is more likely than not that he will seek hysterectomy and breast removal, if not genital surgical masculinization also. If he lives without undergoing masculinizing genital surgery, it is not because of the satisfaction of living as a man with a vulva, but rather because of the cost and imperfect outcome of surgery.

By contrast, it is the satisfaction of living as a lady with a penis that keeps the gynemimetic away from feminizing genital surgery. This satisfaction usually involves extensive attention to cosmetic care, including nongenital cosmetic surgery and electrolysis of the beard, which is protracted and costly. There are some individual cases, however, in which hirsutism is light and easy to manage. Conversely, there are others in which cross dressing as a bearded lady with a penis is a major satisfaction.

Gynemimesis is not a culture-bound phenomenon, but one that occurs in widely divergent cultures around the world, only a few of which have been catalogued and studied systematically. The same applies to andromimesis, although present evidence seems to indicate that it may have a lesser prevalence than gynemimesis.

Ethnographically, the term gynemimesis (and likewise andromimesis) has the advantage of being conceptually large enough to encompass different culturally and historically shaped versions of the same phenomenon. The hijras of India, aforementioned (see Section 4, this chapter), are one example (Nanda, 1984, 1985; Money and Lamacz, 1984).

Another cultural variant of gynemimesis is that reported from the Arabic culture of Oman by Wikan (1977). The local name for the gynemimetic is *xanith* (pronounced han·eeth), the Arabic term that is commonly translated into English as homosexual. The xanith always retains his male given name. He is not allowed to wear the facemask of purdah, nor other female clothing. His clothes are intermediate between male and female: he wears the ankle-length tunic of the male, but with the tight waist of the female dress. Male clothing is white, females wear patterned cloth in bright colors, and xanith wear unpatterned colored clothes. Men cut their hair short, women wear theirs long, the xanith medium long. Men comb their hair backward away from the face, women comb theirs diagonally forward from a central parting, and xanith forward from a side parting, oiled heavily in the style of women. Both men and women cover their heads; xanith go bareheaded. Perfume is used by both sexes, especially on festive occasions and during intercourse. The xanith is generally heavily perfumed and uses makeup to draw attention to himself. This is also achieved by his affected swaying gait, emphasized by his close-fitting garments. His sweet falsetto voice and facial expressions and movements also closely mimic those of women. If he wore female clothes it would, in many instances, not be possible, anatomically speaking, to discern him to be male and not female. Nonetheless, he has no tradition of feminizing the body either by becoming a eunuch or by the contemporary method of taking sex hormones.

The xanith is publicly recognizable in Oman as having the status of neither male nor female, but of xanith. Like his clothing, his role in society resembles but does not replicate that of women. Unlike men, he is permitted to move freely among women behind purdah, and to share their social life, intimate gossip, domesticity, and activities. At a wedding, musical instruments are played by men, whereas the xanith joins the women singers. Unlike women, the xanith is not ruled under the power and dominion of a man. Like a man, he has the right to go about in public unaccompanied. He also has the right, exclusive to the role of xanith, to live alone, to be hired as a house servant, and to be hired by non-xanith men as a prostitute. Female prostitution is outlawed, and like adultery, is subject to severe punishment.

A xanith may gain public status as a man instead of a xanith, provided he enters into a marriage arranged by his family and produces the public evidence of successful vaginal penetration with his virgin bride, namely a postnuptial bloodstained cloth. He gains this status despite the persistence of his feminine demeanor in facial expressions, voice, laughter, and movements. He may relinquish his male status and revert to that of a xanith. The prevalence of xanith in the small town where they were studied was 2 percent of the 3000 adult males.

Still another cultural variant of gynemimesis is that of the North American *berdache*, a name bestowed by early French explorers. Now anglicized, berdache is a French term, derived from the Persian *bardaj* via Spanish *bardage*, that in the seventeenth century was defined as "a young man who is shamefully abused" (Williams, 1986). The role of the berdache was often associated with a special spiritual status as a shaman and healer. The berdache commonly showed the characteristics of gender crosscoding as a boy and, as a youth, received a spiritual revelation while in a divine trance. Thereafter he would dress as a woman, do woman's work, engage in sex with a male, and sometimes be sought after as a berdache wife and provider. From his own ethnographic fieldwork, Williams offers evidence that berdachism has not become extinct, as some had thought, but still lives as a continuing tradition in many tribes from Alaska to Mexico's Yucatan. One of his informants, a traditionalist Navajo woman of the Southwest, spoke of her uncle, a *nadle* (Navajo for berdache):

> Nadle are well respected. They are seen as very compassionate people, who care for their family a lot and help people. That's why they are

healers. Nadle are also seen as being great with children, so parents are pleased if a nadle takes an interest in their child. One that I know is now a principal of a school on the reservation. Everyone knows that he and the man he lives with are lovers, but it is not mentioned. They help their family a lot and are considered valuable members of the community. Their sexuality is never mentioned; it is just taken for granted. No one would ever try to change a nadle. That is just their character, the way they are. Missionaries and schools had a bad effect on stigmatizing homosexuality among more assimilated Indians, so it's not as open as in the past. But among traditionals nadle never even went underground. It has just continued. They are our relatives, part of our family.

The cultural range of gynemimesis, and even more so of andromimesis, has not yet been definitively ascertained. It exists as a widely dispersed tradition in the island cultures of Polynesia, although its range has not been catalogued in detail. In Hawaii, a gynemimetic is known as a *mahu* (Williams, 1985). In Samoa, as in Tahiti, gynemimetics are readily recognizable along the roadside and elsewhere. They are known in the Samoan language as *faa fa' fini*. In Tonga, the family and community recognize the gynemimetic boy as one who is destined to grow up as a Tongan faa fa' fini (unpublished personal data).

According to a recent travelers' report (Coleman, Colgon, and Gooren, 1987), the hijra community of India (see Section 4, this chapter) has a counterpart in Burma, where men who live as women are called *acault* (pronounced a·chow'). Their gynemimetic state is attributed to the power of a female spirit who bestows on them a special spiritual distinction.

In our own culture, the gynemimetic network or community that is present in every metropolitan area is tolerated by society at large, and its police, only if it exists in a quasi-clandestine way. Its members are permitted to earn a living as entertainers provided they enter into complicity with the system by pretending that they cross dress optionally, and only for the purpose of earning a living, not because impersonation is their very way of being. In the bars and clubs that they frequent, they are sought after by men who are gynemimetophiles—men who are sexually and erotically turned on by a lady with a penis, and who may pay them as prostitutes. In some instances, a gynemimetophilic man sets up a long-term pairbonded relationship with a gynemimetic lady with a penis, and they live together.

Urban American gynemimetics neither teach nor learn from the hijras of India, the xanith of Oman, or the berdaches of native American Indians. Worldwide, the patterns of gynemimetic lives have a high degree of overlap (Money and Lamacz, 1984), despite their independent cultural origin and lack of a shared cultural history.

Gynemimesis is not restricted to the human species. There is a parallel in a species of freshwater sunfish. *Leponus machrochirus,* the bluegill sunfish of northeastern North America (Gross, 1984). The female in this species is distinguished by being banded with speckled stripes. All females are the same, but males come in three models. The largest male is bigger than the female, is uniformly colored, and is the one that builds a nest to attract a female. The smallest male is also uniform in color, but matures earlier than the larger one, and is more elongated in shape. He hides in plant growth, biding his time while the other two hover over the nest and prepare to spawn. As the female releases her eggs into the water, he darts in and releases his fertilizing sperms before his larger competitor has had time to fertilize the eggs with his own sperms.

This miniature male has another competitor, the middle-sized male whose advantage lies in being a gynemimetic. He is striped so as to look like a female and is slightly smaller than the female companion who escorts him. Together they approach a large, nesting male. The large male hovers above both of them, waiting to spawn. He loses out to his gynemimetic rival whose position between the male above and the female below gives his sperm priority in reaching the female's eggs as they are released.

7 TRANSVESTISM

In the early part of the twentieth century, at around the same time as Magnus Hirschfeld was writing about transvestism, his great contemporary in sexology, Havelock Ellis (1859–1939), was using the term *eonism*, which he had coined, the eponym being the Chevalier d'Eon de Beaumont (1728–1810) (see Section 5, this chapter). The Chevalier was famous in French eighteenth-century clandestine diplomatic history as a male-to-female cross dresser.

Although eonism is now seldom used, it has great potential as a much needed generic term comprising the four types of gender crosscoding in which cross dressing is a prominent feature (Table 3-1), namely, transexualism, transvestophilia, mimesis (gynemimesis and andromimesis), and transvestism of the type that is not fetishistic. Eonism is needed as a generic term to replace transvestism, which is too amorphously inclusive of acts as well as syndromes of cross dressing.

Transvestism cannot be rehabilitated as a generic term for cross dressing, because it is needed to refer to nonfetishistic manifestations of cross dressing that are not transexual and not mimetic (Table 3-1). Nonfetishistic transvestism represents gender crosscoding that is episodic and partial, though unlimited rather than limited in scope, with respect to clothing style.

Transvestism qualifies as nonfetishistic when, unlike transvestophilia, it is not an essential ingredient of sexuoerotic arousal and attainment of orgasm. Unlike transexualism, it does not involve genital surgery, nor even hormonal changing of the body.

Without either a fetishistic or a transexual supplement, the term transvestism is synonymous with cross dressing. Likewise transvestite is synonymous with cross dresser, and to transvest with to cross dress. Cross dressing has an Anglo-Saxon derivation and has never been used as the name for a clinical syndrome, as has the Latin-derived transvestism. Transvestism alone, however, devoid of an association with fetishism or transexualism, is not a syndrome of cross dressing. Instead it is a manifestation of the act of cross dressing. Since dressing is traditionally gender-coded almost everywhere on earth, cross dressing is one highly specific act of gender crosscoding. Cross dressing by itself does not, however, indicate whether or not it bears a relationship to other variables of gender crosscoding, nor whether it is symptomatic of an accompanying syndrome, in particular transexualism, transvestophilia, or gynemimesis/andromimesis.

Apart from being syndrome related, cross dressing may be associated with religious, shamanistic, occult, or secular ceremony and ritual. In some circles, cross dressing is affirmed as an instrument of sexual politics. It is used as a political statement in affirmation of androgyny and sexual liberation. In espionage and police hunts, it may be used as a disguise for either escape or entrapment. It is in the theater, however, and as entertainment that cross-dressing for disguise and impersonation reaches its apogee and greatest fame.

Cross dressing is a theatrical expediency or necessity if acting is a profession traditionally forbidden to women. Female roles must then be acted by males trained as female impersonators, as in the traditional Japanese Kabuki theater, and in the Shakespearian theater. Theatrical cross dressing also has a long history as a device for the development of plots of amorous and political intrigue calling for males to be disguised as females, or vice versa. Female-impersonating roles do not, per se, require actors who are also homosexually inclined in their private lives, only actors who are dramatically convincing in the role. There is a tradition of homosexual theater, that of comedy or burlesque impersonation, in which all of the actors and musicians are cross dressed. The majority of the roles are for female impersonators, and a minority for male impersonators.

Independently of the professional stage and screen, male homosexuals have a long-established tradition of masquerade parties and balls. Some are scheduled annually for Halloween and New Year's Eve, or to coincide with celebrations like Mardi Gras and the Mummers' Day Parade. These are carnival occasions that offer a splendid opportunity for opulent cross dressing not only for transexuals and transvestophiles, but especially for those who call themselves drag queens and who sporadically cross dress for comic amusement, a virtuoso performance, and the accolade of spectators. Women as male impersonators are not excluded from these carnival occasions, but they do not have a tradition of staging them for themselves. They do not have an institution that corresponds to the drag queens' ball.

8 HOMOPHILIA

The gender-crosscoded entities of Table 3-1 are arranged in order of magnitude from top to bottom and from left to right, so that the extent and/or duration of crosscoding is greater in transexualism than in mimesis or in transvestophilia, and greater in all three than in transvestism. Moreover, in all four, the crosscoding includes cross dressing, which is absent from homophilia, male and female, and from bisexualism (homo/heterophilia).

What this all adds up to is that there may be very little that is crosscoded in homophilia, which is indeed the case in gay men whose gender coding is all masculine, except for the sex of the partner with whom they fall in love, and correspondingly in lesbian women whose gender coding is all feminine, except for the sex of the partner with whom they fall in love. In other words, they are gender-crosscoded (or gender-transposed) only on the criterion of the sex of the lover. Why do I use this criterion? Many people have asked me this question and argued over the answer, which is that one must have some criterion of what is gender-crosscoded and what is not. It is very widely accepted in society and in comparative life sciences that the criterion of sexuoerotically uncrossed gender coding is this: the prevalence of males and females as sexual partners is greater than the prevalence of males and males or females and females as sexual partners. This prevalence applies across species. In the human species it applies also to partners in love affairs and falling in love.

The foregoing characterization of gender coding as being sexuoerotically uncrossed if a sexual partnership is heterosexual, whereas it is crossed (transposed) if a sexual partnership is homosexual, applies specifically and exclusively to the sexuoerotic component of gender coding, considered by itself alone, independently of all the other gender-coded components of identity and role. Any or none of these other components may be either uncrossed or crossed, in either homosexual or heterosexual people.

Thus, for example, it is possible for a woman to have a career as a heavy-machinery operator, traditionally coded as male, to wear a male construction crew uniform to work, to engage in traditionally male recreational and leisure pursuits, to have the same name as a man might have, to fraternize with males more than females, and, nonetheless, to be heterosexually pairbonded to a male lover as her exclusive sexual partner.

Conversely, it is possible for a woman to have a career, recreational and leisure life, domestic and family life, social life, and fashion style that are all traditionally gender-coded as female, and nonetheless to be homosexually pairbonded to a female lover as her exclusive sexual partner.

By changing woman to man, female to male, and her to his, the foregoing two paragraphs apply to men also. Among gay polemicists and theoreticians, the concept of gender crosscoding (transposition) has met with greatest resistance when applied to the man who is gender-uncrosscoded as traditionally masculine on all counts except that the partner in a sexual or a love affair is invariably male. This is the kind of man who is a national football champion, military hero, or matinee idol and who, when he "comes out" and publicly declares himself homosexual, shakes the gender-divided foundations of a social order that relies on him as a role model for youth. Society simply cannot integrate the public masculine image of him with the private image of his having another man, instead of a woman, as a lover and sexual partner, and thus depriving a woman of sexuoerotic access to his body, his penis, and his fertility.

The nonerotically masculine, erotically homosexual man has given rise, among professionals, to the saying that he has a masculine gender identity but a homosexual orientation or object preference (see Section 3, this chapter). The error of this way of saying things is that it robs gender identity of its sexuoerotic foundation. It attributes gender identity to us human beings as if we were Barbie and Ken dolls (see Chapter 2, Section 2), with nothing between our legs.

In the older literature, there was some attempt to recognize that the genitals do exist in male homosexuals of both the Ken and Barbie type by subdividing male homosexuality, and to a lesser degree female homosexuality also, into active and passive, on the basis of the faulty stereotype that the male role in heterosexual intercourse is active and insertive, and the female role passive and receptive. Far too many homosexuals, however, are role interchangeable (vice reversible, to quote one homosexual youth) for the active and passive classification of insertor and insertee to be universally applicable.

For those who are not readily role interchangeable, there is still no reasonable theory of orifices—no theory of why anal penetration is orgasmic ecstasy for some and anorgasmic torture for others, for example. There is a parallel lack of scientifically based information with respect to giving and taking orgasms in oral sex, nipple sex, or any other way—in clitoral sex and vaginal sex, or penile sex and scrotal sex, for example. With respect to the organs and orifices of maximum orgasmic satisfaction, people are different, not only in degree, but also in type. Orgasmic typology applies to both homosexuals and heterosexuals. It is better understood among those who use personal columns of newspapers and magazines to advertise for and find a sexual partner than it is among the theoreticians of sex therapy. Sex therapists today classify all people on the same orgasmic spectrum. The research task ahead is to find out how many different orgasmic spectrums there are, and how to fit each person on the right one with a matching partner.

In the gay vernacular, the so-called active and passive types are recognized among lesbians as butch and femme. Butch is also applied to gay men, to contrast with the more effeminate and swishy or nelly type. The homosexual partner who is a predominantly heterosexual bisexual is also referred to not as butch, but as trade, or rough trade. However, there are no formally recognized names by which to differentiate homosexual men who are masculinely gender-coded, except in their love lives and sex lives, from those whose entire lives are more femininely coded and who therefore are more readily recognized in public by reason of their feminized body language and life-style. Possibly the former could be referred to as Spartan gays, and the latter as Athenian gays.

The same problem with names applies, *pari passu*, to women who are lesbians. Perhaps a nomenclature committee could agree on famous names in history or literature to be used as eponyms for each of the paired subtypes.

Whatever their names, the dual typology of male and female homosexuals represents not a fixed and absolute polarity, but rather extremes on a continuum, with different grades or degrees in between. What the two types share in common is an orientation or status that is exclusively homosexual. The defining characteristic of exclusive homosexuality, male or female, is being erotosexually attracted to and aroused by, and also falling in love with, only a person with the same sexual body morphology and external sexual anatomy as one's own. For such a person, the potential for a bisexual compromise is no greater than it is for the exclusively heterosexual person. The defining characteristic of exclusive heterosexuality is being erotosexually attracted to and aroused by, and also falling in love with, only a person with the body morphology and sexual anatomy not the same as one's own.

9 HOMO/HETEROPHILIA

The bifurcation of gender coding that characterizes the transvestophilic phenomenon of two names, two wardrobes, and two personalities is, in some instances, so complete that it includes genitosexual relationships. There is, for example, such a case (Money, 1970b) as that of a transvestophile who, as a youth, was a member of a young adult bisexual gang. His fellow gang members knew only his male-clothed, male personality, and nothing of his cross dressing and crosscoded feminine personality. Their Saturday night agenda was gay-bashing. They hung out in a park or other section of town known to be a gay male cruising and pick-up area. They used themselves as lures, until one of them picked up a gay man and accompanied him to the gang's clandestine place of rendezvous. He and one or more of his friends may or may not then have used the man's sexual services to achieve their own orgasm. On signal, they proceeded to close in on him in a group assault and robbery that left him wounded, unconscious, or possibly dead. Their ambush completed, the majority of the gang members were in a heightened state of sexual arousal for intercourse with a girlfriend or, if alone, for masturbation.

Not so the transvestophilic member of the gang, however. His arousal was brought about by cross dressing, and then offering his sexual services as an impersonating female to a man with whom he delighted in being sexually submissive—but woe unto the same man had the transvestophile not been in female attire, impersonating a female! Had he been his masculine self in male clothes, he would have met a homosexual advance with assaultive violence. Cross dressed as a female, however, the zenith of his homosexual episode would be reached after he rejoined his girlfriend and engaged in sex with her while still wearing women's lingerie—or, failing that, while having a fantasy of doing so. Otherwise, he might wear women's clothing while masturbating alone. Replayed as a mental tape, the entire experience would engender erotic arousal on future occasions, until finally it would become too worn and faded and would need to be replaced with a new adventure. If it had been recorded not on a mental tape, but on an actual videotape, then the videotape would be classified as personalized pornography. It would engender erotic arousal as pornography for others, only if it matched their own sexuoerotic fantasy.

The foregoing exemplifies transvestophilic bisexuality that is unusual insofar as it expands beyond sexual participation with a partner of each sex to include dualism both of gender-coded clothing and also of behavior that is not specifically sexual and erotic. By contrast, most people who are capable of functioning bisexually with their sex organs are not enmeshed in so extensive a transposition of male and female gender coding.

There are some men and women who are not totally but sufficiently monosexual, either homosexually or heterosexually, so that their sex organs will become aroused for them in the company of the sex less attractive to them only if their arousal is augmented. Thus, for example, a heterosexual male may become disinhibited in the presence of another male only if his arousal is augmented by the presence of a heterosexually responsive female, in a sexual threesome. Alternatively, the augmentation may be supplied by a heterosexual or lesbian movie or videotape. Without either augmentation actually present and perceived, a heterosexual scene mentally replayed as a fantasy may suffice, although it is likely to be insufficient.

In the case of a predominantly homosexual, bisexual man who marries, the failure or insufficiency of erotosexual arousal in the absence of a homosexual stimulus may manifest itself in marital copulatory dysfunction of the hypophilic type; that is, the penis fails to erect, becomes soft too soon, ejaculates prematurely, does not ejaculate at all, loses erotic feeling, or becomes painful. Or, there may be a major loss of sexual interest in the spouse, and in inserting the penis in her vagina— misnamed among sex therapists as inhibited sexual desire, instead of unfulfilled homosexual desire!

There are parallel hypophilic dysfunctions in a married woman whose bisexual inclination is more lesbian than heterosexual. With inadequate arousal to the male stimulus, and without the reinforcement of lesbian stimuli, she also may lose sexual interest in the spouse, and may have an aversion to having his penis in her vagina. She may lubricate inadequately, have premature closure of the vaginal muscles (vaginismus), experience genital pain, lose erotic feeling, or be unable to reach the climax of orgasm. She does not lack sexual desire, but only desire for her male partner.

The role of fantasy, in this instance male heterosexual fantasy, is illustrated in the account given by a young man of his sexual life in prison (Money and Bohmer, 1980). As a young adolescent he had lived in a community where, among the toughest males of his age group, it was acceptable to be given head (fellatio), also known as a blow job, by one of the known homosexual youths or men of the neighborhood. It was accepted sporadically either for fun or for money and did not impede having hetero-sexual contacts or a love affair with a girlfriend. At the time when this man was locked up on a charge of street fighting, he was involved in a very intense, pairbonded love affair with his girlfriend, and had a very active sex life. In prison, he was suffering from intense horniness, he said, in which state, on one occasion, he went to take a shower in the communal shower room. Only one other person was in there, a young new prisoner with smooth, well-formed buttocks. In a split second, this young prisoner's body became a mirage of a woman's body in the eyes of the beholder, whose penis immediately became erect. He rapidly took shelter under a shower head, and facing a corner where he could not be seen masturbat-ing, brought himself through orgasm to flaccidity. To have been seen would have been to invite an assault, for the code among prisoners forbade the uninvited use of the image of someone else's body, as well as the body itself, for sexual arousal.

For the remainder of his months in prison, my informant admitted to synchronizing heterosexual fantasies with fellatio which he coerced his cellmate, more timid than himself, into performing on him. He would not stimulate his cellmate's penis. In the years since his release, he has re-sumed an exclusively heterosexual sex life.

There are some bisexual men and women who do not rely on fantasy to augment arousal by either a man or a woman. They have a sufficiently balanced degree of bisexuality designed into them to ensure an erotic re-sponse to a partner of either sex. If one sex predominates over the other in the extent of the erotic arousal it evokes, then that is the sex of the pairbonded love affair, should one occur. The touchstone for equality of erotic arousal with either sex is the equality of the capacity to fall in love with a member of either sex. Although there are no statistics, the preva-lence of such equality would appear not to be high.

Lack of statistics applies also to the prevalence of sequential as compared with concurrent bisexuality. The prevalence of sequential bisexuality in contemporary Western cultures is masked behind prevalence figures for the occurrence of homosexuality. For example, Kinsey's survey statistics are construed as indicating that the prevalence of exclusive homosexuality in American males is 3–4 percent (and approximately half that percentage in females), and that the prevalence of nonexclusive homosexuality is 10 percent (5 percent in females, and probably underreported by not includ-ing nongenital, romantic body contact). Nonexclusive homosexuality is synonymous with bisexuality, but Kinsey's prevalence figures do not indi-cate how many homosexual contacts occurred, nor whether they were over a brief or a prolonged time span.

Since sexual information has a high probability of being self-incriminat-ing, many informants will be guarded in what they disclose. Thus, it is probable that homosexual activity at the time of puberty and early adolescence is underreported, and that the prevalence of sequential bisexuality, beginning with a youthful homosexual phase, is more prevalent than is generally conceded. In some large American cities, there are a few neighborhoods where, for up to five generations, there has been a tradition for boys between the ages of ten and fifteen to receive financial support by picking up older gay males as sponsors. The boys are not stigmatized among their older friends or family members, many of whom had a similar sexual history. By age fifteen or sixteen, they graduate to having a girlfriend and embark on a heterosexual career.

Among adolescents who circumvent adolescent homosexual activity or who quit it in panic, there are some who coerce themselves into heterosexuality, only to find as husbands and fathers (or wives and mothers, in the case of females) that the lid on Pandora's box springs open. These are the people who, when young adulthood advances into midlife, begin the homosexual phase of sequential bisexuality. For some, the transition is to homosexual relations exclusively, whereas for others heterosexual relations also may continue. The transition may take place autonomously, or it may be a sequel to the divorce or death of the spouse or to sexual apathy in the marriage. When the youngest child leaves home, there may be a degree of freedom hitherto unavailable. The bisexualism of a parent is not transmitted to the offspring, and is not contagious. However, to avoid offending a heterosexual child, a bisexual parent may be self-coerced into suppressing homosexual expression.

The late expression of homosexuality in sequential bisexuality may be associated with recovery from illness and debilitation (e.g., recovery from alcoholism) that had masked the homosexual potential. Hypothetically it might, conversely, be associated with premature illness and deterioration from brain injury or disease, as in temporal lobe trauma and Alzheimer's disease. However, although brain pathology may release the expression of sexuality formerly strictly self-prohibited as indecent or immoral, it is not especially associated with releasing bisexuality.

In sequential bisexuality, the transition from homosexual to heterosexual expression is also known to occur autonomously in adulthood. Since this transition is socially approved and not registered as pathological, it is not likely to be recorded. If the individual were at the time in some type of treatment, the transition might be wrongly construed as a therapeutic triumph.

More than sequential bisexuality, concurrent bisexuality may be jocularly considered as having the best of two possible worlds. But it has a dark and sinister potential also. Its most malignant expression is in those individuals in whom it takes the form of a Dr. Jekyll and Mr. Hyde. The split applies not simply to heterosexuality and homosexuality, but to good and evil, licit and illicit, as well. The two names are not gender-coded as male and female as they are in the two names of the transvestophile, nor are the two personalities and the two wardrobes. Instead, the two names, wardrobes, and personalities are both male (or in the less likely case of women, female), but one, the given name with its wardrobe and personality, is for the heterosexual, and the other, an alias or a nickname, for the homosexual. The heterosexual personality is the servant of righteousness and the acolyte of a vengeful God. The homosexual personality is the servant of transgression and a fallen angel in the legions of Lucifer. The heterosexual personality has the pontificating mission of a sadistic grand inquisitor, bent on the exorcism of those possessed of homosexuality, himself included. The homosexual personality has the absolving mission of officiating indulgences in the place of masochistic penances for homosexuality, but only for himself and nobody else.

The absolute antithesis of homophobia and homophilia in this malignant form of bisexuality is not evident to those who know the individual in only one of his personalities, but not both. For those who know him only in his heterosexual guise, he is a standard-bearer of traditional sexual values, conservator of virtue, and exterminator of vice. For those who know him only in his homosexual guise, he is a standard-bearer of idealized masculine lust, a devil-may-care playmate, and a rebel fearless of consequences.

The malignancy inherent in the antithesis of homophobia and homophilia in this type of bisexuality takes its toll in self-sabotage and the sabotage of others. Self-sabotage is an ever-present threat that materializes if there is a leakage of information from those in one antithetical world to those in the other. The greater danger is, of course, that knowledge of the illicit homosexual existence will leak out to the society that knows only of the heterosexual existence. The ensuing societal abuse and deprivation, legal and social, may be extreme.

The sabotage of others is carried out professionally by some individuals with the syndrome of malignant bisexualism. Their internal homophobic war against their own homosexuality becomes externalized into a war against homosexuality in others. The malignant bisexual becomes a secret agent, living in his own private and secret homosexual world, while spying on its inhabitants, entrapping them, assaulting and killing them, or, with less overt violence, preaching against them, legislating against them, or judicially depriving them of the right to exist.

The malignant bisexual is the perfect recruit for the position of homosexual entrapment officer or decoy in the employ of the police vice squad. Supported by clandestine operations, blackmail, and threats of exposure, in espionage or in the secret police of governmental surveillance, he may achieve legendary power, such as that attributed to the J. Edgar Hoover of mythical FBI fame.

People in high places may have the power to keep under cover for a lifetime, with the homosexual manifestations of their bisexuality never exposed. Others have their career blown, as did the bisexual former U.S. congressman from Maryland, Robert E. Bauman, a fanatical homophobic ultraconservative of the religious new right, who subsequently published a biography of his own downfall (Bauman, 1986).

Bauman was exposed by a combination of surveillance and the testimony of a paid informant and blackmailer. Nowadays there is a hitherto nonexistent way of being suspected or exposed, namely by dying of AIDS. This is what happened to Roy Cohn (*New York Times*, August 3, 1986), the malignantly bisexual legal counsel for the homosexual witch hunter from Wisconsin, U.S. Senator Joseph McCarthy, himself suspected of malignant bisexuality. Together, they destroyed the lives of many American citizens, simply by publicly accusing them of being homosexual, falsely or otherwise.

Religious leaders are not exempt from the homophobic fanaticism of malignant bisexualism; witness the case of the Reverend Billy James Hargis (*Time*, February 16, 1976), the television evangelist and new right fundamentalist. By a young couple of his congregation whom he married, he was unmasked as practicing what he vehemently preached against. They revealed to one another on their wedding night that the evangelist had formerly had sexual relations with each of them. Another bisexual television evangelist who did not practice what he preached is the Reverend Jim Bakker (*Time*, August 3, 1987), although in his case his preaching was not stridently antisexual. Nonetheless, his failure to conform to the rigid standards of fundamentalist sexual orthodoxy required him to relinquish his electronic pulpit.

Scratch the surface of the self-righteous and find the devil. This is a maxim of widespread applicability, not only to the self-righteous in high places of homophobic power, influence, and authority, but also to the homophobic, gay-bashing hoodlums who, as in the case with which this section began, pick up or are picked up by a gay man, have sex with him, and then exorcise their own homosexual guilt by assaulting and maybe killing him. Both versions of homophobia are manifestations of malignant bisexuality that, in an interview with the journalist, Doug Ireland, for *New York Magazine* (July 24, 1978), I called the *exorcist syndrome*.

There must be a very widespread prevalence of lesser degrees of the exorcist syndrome in the population at large. If it were not so, otherwise-decent people would not persecute their homosexual fellow citizens nor tolerate their persecution. Instead they would live and let live those who are destined to have a different way of being human in love and sex. They would tolerate them as they do the left-handed. Tolerance would remove those very pressures that progressively coerce increasing numbers of our children and grandchildren to grow up blighted with the curse of malignant bisexuality.

10 POSTPUBERTAL HORMONAL THEORIES

Endocrinology is a young science (Young, 1961). The sex hormones were not isolated and synthesized until the 1920s, and were first commercially marketed for widespread clinical use in the 1930s and 1940s. In animals they had been shown to govern not only fertility but also mating behavior, especially the receptivity of the female at the ovulatory phase of being in heat. (Proceptivity had not been conceptualized in that era.) From male- and female-hormonal control of male and female mating behavior, specifically, the logical next step was to the male- and female-hormonal control of, respectively, everything masculine and feminine globally. The next step was to look for an excess of female hormones in male homosexuals and an excess of male hormones in female homosexuals. That the crosscoding of hormones would cause the crosscoding of sexual orientation was a popular hypothesis of the 1940s, and it continues to be so in newsprint and magazine science today.

The first round of investigations (reviewed in Money, 1961a,b, 1970a) produced inconsistent and inconclusive findings, in large part because of the cumbersome and imprecise technology for measuring hormones in blood and urine. Enthusiasm for hormones and homosexuality research waned until the arrival, in the mid-1960s, of the precision technology of radioimmunoassay for measuring even minute levels of hormones circulating in body fluids, and taken up by hormone-hungry cells.

The new round of research (reviewed in Money, 1980a, 1986b) also produced findings that were inconsistent and inconclusive, chiefly because of insufficient attention to diagnostic homogeneity of the sample subjects or insufficient attention to the possible significance of intervening or contaminating variables. There are only two studies that cannot be faulted on these counts, one by Parks et al. (1974) and one by Sanders, Bain, and Langerin (1985). The evidence of both of these studies is that there is no difference in the circulating levels of sex hormones in the bloodstream of homosexual and heterosexual adult males. The absence of lesbian studies can be attributed to the confounding factor of fluctuation of hormonal levels in synchrony with the menstrual cycle.

Another approach to hormones and male homosexuality in adulthood pertains not to endogenous hormone levels, but to changes in them after administering an injection of exogenous hormone. The injected hormone is estrogen (Premarin, or estradiol benzoate). The rationale for giving the injection is that it has an effect that differs in women and men. The effect is on the pituitary gland, which secretes luteinizing hormone (LH). In phase one of the response, the influx of injected estrogen signals the pituitary to shut off the secretion of LH, until blood estrogen level lowers toward normal. In phase two the pituitary resumes secreting LH. In females it overshoots, so that the amount of LH entering the bloodstream is transiently higher than normal. Doerner and associates in East Berlin measured this LH overshoot or rebound effect not only in women, but also in heterosexual, homosexual, and bisexual men (Doerner et al., 1975; Doerner, 1976). They found that all the men had a lowered LH level in phase one. In phase two, LH returned to its normal level without a transient rebound effect in heterosexual men, whereas in homosexual men there was some rebound, but not as much as in normal women.

Doerner construed his finding to mean that the pituitary gland in homosexual men was partially able to simulate a female response because its regulator mechanism in the nearby hypothalamus of the brain was incompletely masculinized. Going one step further, he conjectured that the hypothalamus had been left incompletely masculinized in prenatal life through an insufficiency of the male hormone testosterone. Therefore, he proposed that pregnant mothers in East Germany should have the sex of their unborn child tested. If male, then the fetus should be given the benefit of testosterone injections (which would masculinize the mother, if strong enough) to ensure that the baby would not grow up to be a male homosexual. This proposal met with a storm of protest at international meetings and has not been further pursued. However, it did provoke a need for Doerner's findings to be replicated.

There have been three replication studies. One, by Gladue, Green, and Hellman (1984) at Stony Brook, New York, was published with the claim that it had indeed confirmed Doerner's findings, although the authors glossed over a subsidiary and preliminary new finding in their data that pertained to the gonadotropin factor—LH and its companion hormone, FSH (follicle-stimulating hormone)—which together are the gonadotropins secreted by the pituitary gland in response to signals from the testicles or ovaries.

This gonadotropin factor received special attention in the second replication study, conducted by Gooren (1986) in Amsterdam. Independently of the estrogen test, Gooren put all of his subjects (male heterosexuals and homosexuals, and untreated male-to-female transexuals) through a gonadotropin test. They all received an injection of chorionic gonadotropin, which stimulates the testicles to increase their secretion of testosterone. The injection did have this expected effect in some of the homosexual men as well as in some of the heterosexual men, and in all of the male-to-female transexuals. Those homosexual and heterosexual men whose testicles showed only a weak response to the gonadotropin injection also showed an LH rebound response when given an injection of estrogen. The conclusion is that the LH rebound effect is not specific to homosexuals, since it was found in heterosexuals also, and that it is an indicator not of sexual orientation, but of whether or not the testicles have a normal or impaired responsivity to stimulation by gonadotropin. Next it will be important to ascertain the prevalence of impaired gonadotropin response in the testicles of a random sample of homosexual and heterosexual men. Hypothetically, it is possible that there is an as yet unidentified syndrome of testicular impairment, and maybe other symptoms (Kolodny et al., 1971, 1972), that predisposes a boy to grow up as a homosexual. It is already quite clear, however, that the majority of homosexual men have normal testicles that respond with a normal male hormonal response to gonadotropic hormones.

The third replication study was done at the University of Nebraska by Hendricks, Graber, and Rodriguez-Sierra (1986). They investigated the effect of three different quantities (10, 20, and 30 mg) of injected estrogen (Premarin). All three dosages had the expected effect of lowering the blood level of LH, but only after the smallest dose of estrogen did the expected high LH rebound effect occur predictably. After the intermediate dosage, the effect was unpredictable and, after the highest dosage, negligible. These findings were the same for homosexual as for heterosexual men.

As presently measured and tested, hormonal secretions from the endocrine glands (as compared with other hormone-secreting cells), definitely are not the key to understanding the origins of homosexuality, bisexuality, or heterosexuality. My construing of the current evidence is that the experimental and investigative endocrinology of sexual orientation is at an impasse. The next advance in knowledge will come from further study not of the gonadal and pituitary hormones, but of the newly recognized peptide hormones, neuromodulators, and neurotransmitters that have been found, or will be found, differentially housed in various parts of the reproductive system and the genitalia, and in the autonomic and the central nervous systems, both peripherally and in the sexual centers and pathways of the spinal cord and, above all, the brain.

Another version of the attempt to explain homosexuality by hormones, more a doctrine than a hypothesis, deserves to be left scientifically buried, but gets occasionally disinterred (Manosevitz, 1970; Tripp, 1975; Storms, 1981). According to the doctrine of this attempted explanation, boys who will become homosexual are more sexual than other boys of the same age because of either the larger size of their penises or the earlier onset of puberty, or both—but they are more sexual only with boys of their own age, not girls. The unstated premise in the logic of this doctrine is that each stage of psychosexual development is determined by chronological age alone, and bears no relationship whatsoever to hormonal and physique age—which is manifestly absurd. An accompaniment of the onset of hormonal puberty, irrespective of age, is the onset of erotic interest. In those boys who are destined to be heterosexual, the interest is in girls. In those who are destined to be homosexual, it is in boys. Enlargement of the penis is one of the signs of the onset of puberty, but its adult size is not related to either early or late puberty. It is as erroneous to relate homosexuality to penis size as it is to left and right sidedness of the positioning of the penis in the trousers (homosexual to the left, heterosexual to the right) Both are without substantiating evidence.

There is no alarm bell that sounds to signal the onset of puberty. It is a protracted process with hormonal origins three or more years in advance of the first visible evidence, the signs of which develop insidiously, and not inevitably in the same sequence. Moreover, boys do not keep detailed written records of the progressive signs of pubertal development, and retrospective recall is not reliable. Even the first ejaculation may not be recalled. It may have occurred in sleep, without waking.

Precise documentation is not, however, a serious consideration to the proponents of the doctrine of early puberty as a cause of homosexuality. Its premise is that when puberty is early, boys are still at the age of fraternizing only with other boys to whom, therefore, they become sexually attached. Once popular, this is the sex-segregated explanation of homosexual attachment based on institutionalized life in an all-boys' boarding school, a seminary, a Boy Scouts' camp, a military barracks, a reformatory, or a prison. For most participants, it is the first phase of sequential bisexuality, not long-term homosexuality. Its error is perpetuated by lack of follow-up statistics to show the proportion of boys who are sex-segregated at puberty and become heterosexual as adults. Homosexual activity in a sex-segregated adolescent population, representing the homosexual phase of sequential bisexuality for the majority of boys, is quite unrelated to the age of the onset of puberty. The important variable is the effectiveness of the social sanctions that keep the sexes segregated.

In societies where juvenile sexual rehearsal play is not negatively sanctioned, boys and girls at puberty are not heterosexually phobic and do not sexually self-segregate. They fraternize heterosexually. There is no imperative homosexual phase of boys fraternizing only with boys, and girls only with girls. Sex hormones regulate the onset of puberty, but puberty does not, by its timing, determine either homosexuality or heterosexuality. The sex of the partner is determined partly by social availability and partly by personal attraction to one sex more than the other, which has been designed into the G-I/R in the prepubertal years of childhood.

Attribution of homosexuality to precocious onset of puberty is not substantiated in cases of genuinely precocious puberty—that is, puberty that has its onset as early as age three, and no later than age eight in girls and nine in boys (Money and Hampson, 1955; Hampson and Money, 1955; Money and Alexander, 1969; Money and Walker, 1971). At these early ages of pubertal onset, heterosexual imagery and ideation prevail almost without exception. Heterosexuality is manifested in dreams and fantasies, including masturbation fantasies. Its precise details are contingent on what sexual learning the pubertally precocious child has assimilated: cuddling, hugging, breast suckling, and kissing precede genital contact. Genital sexuoeroticism makes its appearance developmentally not in a void, but in the context of social traditions that define the rules of sexual learning and sexual expression from the earliest phases of infantile and juvenile sexual rehearsal play onward. There is no automatic biological clock signaling that a child's development should be either homosexual or heterosexual; nor is there an automatic mechanism of sociosexual conditioning and learning that does so. Neither biological teleology nor the mechanics of stimulus-response alone have the power to determine sexuoerotic status. Biology and social input interact at a crucial phase of maturation. It is their interaction that determines the outcome.

11 CONCEPTS OF DETERMINISM

Sexologically, biological teleology translates into evolutionary teleology in comparative sexology, and into motivational teleology in clinical sexology.

Mechanistic determinism translates into various forms of somatic determinism in comparative sexology, and into stimulus–response determinism in clinical sexology.

In this book, and in all of my writings, I have avoided adopting the teleology of motivation as a primary explanatory concept, and likewise stimulus–response mechanism. For me, motivational drives, instincts, or needs belong in history's storage closet along with astrology, phlogiston, vital forces, and demonic possessions. They explain everything, and they explain nothing. Of course, I am able to converse with patients and other people who do use these idioms. In fact, I may even reciprocate their use in interviewing for a sexual history. Nonetheless, an idiom is not an organizing principle or concept on which a science is built, and it is as an organizing principle that I reject instincts, drives, needs, and motivations.

In rejecting teleology, I know, of course, that for many sexologists the only fashionable alternative is the behavioral determinism of either Pavlovian conditioning or Skinnerian operant conditioning. However, I do not substitute a mechanistic stimulus–response principle whereby sexual man and woman become scientistic robots—not at all. As a first principle, I accept sexual behavior, like all of human behavior, as a kinetic or dynamic system by definition. Like the solar system, it goes; that is the scheme of things. Parenthetically, I can be a little facetious and say that I must figure out its "go-itivity" or its "go-ationality,"—to use bastard graftings of Latin suffixes. Without Latin and Greek suffixes most of motivation theory, in the English language, would have had no vehicle for its existence.

Some years ago I wrote a short paper on linguistic resources and psychodynamic theory (Money, 1955b). It is fascinating to see that we are victims of language when it comes to basic principles. For example, one always has to use some other psychic force or drive to explain dreams, because one does not have words like "dreamivity" or "dreamuance" that explain something else. Anything that is known to us by a word of Anglo-Saxon or earlier Nordic origin has to be explained by something else that has a Latin or Greek root.

I have found it possible to make headway if I substitute for motivation the concept of *threshold*—threshold for the release or inhibition of behavior (see Chapter 2, Section 6). Then I can classify the types of behavior released or inhibited, the primary types being lexical versus gestural. In another way one might say imagistic versus signalistic or, in simplest English, voice talk versus body talk. The concept of threshold is really an extraordinarily useful one. It conveys a great advantage of continuity and unity to what would otherwise be disparate and divided. Thus one may look for threshold differences in the release or the inhibition of sexual behavior. The threshold may apply to behavior attributable to genetic programing, or to prenatal hormonal programing, or to toxic programing, or to circulating hormonal programing at puberty, or to pheromonal programing—pheromones being stimulating odors.

One may look also for differences of threshold with regard to visual-image programing of erotic arousal. There is an implication for sex differences here, in that more men are girl watchers than women are boy watchers. Males at puberty have nature's own presentation of a pornography show in their wet dreams and their masturbation fantasies, whereas females are not so programed for visual imagery (see Chapter 2, Section 6). One could go one step further up the ladder and say that thresholds can be studied with regard to activation or inhibition in social-biography programing. The top of the ladder would represent traumatic or deteriorative change in the central nervous system—change in the threshold for release or inhibition of sexual behavior. In that respect the temporal lobes of the brain and its limbic system are particularly important. A temporal lobe lesion is very likely to change sexual behavior thresholds in some way or another. But the deteriorative process could also be a matter of nervous system disease in the pelvic genitalia themselves, and not simply of sexual pathways in the brain.

The concept of threshold does indeed have great value because of the wide spectrum to which it applies. It helps to tie what would otherwise be a lot of loose ends together. It also allows one to think developmentally or longitudinally, in terms of stages or experiences that are programed serially, or hierarchically, or cybernetically (i.e., regulated by mutual feedback).

No longer does one need to be enslaved to such worn-out platitudes of dichotomy as nature versus nurture, the biological versus the social, the innate versus the acquired, or the physiological versus the psychological. All these dichotomies capitalize on the very ancient, pre-Platonic, prebiblical dichotomy of the body versus the mind, or the physical versus the spiritual. This body/mind dichotomy is now so ingrained a principle of our vernacular or folk metaphysics that it is something very difficult for us to get rid of. Yet as scientists I believe we have to find our way around it. Otherwise it spells total disaster to the development of sexual science today, tomorrow, and in the future.

In order to circumvent the platitudes of nature versus nurture, I needed a concept that would not only encompass both, but also transcend both. I formulated this concept as irreducible exigencies of being human that apply universally, transculturally, and transhistorically. They are not causal in either the teleological or mechanistic sense of causality. They are, instead, phenomenological verities of existence to be taken into account by any and every theory of the causality of what human beings do, sexologically or otherwise. There are five universal exigencies of being human, named and briefly characterized, as follows.

Pairbondage

Pairbondage means being bonded together in pairs, as in the parent–child pairbond, or the pairbond of those who are lovers or breeding partners. In everyday usage, bondage implies servitude or enforced submission. Although pairbondage is defined so as not to exclude this restrictive connotation, it has a larger meaning that encompasses also mutual dependency and cooperation, and affectional attachment. Pairbondage has a twofold phyletic origin in mammals. One is mutual attachment between a nursing mother and her feeding baby, without which the young fail to survive. The other is mutual attraction between males and females, and their accommodation to one another in mating, without which a diecious species fails to reproduce itself.

Male–female pairbonding is species specific and individually variable with respect to its duration and the proximity of the pair. In human beings, the two extremes are represented by anonymous donor fertilization versus lifelong allegiance and copulatory fidelity.

Troopbondage

Troopbondage means bondedness among individuals so that they become members of a family or troop that continues its long-term existence despite the loss or departure of any one member. Human troopbondage has its primate phyletic origin in the fact that members of the troop breed not in unison but asynchronously, with transgenerational overlap, and with age-related interdependency. In newborn mammals, the troopbonding of a baby begins with its pairbonding with its mother as the phyletically ordained minimum unit for its survival and health. After weaning, it is also phyletically ordained for herding and troopbonding species that isolation and deprivation of the company of other members of the species or their surrogate replacements is incompatible with health and survival. Nonhuman primate species are, in the majority of instances, troopbonders like ourselves.

Abidance

Abidance means continuing to remain, be sustained, or survive in the same condition or circumstances of living or dwelling. It is a noun formed from the verb, to abide (from the Anglo-Saxon root, *bidan*, to bide). There are three forms of the past participle, abode, abided, and abidden.

In its present usage, abidance means, like its synonym, sustentation, to be sustained in one's ecological niche or dwelling place in inanimate nature in cooperation or competition with others or one's own species, among other species of fauna and flora. Abidance has its phyletic origin in the fact that human primates are mammalian omnivores ecologically dependent on air, water, earth, and fire, and on the products of these four, particularly in the form of nourishment, shelter, and clothing, for survival. Human troops or individuals with an impoverished ecological niche that fails to provide sufficient food, water, shelter, and clothing do not survive.

Ycleptance

Yclept is an Elizabethan word, one form of the past participle of to clepe, meaning to name, to call, or to style. Ycleped and cleped are two alternative past participles. Ycleptance means the condition or experience of being classified, branded, labeled, or typecast. It has its phyletic basis in likeness and unlikeness between individual and group attributes. Human beings have named and typecast one another since before recorded time. The terms range from the haphazard informality of nicknames that recognize personal idiosyncrasies, to the highly organized formality of scientific classifications or medical diagnoses that prognosticate our futures. The categories of ycleptance are many and diverse: sex, age, family, clan, language, race, region, religion, politics, wealth, occupation, health, physique, looks, temperament, and so on. We all live typecast under the imprimatur of our fellow human beings. We are either stigmatized or idolized by the brand names or lables under which we are yclept. They shape our destinies.

Foredoomance

Doom, in Anglo-Saxon and Middle English usage meant what is laid down, a judgment, or decree. In today's usage it also means destiny or fate, especially if the predicted outcome is adverse, as in being doomed to suffer harm, sickness, or death. A foredoom is a doom ordained beforehand. Foredoomance is the collective noun that, as here defined, denotes the condition of being preordained to die, and to being vulnerable to injury, defect, and disease. Foredoomance has its phyletic origins in the principles of infirmity and the mortality of all life forms. Some individuals are at greater risk than others because of imperfections or errors in their genetic code. Some are at greater risk by reason of exposure to more dangerous places or things. All, however, are exposed to the risk, phyletically ordained, that all life forms, from viruses and bacteria to insects and vertebrates, are subject to being displaced by, and preyed upon, by other life forms. Foredoomance applies to each one of us at first hand, in a primary way, and also in a derivative way insofar as it applies also to those we know. Their suffering grieves us; their dying is our bereavement.

Coping Strategies

The human organism has three generic strategies for coping with the five universal exigencies: adhibition, inhibition, and explication. These strategies are under the governance of bodymind and should not be attributed to such inferential entities as unconscious motivation, voluntary choice, or willpower.

Adhibition and inhibition derive etymologically from the same Latin root, *habere*, to have or to hold. The verb, adhibit, means to engage, take, let in, use, or apply. Inhibit means to restrain, hinder, check, or prohibit. Thus adhibition is characterized by actively becoming engaged in doing something, gaining mastery or control of a situation, accomplishment, and fulfillment. Inhibition is characterized by becoming actively disengaged, avoiding or circumventing a situation, yielding, and being thwarted or deprived.

Explication derives from the Latin, *explicatus*, meaning unfolded. To explicate means to explain, interpret, or attribute meaning to an experience, situation, signal, or stimulus. Thus, explication as a coping strategy is characterized by actively construing, inferring, conceptualizing, formulating, designating, evaluating, confabulating, and, in general, trying to make sense of what happens.

The aforesaid three coping strategies are generic insofar as they are inferential abstractions and conceptualizations derived from particular coping strategies, stratagems, or tactics. Any particular example of coping is classified as being primarily adhibitory, inhibitory, or explicatory, but each has the other two strategies represented as either secondary or tertiary, respectively. The ratio of the mix allows each particular strategy, stratagem, or tactic to have a three-way interpretation. Thus a major episode of transvestophilia associated with depression—although it may be primarily inhibitory and incapacitating from the viewpoint of the sufferer—is secondarily adhibitory, insofar as it has a manipulatory, tyrannical effect on the partner. It is tertiarily explicatory insofar as its genesis may be incorrectly attributed by the sufferer, perhaps to the extent of his being quasi-delusionally suspicious of being persecuted by others. The coexistence of these three interpretations constitutes the basis upon which psychodynamic hypotheses are constructed by scholars of sexology as well as other sciences.

With each of the generic categories of coping strategy, there are several recognizably different particular strategies, stratagems, or tactics for coping with the various demands subsumed under the five universal exigencies. A provisional listing of them is adapted from previous writings (Chapters 3–5 in Money, 1957; Chapter 9 in Money, 1986b), as follows.

Adhibitory Strategies. Perseveration; orderliness, hoarding and ritual; constant exertion; risk exploits; protest exploits; mating protests; surrogate displacement; impersonation; addiction.

Inhibitory Strategies. Fixation and regression; disownment; phasic disownment; phobia; sleeping spells; depression; suicide; mutilatory sacrifice of body parts; organs and limb amnesias; visceral amnesias; autonomic dysfunctions; gestural and vocal automatisms; seizures and paroxysmal states.

Explicatory Strategies. Causal explanation; mirth and the comic; fantasy; dream; hallucination; depersonalization.

The five universal exigencies of being human, and the strategies of inhibition, adhibition, and explication constitute a conceptual or theoretical system to apply to sexological research in society and culture, as well as in the clinic. The system applies also to sexological diagnosis and prognosis in sex counseling and therapy. In the history of sexology, it is a system of post-Freudian, postmotivational psychodynamics. It is post-Pavlovian and post-Skinnerian as applied to stimulus–response theory. It is not univariate but multivariate. In the clinic it has the special virtue of freedom from the idioms of judgmentalism that haunt motivation theory: It allows the patient and the sexologist to be allies aligned against the syndrome, and not against one another as adversaries. It is a system that protects sexologists from the trap of motivational language that surreptitiously attributes to a patient personal guilt, blame, and responsibility for his or her syndrome. For that, patients are greatly appreciative. They are not helped by being judged and condemned, even covertly, for being deficient in health and well-being.

12 EPILOGUE AND SYNOPSIS

There are no absolute criteria of what is male and what is female in gender coding. Therefore, there are no absolute criteria by which to identify gender crosscoding. Consequently, in human sexology, one tolerates the penis/vulva criterion as a satisfactory approximation of the male/female criterion for the purpose of stipulating that masculine is what males do and feminine is what females do.

One must guard against cultural chauvinism, since a great deal of what is gender-coded is not intrinsic to male or female, but extrinsic and culture bound. There are no culture-free definitions of masculine and feminine. Thus, there is always a significant cultural component that becomes incorporated into childhood gender crosscoding when it occurs. However, the cultural component does not account for everything. It is grafted onto a prenatal proclivity or compliancy, and reinforces or endorses it.

In conventional psychoanalytic theory applied to boys who are stigmatized in the vernacular as sissy, the mother (close-binding or domineering) has been held more directly responsible than the father (meek, distant, absent, or abusive) for the child's gender crosscoding. However, in some cases, if not all, fathers may also contribute more positively insofar as a father may covertly court his son's allegiance when there is an adversarial relationship between the husband and wife. To replace what is missing in his relationship with his wife, he may cast the boy in the role of an understudy for an alternative wife in the future. The son, in turn, may be readily compliant and enter into a collusion that keeps his daddy in the household or, if he has gone, brings him back home.

Gender transposition is a synonym for gender crosscoding. Both are descriptive terms only, and do not signify causality, nor do they indicate the degree of either the penetrance or the immutability of the crossover. All three must be specified independently.

The variations of gender transposition differ as to how long they last, and how many facets or components of G-I/R are transposed. The most extensive and long-lasting transposition is transexualism. Transexualism is the syndrome in which, with hormonal and surgical sex reassignment as a warranty, a person changes officially and permanently to live in the sex into which his/her G-I/R has already been crosscoded.

Transvestism means literally cross dressing, which usually goes together with at least some degree of gender-crossed impersonation, even though only transiently in carnival spirit or at a masquerade. Transexuals cross dress or transvest, in which sense they are transvestic on a full-time basis, but they are not transvestophiles. Transvestophilia is a syndrome that might be called episodic transexualism, but with a major difference from transexualism; namely, no surgical change and no hormonal treatment is required. Transvestophilia is a paraphilia, believed to occur only in men, in which the man is dependent on wearing women's clothes, or the recall of having recently done so, in order to become sexually aroused and to attain orgasm.

Sometimes in middle or later life, transvestophilia becomes no longer episodic, but full-time gender crossing, requiring hormonal and surgical sex reassignment, and thus showing the close relationship between the two conditions, transvestophilia and transexualism. Another closely related condition is gynemimesis and its counterpart andromimesis, in which gender crossing includes hormonal treatment and is full-time and complete, except for genital surgery, which is not required. In gynemimesis a natal male mimes or impersonates a woman's life, and, correspondingly, in andromimesis a natal female, a man's life. In the vernacular, a gynemimetic is known as a drag queen; and an andromimetic is occasionally known as a butch dyke or a diesel dyke. In neither case is cross dressing related to becoming sexually aroused and reaching orgasm, as it is in transvestophilia.

The gynemimetic is homophilic and has a male as a lover or sexual partner, and thus represents a very extensive degree of both homosexuality and effeminacy. Correspondingly, the andromimetic represents an extensive degree of homosexual masculinacy. Homophilia ranges from the gynemimetic and andromimetic extreme, in which not only the sexuoerotic but also the major part of the G-I/R is gender-transposed, to the other extreme in which the major part of the G-I/R is not gender-transposed, whereas the sexuoerotic part is, specifically and exclusively.

Homophilia and homosexuality are almost synonymous insofar as homo- means the *same*, and -philia means *love*, and sex means *sex*. Thus homophilia signifies same-sex loving, or having a lover of the same sex, and homosexuality means being or having a sexual partner of the same sex. Each may signify being erotically attracted to a same-sex partner. However, homosexual may also apply to a single sexual act, perhaps even under coercion, with a partner of the same sex, but without being erotically attracted to a same-sex partner as lover.

In homophilic homosexuality, gender transposition may be limited exclusively to transposition of the sex of the partner from other sex to same sex.

The transposition is manifested in the sexuoerotic imagery and ideation of dreams, fantasies, and practices of love life and sex life. When no other gender-coded aspects of living are crosscoded (i.e., transposed), then the homosexual person, if a male, appears masculine in toto, except to those privy to his sexuoeroticism. Correspondingly, the lesbian would appear totally feminine. Many people are astonished when a national hero, sports champion, film star, co-worker, or neighbor is discovered to be a homosexual of this type, because it is a common and popular misconception that all homosexual men are swishy, unmanly, and easily recognized in public because of their effeminate ways and exaggerated stereotyping of femininity. Correspondingly, a lesbian is misconstrued as always being mannish in bearing, speech, and dress, and publicly recognizable because of masculine accounterments, crudity, and exaggerated toughness.

The mannish lesbian and the effeminate male homosexual would both qualify for a rating of six on the Kinsey zero-to-six scale of heterosexuality/bisexuality/homosexuality. So also would a macho gay male whose sexual attraction was exclusively to male lovers, and a femme lesbian whose lovers were exclusively female. The Kinsey scale is a unidimensional ratio scale that is not designed to take into account multidimensional, qualitative differences and to discriminate between different varieties and/or syndromes of gender transposition. Nor does it discriminate bisexuality that is synchronous or concurrent from that which is sequential, i.e., with one period of the life span being heterosexual and another homosexual.

A bisexual rating on the Kinsey scale is three, provided the bisexual or homophilic/heterophilic ratio is exactly 50:50. It seldom is so exact, but more likely disproportionate, such as 60:40, or 20:80, favoring one sex more than the other. The more disproportionately the ratio is weighted toward either homosexual or heterosexual, the more is it likely that a bisexual will be able to have a full-blown love affair with a member of one sex rather than the other, respectively. In the absence of specific sexuoerotic information, usually it is not possible to know whether a person is bisexual or not, provided the vocational, recreational, and other nonerotic components of the G-I/R are not ambisexual or androgynous.

Sexological science has not yet advanced to being able to formulate a causal explanation of gender transposition, specifying all necessary and sufficient determinants in the degree of detail that would permit its prediction, induction, prevention, or reversal. Consequently, special-interest groups adopt their own dogmas, doctrines, hypotheses, theories, and ideologies, and set themselves up as religious, legal, moral, political, or professional authorities.

Currently, the innate versus acquired is prominent in arguments about the cause of homosexuality. It is the old nature/nurture debate all over again—or, more correctly, the debate that has never ceased since last century, and is now hackneyed in the media, under the guise of biological determinism versus being "all in the mind." The up-to-date formulation is a three-term one: nature/critical period/nurture. Nature and nurture interact at a critical period of development and produce an effect that is immutable or, at least, long-lasting.

There is some public interest regarding the origin of transexualism because transexualism gets headlines, even though rare in the population at large. Whereas homosexuality is not rare, there is a great deal of public interest in what causes it, and much impassioned argument over changing it. Many wrongly assume that whatever is biological cannot be changed, and whatever mental can be. Both propositions are in error.

Homosexuality is always biological and always mental, both together. It is mental because it exists in the mind. It is biological because the mind exists in the brain. The sexual brain through its extended nervous system communicates back and forth with the sex organs.

In the causation of homosexuality, the basic principle is not biological determinism versus social, mental, moral, or occult determinism. The basic principle is developmental determinism, which pertains to the developmental history of when the brain becomes homosexualized (or correspondingly heterosexualized), to what degree, for how long, and how immutably. Whether the determining agents of homosexuality are innate and biological or acquired and social is beside the point. The point is that they are determinants, no matter where they come from, or when they occur. The principle of developmental determinism permeates everything that is written in this book.

On the basis of today's store of scientific knowledge, the best answer that can be given today to the question of causation is that homosexuality and heterosexuality develop in stages, and have more than one contributing cause. The first stage is prenatal, when sex hormones are the causative agent. In the unborn brain of both sexes, male sex hormone masculinizes but does not simultaneously defeminize. Insufficiency of male hormone demasculinizes, but it does not simultaneously feminize. At the prenatal and early-newborn stage of development, when the brain is influenced by male sex hormone, it is apparently indifferent to female sex hormones circulating in the bloodstream.

No one has yet recaptured the prenatal hormonal history of adult homosexual men and women. There is no way of being able to measure or estimate prenatal hormonal levels retrospectively. Direct evidence comes from animal experiments and from human beings born with a known prenatal history of abnormal hormone levels. From this direct evidence it is inferred that genitally normal boys and girls who develop as prehomosexuals had a prenatal hormonal history that produced a proclivity toward, but not a predestined certainty of developing a postnatal homosexual history.

From infancy through childhood, the hypothalamic-pituitary-gonadal system responsible for the secretion of sex hormones goes into a period of inertness or dormancy, until it becomes activated again at puberty. During the stage of infancy and early childhood, the influences that become causative in the development of homosexuality in the G-I/R, and also of heterosexuality or bisexuality, enter the brain through the skin senses, vision, and hearing, and to a lesser degree, maybe, through smell and taste. The process is usually named social learning or conditioning, although it is as much a process of apperceptive assimilation, as of didactic instruction and training. The two principles involved are identification with exemplars of one sex, and complementation with exemplars of the other sex. In identification, the sex of exemplars usually matches one's own, and in complementation it does not match, but reciprocates. In that case, postnatal gender coding develops or evolves in concordance with the natal sex of the genitalia. Postnatal gender crosscoding or transposition develops or evolves in discordance with the natal sex of the genitalia. The degree of discordance is individually variable. When discordance is complete, the outcome of specifically sexuoerotic gender crosscoding is homosexuality in adulthood. When less than complete, the outcome may be bisexuality of either the synchronous or the sequential variety. Individuals vary as to when the outcome makes itself fully evident. Some "come out" later than others.

In sexology, application of the scientific maxim or law of parsimony decrees that a sexual effect has a sexual cause. Therefore, in childhood, the postnatal developmental cause of homosexuality has its most likely source in the development of juvenile sexual (sexuoerotic) rehearsal play. There are various ways in which a child's rehearsal play can be thwarted or warped: play deprivation, as when a child is too closely bonded with a parent and too isolated from playmates, for example; wrong timing, either too early or too late; being excessively prohibited and abusively punished for engaging in sexual rehearsal play; being sexually coerced and injured; and being forced into the double bind of conspiratorial secrecy, that is by being damned if you do disclose what you play sexually, and damned if you don't.

Sexological science continues to have an insufficient data base on the relationship between sexual rehearsal play and the development of homosexuality. The ethnographic evidence on record indicates that in societies where boy–girl sexual rehearsal play is not punished or prevented, adult homosexuality is absent or rare. Boy–boy or girl–girl sexual rehearsal play, where it is by custom not illicit, does not lead to homosexuality in adulthood, although it may lead to bisexual adaptability. Participant homosexuality at the time of puberty and early adolescence does not foreordain continued homosexuality, but is compatible with heterosexuality in adulthood.

Overall, it would appear that the most important formative years for homosexuality, bisexuality, and heterosexuality are those of late infancy and prepubertal childhood, and not those of puberty and adolescence. The hormones of puberty activate what has already formed and is awaiting activation. Homosexuality of orientation, imagery, and ideation is not caused by sex hormone levels at puberty or thereafter. However, the onset of overt homosexual behavior may be initially postpubertal, or later. The same applies to heterosexuality. The various investigative attempts to find a hormonal difference between adult homosexuals and heterosexuals have all failed or been discredited. If the hormonal story has any validity, it will lie in the prenatal and early neonatal phase of development, when hormones influence the sexualization of the brain, not in the pubertal and postpubertal phases. The next advance in research on the chemistries of homosexuality will not pertain to the hormones of endocrine glands but to neurohormones and other neurochemical substances that govern and regulate the development and function of the cells and messageways of the sexual brain and its special centers.

Exigency theory, with its five universal exigencies of being human, goes beyond either motivational theory or stimulus–response theory. It is exceptionally well suited to serve as a unifying theory that accommodates not only hormonal sexology but all other aspects of sexology into the same universe of discourse.

FOUR

Lovemaps and Paraphilia

1 FROM GENDER TRANSPOSITION TO LOVEMAPS

The foregoing three chapters of this book constitute a survey of what today's science of sexology is able to teach about how and why our children
grow up to be homosexual or bisexual, instead of heterosexual. The rationale for focusing on this topic and devoting the best part of an entire book
to it is that, in the sexual ideology or sexosophy of our civilization, it is a
topic of inordinate concern that we have children who grow up to be
heterosexual—so much so, that we wear the mantle of invincibility and are
piously complacent in our conviction that only other people have children
who grow up to be homosexual. They are not our own, and so we turn on
them as adversaries, and take vengeance against them for being in our
midst. That relieves us, as a society, of the moral responsibility of paying
the scientific cost of discovering causation because, indeed, we claim to
know the answer already: homosexuality is a preference, an option, voluntarily chosen.

Homosexual activists themselves echo the dogma of their adversaries
and say that their sexual orientation is a preference, and one that, like a
religious preference, deserves civil respect of the right to be different. In
the politics of civil rights, it is necessary to have a constituency that, no
matter how great the range of individual differences, shares one factor in
common—like being black or being homosexual. Having a shared common
factor is not the same as being identically alike, but it is easy to drift into
that position. In the gay activist movement, that drift has manifested itself
as a tendency to claim that, since all manifestations of homosexuality are
equal on the criterion of the political fight for gay rights, they are also equal
on other criteria, for example, personal health. According to this proposition, there is no basis for differentiating sexual practices that are kinky and
bizarre from those that are not, simply because they are engaged in homo-

sexuality instead of heterosexually. Then the next logical step is that there are no kinky and bizarre sexual practices, homosexual or heterosexual—which is somewhat like saying that there are no sexual practices that transmit the deadly AIDS virus.

In the urgency and intensity of the campaign for gay rights, it is understandable that gay activists, writers, and theoreticians, seeing the enemy lurking everywhere, including in science and medicine, have neglected to recognize that the pros and cons of kinky and bizarre sex affect individual homosexuals as much as they do heterosexuals. For example, homosexual pedophilia is no different than heterosexual pedophilia, both vindictively referred to as child molesting, in evoking society's vengeance and reprisals.

The authors and readers of gay strategy in politics, law, and health have rights and responsibilities equal to those of everyone else with respect to medical sexological knowledge. That is why this chapter is about the new concept of *lovemaps*, first formulated in Money (1986a), and the theory of how a lovemap may develop to be either homosexually or heterosexually *normophilic* or defaced and *paraphilic* (see Section 3, this chapter).

2 NORMOPHILIC AND PARAPHILIC LOVEMAPS

A lovemap is defined as a personalized, developmental representation or template in the mind and in the brain that depicts the idealized lover and the idealized program of sexuoerotic activity with that lover as projected in imagery and ideation, or actually engaged in with that lover (Money, 1983, 1986a). A lovemap is rated as normophilic on the basis of what is ideologically defined by those with ideological authority as sexuoerotically normal and acceptable. Ideological norms vary historically, regionally, and by community. The ideological norm may or may not agree with the statistical norm, which is calculated as typifying at least half of a population in the midrange between the extremes. Statistical norms also vary historically, regionally, and by community. The larger the variability of people used in calculating a statistical norm, the wider the range of what constitutes normal.

A lovemap that is not normophilic may be rated as hypophilic, meaning incomplete or insufficient; as hyperphilic, meaning too dominant or prevalent; or as paraphilic, meaning unlikely love, or love that is too peculiar and divergent from a given norm. Paraphilias formerly were termed perversions or deviations in medicine and social science, as they still are in the law. On the street they are termed kinky or bizarre sex.

Everyone has a lovemap, in the mind and in the brain. Your lovemap is as personalized as your face or your fingerprint. It is both a repository and a readout of your sexuoerotic credenda and agenda. A *credenda*, in its literal meaning, is a memorandum of doctrinal beliefs or articles of faith, and an *agenda* is a memorandum of things to do. In its sexuoerotic application, a credenda is a memorandum of the complete inventory of imagery and ideation, separated or interconnected as in the story line or drama of a dream or fantasy, that may either induce or augment personal sexuoerotic arousal, heightening its intensity and facilitating the achievement of orgasm.

Credenda and agenda are sexuoerotically related in the same way as are a rehearsal and an actual dramatic performance: one precedes and then becomes the other. The sexuoerotic agenda is the credenda with movements, gestures, and vocalizations. They cohere together into the scenes and acts that constitute the lovemap drama or ritual materialized from a dream or fantasy into a live performance. The live performance may be solo, or autosexual. With one partner, it may be heterosexual or homosexual, and with two or more partners, it may be bisexual.

Nature has evolved the human species so that individuals have the ontogenetic or life-history capacity to develop highly personalized lovemaps, with an extensive range of variation from one person to another. In other species, individuals conform more closely to a uniform courtship and mating pattern that is phylogenetically determined, and typical for the species. Subprimate species, especially, have what may be called a phyletic lovemap, that is, one that, in terms of new phylism theory (Money, 1981), is phylogenetically programed into the brain, without much flexibility for the subsequent influence of ontogenetic learning and experience.

In the human species, ontogenetic personalization of the lovemap applies predominantly to the courtship phase of mating, also called the proceptive phase. Proception typically progresses to the acceptive phase. Acception typically progresses from body-to-body skin contact and rubbing to orifice contact (see Chapter 3, Section 8). The body's orifices are used for taking into and putting into, admitting and intromitting. The mouth is used for tongue kissing; in fellatio, cunnilinguism (in the vernacular, "giving head" or "eating out") or anolinguism; and in sucking and licking other protrusions and surfaces of the body. Like the mouth, the anus and the vagina are orifices of insertion. They admit protruding organs or erotic artifacts, especially the penis. Genital union augments the buildup of erotic ecstasy. It is one way, but not the exclusive way, of achieving orgasm.

The conceptive phase follows the acceptive phase, but only if egg and sperm have encountered one another. To the extent that conception is a sequel to acception, genital union would appear to be ontogenetically less variable, and more phylogenetically programed into the brain than are other activities of both the acceptive and the proceptive phases. There is no consolidated sexological theory to explain why various activities that are an immense sexuoerotic turn-on for some are an immense turn-off for others. Thus, for example, there is no better way to explain the erotic ecstasy of anal penetration for some, but not others, than the maxim of a black woman regarding her son when she explained that "he must have his nature in his hind parts."

Despite its flexibility and individual variability, the progress and activities of proception or courtship are not randomly haphazard. When couples are, in the vernacular, "putting the make" on each other, there is, world-wide, a degree of phyletically predictable orderliness in the progress of their mutual romantic and erotosexual interest. The following list of how it is done is indebted in part to the field research of Perper (1985) in singles bars in Philadelphia and nearby, and to cross-cultural observations of Eibl-Eibesfeldt (quoted in Donahue, 1985). Read the left column first.

- Establishing eye contact
- Holding the gaze
- Blushing
- Averting the gaze, eyelids drooping
- Shyly returning the gaze
- Squinting and smiling
- Vocal intonation animated
- Vocal acceleration and breathiness
- Vocal loudness

- Vocal exaggeration of trivialities
- Laughter
- Rotating to face one another
- Moving closer to one another
- Wetting the lips
- Garment adjustment exposes more skin
- Gesturing and touching, as if inadvertently
- Mirroring each other's gestures
- Synchronizing body movements

In addition to these observable signs, those that are subjectively experienced are increasing heart rate and breathing rate, perspiring, and feeling butterflies in the stomach. Over a prolonged period of time, there may also be changes in eating, sleeping, dreaming, and fantasying.

This proceptive ritual is engaged in by homosexual as well as heterosexual couples on the make. There are, of course, many embellishments that may be added, according to local custom, such as exchanging gifts, writing poems, singing lovesongs, and dancing, before the more erotically explicit genital activities of foreplay get under way. The process may also be short-circuited. In Tahiti, for instance, when groups of young people socialize, a young woman indicates her availability by wearing a cluster of scented frangipani flowers in her hair, over the ear; and a young man by wearing a headband of the same flowers.

There is even more short-circuiting when, as in establishing contact with a hustler or prostitute, both parties know ahead of time that they will meet at a certain time and plan to establish a sexual contract commercially. Anonymous sex on a promiscuous, noncommercial basis is similarly direct insofar as people who meet at known cruising or gathering places know why they are there, and can reduce protocol to a minimum. Except for prostitutes, women have a lesser tradition than men do of engaging in casual sex, and this tradition extends to lesbian women as compared with gay men.

The greater ontogenetic plasticity of the proceptive phase in the human as compared with subhuman species has its analogue in language. For each individual, the possibility of having a human language is phylogenetically programed into the healthy, unimpaired brain of the newborn. But the language itself is not. If it were, there would be no fable of the Tower of Babel, only one universal human language. In human phylogeny, language and symbolic conceptualization are inextricably combined. Phylogeneti-cally, the design of a conceptualizing brain required the sacrifice of a univer-sal human language. Since time immemorial, the conceptualizing brain con-ceptualized, *inter alia*, a flux of divergent and ever-changing languages. Phylogenetic release of the human brain from restricted to unrestricted sym-bolic conceptualization involved, according to a likely hypothesis, not only the contingent release of language but also of lovemap formation, and proba-bly of dietary selection, from a species-fixed expression to an individually variable one. Just as there are many different languages and dialects on earth, so also there are many different lovemaps and variations of sexuoerotic turn-on, some of them paraphilically exotic and eccentric. Whereas the reconstruction of phylogenetic history is always more or less science-fictional, there is no fiction in the present-day evidence that there is not one human lovemap but a diversity of them. Their diversity is not simply that they are personalized but also that, like faces and fingerprints, they can be classified into types.

The first principle of classification is, like beauty and ugliness of appear-ance, into the categories of social approval and disapproval. Regardless of who assumes the power of authorization, a normophilic lovemap is socially approved, and a paraphilic lovemap is not. The criterion of social approval automatically signifies that the criterion of normal will be ideological, no matter whether it is consistent or inconsistent with the statistical norm (see Section 1, this chapter). Normophilia is culture bound and subject to a high degree of historical and cross-cultural variability. For example, in Maryland and the District of Columbia, as well as elsewhere in the United States, citizens whose lovemap includes oral sex, if they translate oral sex into practice, are legally defined not only as abnormal but as deviant and crimi-nal. In Maryland, the penalty for expressing the oral-sex component of a lovemap is ten years of imprisonment or a 1000-dollar fine, or both. The 1986 Supreme Court ruling on the Georgia sodomy law upholds the right of all states to have laws that criminalize oral and anal sodomy between consenting partners of either sex, married or unmarried, heterosexual or homosexual, regardless of age.

Restrictive laws invite dissidence. The troubadours sang of erotic passion and the "mystical code of love" in the age of Chaucer (Kelly, 1975). Histori-cally, however, in the Christian culture of the West, the only lovemap tolerated as officially and bureaucratically normophilic was, and in some religions still is, the lovemap of total premarital chastity; no masturbation; monogamous heterosexual fidelity for life with, until recently, no divorce; no limitation on conception; and intercourse in the missionary position, devoid of passion so as to prevent wantonness, conserve semen, and pre-vent self-degeneracy (Money, 1985).

This restrictive, heterophilic prescription of the normophilic ideal re-quired that both autophilia (masturbation) and homophilia be classified as paraphilia. It is only within the era of very recent history that both have been declassified. Nonetheless, there are many archconservatives who still vigorously resent the new status of both masturbation and homosexuality as normophilic. They adduce the acquired immune deficiency syndrome (AIDS) as proof of God's wrath against homosexuals. Meanwhile, like Nero fiddling while Rome burned, they watch as the virus spreads into the heterosexual population and prepares to invade and kill their own progeny.

There is no logic whatsoever in classifying masturbation as paraphilic, insofar as it is compatible with heterophilia as expressed in the masturbation fantasy as well as in actual experience. In addition, it is normal according to the statistical criterion of normality. It is compatible with homophilia as well as heterophilia. The once widespread doctrine that masturbation causes homosexuality is based on a peculiar dogma of last century's fanatical crusaders against "self-abuse or the secret vice," namely that boys learned the vice possibly from depraved nursemaids, but chiefly from depraved older boys or men (Money, 1985). Thus, male homosexual relationships were defined as lessons in masturbation, without reference to male bonding and mutual erotic attraction. Female homosexual relationships were more commonly attributed to unhealthy friendships, especially between unmarried girls of idle wealth and luxurious, featherbedded leisure.

The criterion of bonding and mutual erotic attraction is applicable to both homophilia and heterophilia. Insofar as mutual attraction and bondedness are able to exist in homophilic as well as heterophilic couples in the mutually responsive, love-smitten limerence (Tennov, 1979; refer to Glossary and see Sections 7 and 8, this chapter) of a pairbonded relationship, there is no logic, on the basis of this criterion, in defining homophilia as a paraphilia instead of a normophilia. Paraphilia is an opportunistic trespasser into the lovemaps of either heterophilia or homophilia, or of those lovemaps that combine both, bisexually.

The following example is of a paraphilia that trespassed into a boy's lovemap at a time when it was developing through a phase of homosexual sexual rehearsal play. The person who doomed his son's lovemap to be neither homosexual, bisexual, nor heterosexual, but only paraphilic, was the misguided father himself. The son was a vulnerable candidate. He had a history of shyness and masculine inadequacy among the rough boys at school. At age nine, he turned instead to a hobby, namely, "a little zoo" of ants. The ticklish feeling of having them crawl on his legs and thighs was destined to become the stratagem of his paraphilia (formicophilia). His little zoo, expanded to include snails and cockroaches, became a private source of consolation after his mother died of cancer when he was eleven, leaving him devastated by grief. One year earlier, he had been deprived of his only close friend, a houseboy employed as a domestic servant. The story is as follows (Dewaraja and Money, 1986).

> The houseboy had taught him how to masturbate, and how to have nonpenetrative, interfemoral intercourse with him. The older boy was the insertor. When the patient's father found out about the relationship, he had the older boy taken to the local police station, severely

beaten in front of the patient and dismissed from his employment. The father also gave his son a severe beating. This incident left a deep impression on the son. He blamed himself for the predicament of the servant boy, whom he believed he had gotten into trouble because of his own "dirtiness."

By the time he reached puberty, at age thirteen or fourteen, the patient added to his practice of having his insects crawl over his legs and thighs by masturbating at the same time. He recalled having derived a great deal of pleasure from doing this. By the time he was eighteen, he had developed a paraphilic pattern of masturbating which would continue until, at age twenty-eight, he came to the clinic: three or four times a week he would be overtaken by an irresistible urge or feeling which required him to lock himself in his room and go through his masturbation ritual. After removing all his clothes, he would take a few snails and cockroaches from his zoo cupboard. He would then lie on the floor and have the cockroaches crawl over his thighs and testicles, while the snails slid over his nipples and the tip of his penis. He claimed he derived a great deal of pleasure from the sensation caused by the snails biting the tip of his penis, "as if they were eating a leaf with their little mouths." He also enjoyed the sensation of the cockroaches crawling around his perineum and anus. On such occasions he would masturbate to orgasm as often as four or five times in the space of two or three hours. On some occasions he used a frog. He would hold the frog in the palm of his hand and squeeze it lightly. The frog, attempting to escape, would vibrate. He found that it produced a very pleasant sensation when he held the vibrating frog against his penis and testicles.

At the age of eighteen, the patient unexpectedly found his father having sexual intercourse with a woman who was a family friend. He was both surprised and disgusted by what he saw. He claimed that he had never imagined that women behaved like that, "just like an animal." Around this time he first attempted to masturbate to pornographic pictures of nude women and couples. Though he tried on several occasions, he was unable to attain an erection from these pictures. He claimed that he found pornographic pictures disgusting and offensive.

At the age of twenty-five, he had his first heterosexual encounter. The woman was thirty, and had apparently led him on: "She tempted me and made me do dirty things with her." Though he was able to achieve intromission and ejaculation, it was not a pleasurable experience for him. Though this woman remained available to him, he subsequently avoided her. On several occasions he dreamed that his mother was watching him have intercourse with a woman, "with an expression of horror on her face." Except for the one heterosexual encounter and the brief homosexual affair in childhood, his entire sexual history has consisted of his paraphilic activities.

A special feature of this case is that it is transcultural, thus demonstrating that paraphilia is not a culture-bound phenomenon: the boy grew up in Sri Lanka under the authority of a father whose antisexualism was atypical for a practicing Buddhist.

3 LUST, LOVE, AND PARAPHILIA

Paraphilia is defined as a condition occurring in men and women of being compulsively responsive to, and for optimal initiation and maintenance of sexuoerotic arousal and the facilitation or attainment of orgasm, obligatively fixated and dependent on an unusual, personally or socially unacceptable stimulus either perceived directly, or in the imagery or ideation of fantasy (from Greek, *para-*, beyond, amiss, and by implication altered + philia, love). The antonym is normophilia. Synonyms are, in the law, perversion; in the vernacular, kinky sex.

Transvestophilia (Table 3-1) is an example of a paraphilia with gender crosscoding as an incorporated feature. It is a paraphilia insofar as the transvestophile's lovemap requires that sexuoerotic arousal, genital performance, and orgasm are contingent upon wearing women's garments. In the intervals between episodes of cross dressing, replay of a mental tape of being cross dressed may suffice as an attenuated substitute for the actual experience.

The complete scientific story of how a lovemap develops so as to become a paraphilic lovemap has not yet been ascertained. It is likely that there is a vulnerability factor such that, other things being equal, some individuals more than others have a brain that has become predisposed to elaborate a paraphilic lovemap during the early developmental period of childhood sexual rehearsal play. The nature, cause, and time of functional onset of the vulnerability factor remains unknown. It could be either prenatally or postnatally induced, and it could be either internal or external in origin. Whatever this vulnerability factor may ultimately prove to be, the best present hypothesis is that it will be proved to be related to temporal lobe or limbic brain epileptic dysfunction, or perhaps to be a special form of it. The substantiating evidence is the dissociative or fuguelike state (the paraphilic seizure), instances of which have been directly observed and recorded in some paraphiles. In his own unrehearsed words and idiom, a paraphile commonly describes what is, in effect, a trancelike state or fugue (for definition refer to Glossary), during which each paraphilic episode takes place. As this trancelike state overtakes a transvestophile changing from his male to his female personality, name, and clothing, it can be recorded on videotape. There is new and preliminary evidence that it may also be recorded on a PET scan of the brain (Frost et al., 1986).

Being predisposed or vulnerable to the possibility of developing a paraphilic lovemap is not sufficient to ensure that one will actually develop. There must also be social-developmental input. The retrospective biographies of adolescent and adult paraphiles point to the years of childhood sexual rehearsal play as the vulnerable developmental period. Prospective biographies of paraphilic lovemap development are an almost zero commodity, because there are no adequate criteria by which to identify likely prospects. Serendipitously, however, some paraphilic lovemaps have emerged in individuals whose developmental biographies were being recorded progressively from early childhood onward as part of a longitudinal outcome study of chromosomal and endocrine disorders in pediatrics (Money and Lamacz, unpublished data). These biographies are being prepared for publication. They demonstrate the early-childhood genesis of paraphilia in the lovemap, and thus confirm the evidence of retrospective biographies.

Developmentally, a paraphilia is a devious and circuitous stratagem by which lust is rescued from extinction, and preserved in the lovemap, by the subterfuge of making it the antithesis of love. The lovemap is warped by this antithesis, which declares love to be saintly and God-fearing, and lust to be sinful and of the devil. Love is pure, clean, and wholesome, whereas lust is impure, dirty, and unwholesome. Love is lyrical, romantic, and spiritual. Lust is epic, animal, and carnal. Love is above the belt, tender, affectionate, and permitted in public. Lust is below the belt, brutal, pornographic, and prohibited in public. Love is grooming and erotic. Lust is copulative and orgasmic. Love is long-term commitment and fidelity. Lust is short-term exploitation and promiscuity. Insidiously, and far-reaching in its cross-gender implications, love is feminine and refined, and lust is masculine and crude.

The antithetical attributes of love and lust permeate the lovemaps not only of paraphiles, but of everyone, in variable degree, for they are part of the sexual philosophy or sexosophy of the heritage of our entire society. The difference between the paraphilic and nonparaphilic lovemap lies in the degree of developmental traumatization to which it has been subjected by reason of the antithesis between love and lust, saint and sinner, madonna and whore, provider and playboy.

The possibility of lovemap traumatization in childhood exists against the background of the ancient sexual taboo, still very powerful today, which prescribes planned neglect of children's sexual learning, and organized opposition to formal sex education. The harsh truth is that as a society we do not want our children to be lustfully normal. If they are temerarious enough to be discovered engaging their lust in normal sexual rehearsal play or in masturbation, they become, in countless numbers, the victims of humiliation and abusive violence. Even the most decent of parents and care-givers go beserk and become antisexual monsters of child abuse when they see the Satan of original sin showing his serpent head. They must destroy the serpent in obedience to the myth of the asexual innocence of childhood. They do not know that what they destroy, or vandalize, is the incorporation of lust into the normal development of the lovemap. The expression of lust is diverted or detoured from its normal route. Thus, to illustrate: those adults who humiliate and punish a small boy for strutting around with an erected penis, boasting to the girls who watch him, do not know that they are thereby exposing the boy to risk of developing a lovemap of paraphilic exhibitionism (peodeiktophilia).

The trauma of humiliation and punishment becomes an insidious and long-term warning against lust. All sexual rehearsal play, including mastur-bation, is subject to the "catch-22" of being damned if you do admit to it, and damned if you don't. There is no escape from sin if you are burned at the stake for confessing it now, and burned forever in hell if you don't.

The catch-22 dilemma forces children to be clandestine about everything they know and do sexually that is socially forbidden. Because it is forbid-den, lust becomes in the literal sense unspeakable—like the unspeakable crime against nature, as defined by the law. So it is that children keep their silence about even those sexual experiences that traumatize their lovemaps by reason of not being talked about. The same experience, when not un-speakably secret, loses its traumatizing effect (Money and Weinrich, 1983).

In addition to the traumatization of humiliation and abusive punish-ment, a lovemap may also be traumatized by reason of being at a stage of development that is out of synchrony with that of a partner of disparate, usually older, age. Here again the catch-22 dilemma is paramount, for the very request for assistance, if it is needed to dissolve the partnership, is self-incriminatory. According to the ethnographic evidence from societies in which sexual rehearsal play is not obliged to be clandestine, and is not coerced, some degree of age disparity between partners is compatible with normal, nontraumatized lovemap development. The evidence from subhu-man primates is confirmatory. The limits of age disparity need to be estab-lished empirically.

Irrespective of age disparity, coercion and force are, so far as is known, incompatible with normal lovemap development. Normal sexual rehearsal play takes place between consenting playmates whose lovemaps are recip-rocally matched, not mismatched, in content. When lovemaps are mis-matched and there is no way for the dissenting partner to escape, then the risk of lovemap traumatization is high, and more so if the catch-22 dilemma applies. For example, the lovemap of a boy of pubertal age that reciprocally matches the lovemap of a youthful pedophile will not be at risk for traumatization, whereas the risk will be high for a boy with a lovemap that reciprocally mismatches the lovemap of a pedophile, in an enforced rela-tionship from which there is no escape.

If the traumatic history of a paraphilic lovemap can be retrieved, it is likely to hold the key not to the existence of the paraphilia, but to its contents. To illustrate: klismaphilia is the enema paraphilia. For the klismaphile, receiving an enema induces the high peak of erotic excitement and orgasm. The klismaphilic history typically includes, in childhood, an excessive dedication of a parent or guardian to administering enemas. Inter-nal pressure of the water affects internal genital nerve endings directly and independently of external genital stimulation. However, the adult giving the enema may contrive, more or less surreptitiously, to stimulate the genitalia also, and may herself or himself become erotically aroused by doing so.

4 SIX GRAND PARAPHILIC STRATAGEMS

There are more than forty entries in the list of the paraphilias (Money, 1986a; see also Section 15, this chapter, and Glossary). The number varies according to the specificity with which subtypes are separated and named.

Each paraphilia has its own lovemap, and each paraphilic lovemap incorporates a stratagem for saving lust from extinction by cleaving it from love. The term stratagem is used, rather than strategy, because a stratagem has the quality of a ruse or trickery. It deceives and circumvents the enemies of lust, regardless of the costs, which may be exorbitant. Each specific stratagem can be subsumed under one of six grand stratagems: sacrificial/expiatory, marauding/predatory, mercantile/venal, fetishistic/talismanic, stigmatic/eligibilic, and solicitational/allurative.

Each grand stratagem represents a way of wresting triumph from the jaws of tragedy. Developmentally, the jaws of tragedy are the threat that sinful lust will be exterminated from the lovemap and become extinct, which is precisely what does happen in extreme cases of hypophilia. The triumph over tragedy is that sinful lust is rescued and retains a place in the lovemap. Because it is sinful, lust irrevocably defiles saintly love. Therefore, its retention in the lovemap is contingent upon not defiling saintly love but being separated from it. Each of the six grand paraphilic stratagems is a formula that satisfies the conditions of keeping the defilement of sinful lust away from saintly love—of keeping lust for the whore or the playboy separate from love for the madonna or the provider. Lust and love together cannot converge on the person of either the saint or the sinner.

The six grand stratagems for cleaving lust from love in the lovemaps of the paraphilias are as follows.

The sacrificial/expiatory stratagem requires reparation or atonement for the sin of lust by way of penance and sacrifice. The extreme sacrifice is lust murder: erotophonophilia when the partner is sacrificed, and autassassinophilia when a person stage-manages the sacrifice of the self. Excluding death, there are varying degrees, from major to minor, of sadomasochistic sacrifice and penance for the sin of lust.

The *marauding/predatory stratagem* requires that, insofar as saintly lovers do not consent to the sin of lust, a partner in lust must be stolen, abducted, or coerced by force. The extreme case of this stratagem is the syndrome of assaultive and violent paraphilic rape (raptophilia or biastophilia). The spectrum of coercion ranges from major to minor. In statutory rape there may be no coercion, but a consensual and pairbonded love affair, one of the partners being below the legal age of consent.

The *mercantile/venal stratagem* requires that sinful lust be traded, bartered, or purchased and paid for, insofar as saintly lovers do not engage consensually in its free exchange. The very existence of this stratagem gets masked by reason of its place in the orgasm trade. Nonetheless, there are some hustlers and prostitutes, as well as their customers, whose paraphilia is chrematistophilia, marketing and purchasing sex. Some chrematistophiles, not in the commercial orgasm trade, pretend with play money, or have the partner impersonate a whore or a hustler with a third person. Some set themselves up to be victims of blackmail or robbery, and some are blackmailers or robbers. The popular military and judicial dogma that homosexuals are more vulnerable to blackmailers, paraphilic or otherwise, applies equally well to heterosexuals caught in clandestine adultery, and to paraphiles of any type whose paraphilia is exercised clandestinely. Homosexuals who have come out of the proverbial closet and have nothing to hide may be subject to discrimination, but not to blackmail.

The *fetishistic/talismanic stratagem* spares the saintly lover from the sin of lust by substituting a token, fetish, or talisman instead. Fetishes are predominantly either smelly (olfactophilic) or touchy-feely (hyphephilic), and both are derived from the smell and feel of parts of the human body. Devotion to the fetish may be all-consuming or minor.

The *stigmatic/eligibilic stratagem* requires that the partner in lust be, metaphorically, a pagan infidel, disparate in religion, race, color, nationality, social class, or age, from the saintly lovers of one's own social group. Morphophilic disparity pertains to disparity in the appearance of the body, and chronophilic disparity to age disparity. An exceptional example of morphophilia is acrotomophilia, in which the partner must have an amputation stump. The extremes of chronophilia are pedophilia, in which only juveniles (or babies, in nepiophilia) are eligible as lust partners, and gerontophilia in which the eligible partners are of parental or grandparental age. Age eligibility limits the duration of a partnership. In pedophilia, for example, the pedophile's own sexuoerotic age remains permanently juvenile and out of synchrony with his or her advancing chronological age. Correspondingly, the partner's eligibility is abolished by the odors and maturational changes of puberty. There is a corresponding limitation on the duration of relationships in, not only ephebophilia (attraction to adolescents) and gerontophilia, but also in what might be called "twentiophilia," "thirtiophilia," and so on. These latter underlie the broken relationships, homosexual as well as heterosexual, and the divorces of many couples in the decades of middle adulthood.

The *solicitational/allurative stratagems* protect the saint by displacing lust from the act of copulation in the acceptive phase, to an invitational gesture or overture of the proceptive phase. This might be called in the vernacular the paraphilia of the cockteaser or, in gay argot, of the loving queen. Among primates, exhibiting the genitals and inspecting them are prototypic invitations to copulate. In paraphilic exhibitionism of the penis (peodeiktophilia) and voyeurism (being a Peeping Tom), the preliminary overture displaces the main act in lustful importance. Displacement in this stratagem is the counterpart of inclusion of something in the other five stratagems. Paraphilic female exhibitionists who expose their genitalia to men almost never get reported to the police, so that their prevalence is unknown. Genital exposure under licit circumstances, as in a nudist resort, is not sexuoerotically arousing to exhibitionists and voyeurs. Their arousal is contingent on the illicitness of their paraphilic actions. Narratives and pictures also may feature as invitational stratagems.

One shared feature of all six grand stratagems is that they are not exclusive to the paraphilias but have much broader significance in the cultural heritage of our existence: sacrifice and expiation in religion, marauding and predation in warfare, mercantilism and venality in commerce, fetishes and talismans in magic, and stigmata and eligibility in kinship.

Another shared feature of the six grand stratagems is that each paraphilia subsumed under them is able to exist in members of the human species not only because of their personal developmental histories, but also because there is a phyletic basis from which personal development originates. To illustrate: pedophilia has its phyletic origins in parentalism. What happens developmentally is that parentalism becomes paraphilically diverted into the service of lust. Parent–child pairbonding and lover–lover pairbonding become merged together, as do parental love and erotic love. The neurobiology of the merger still remains unascertained, as do most of the necessary and sufficient causes in the social biography. The complete range of phyletic mechanisms that may become entrained in the service of paraphilia is examined in *Lovemaps* (Money, 1986a).

5 PARAPHILIC PATHOLOGY VERSUS PLAY

Encroachments and assaults on lust in the developing lovemap differ in their degree of effectiveness in suppressing or eradicating it. Correspondingly, the power of the stratagem for rescuing lust from extinction also differs in the degree of its enforcement. In instances in which enforcement is weak, the lovemap manifests itself as paraphilic in only an attenuated way—perhaps, for example, only as imagery and ideation in a masturbation or copulation fantasy, but not put into actual practice. Alternatively, if actually carried out in practice, then the performance will qualify as more playful and entertaining than burdensome and duteous, and more elective and revisionable than compulsory and dictatorial. Sadomasochism in the lovemap is an example of a stratagem that may be practiced as a mild and benign erotic sport, or as a brutal and injurious erotic combat, ending possibly in manslaughter or self-staged management of one's own masochistic death.

The two extreme degrees of sadomasochism raise the vexed issue of the dividing line between paraphilia as a harmless sexuoerotic diversion, and as a noxious pathology or criminal offense. This is really a two-part issue of which the first part pertains to quantitative and the second to qualitative difference between pathology and lack of pathology. Quantitatively, no paraphilic lovemap is pathological if its expression is attenuated, mild, and not compulsory, but elective. For example, its expression may be exclusively in private fantasy or, if shared in performance with a partner, only with one who reciprocates. Thus, paraphilia in the lovemap may be expressed as a sexuoerotic embellishment of, or alternative to the official, ideological norm.

Qualitatively, the issue is whether some paraphilias are pathological and others not. The law, in its omnipotent majesty, declares by fiat which paraphilias, if enacted, are criminal offenses. In the quaint language of a former era, they are called crimes against nature because they break what the medieval church defined as God's natural law which, in this instance, is specified as God's natural law of procreation.

The law is presently engaged in reluctantly handing over the crimes against nature to medicine, so that they can be reclassified as illnesses instead of crimes. At this moment in history, they are classified as psychiatric disorders. In 1980, in the third revision of the *Diagnostic and Statistical Manual* (DSM-III) of the American Psychiatric Association (APA), the legal term, perversion, was dropped, and the biomedical term, paraphilia, adopted.

In becoming the paraphilias, perversions found their way from the criminal justice system into psychiatry as forensic entities. Their new classification as illnesses was contingent on their having been previously singled out legally as crimes: zoophilia because of a forbidden species as a partner, pedophilia (or ephebophilia) because of a forbidden age as a partner, exhibitionism and voyeurism because of acts forbidden in public, masochism and sadism because of their potential for assault and battery, transvestism because of potential imposturing, and fetishism because of potential theft of the fetish. All other paraphilias were coalesced, unnamed, under the term, atypical. DSM-III Revised, added frotteurism to the list, changed transvestism to transvestic fetishistism, and reclassified zoophilia as not otherwise specified, along with necrophilia, telephone scatologia (telephonicophilia), partialism (fetishism not for an object but for a limb or part of another person's body), coprophilia, urophilia, and klismaphilia (refer to Glossary for definitions). The proposal to add paraphilic rape (raptophilia) had to be scuttled because of the militant resistance of radical feminists in psychiatry and psychology who objected to the possibility of an illness or insanity defense for accused raptophiles, and to the possibility of treatment instead of vengeance and the death penalty—they do not differentiate paraphilic rape from date rape and spouse rape (i.e., copulation as a sequel to cajoling and coercion after the female dating partner, lover, or wife has said no). There is no mention of lust murder (erotophonophilia). Hypoxyphilia (self-asphyxiation) did not get beyond the proposal stage.

In DSM-III Revised, the psychiatric nosology of paraphilia fails the test of being both exhaustive and mutually exclusive, and its criterion for inclusion, insofar as there is one, is forensic and not biomedical. It is the classification of a forensic priesthood, not of a committee of scientists, perhaps because it is beyond the capability of the APA and its committees to find a criterion by which to separate nonpathological from pathological paraphilia.

The criterion that I have found to serve me well, and that guarantees equal sexual rights for all, homosexual as well as heterosexual, while safe-guarding societal rights in a genuine sexual democracy, is the criterion of personal inviolacy (Money, 1979, 1986a). According to this principle, no one has the right to infringe upon someone else's personal sexual inviolacy by imposing his or her own private ideological version of what is or is not erotic and sexual, without the other person's informed consent. It is possi-ble to give informed consent, and to enter into a consensual contract, only if the terms of the contract are known in full, and not taken for granted. They can be known in full only if the end is predicated by the beginning. In a sexual engagement, that means no unexpected ending, unilaterally im-posed on one partner by the other.

Whereas leaving a singles bar in the company of a pickup ordinarily predicates participation in lust, it does not predicate a lust death by strangu-lation. That outcome would be unpredictable to the intended victim so long as the other person's proclivity as a lust murderer remained undisclosed. Without the murderer's advance warning of this proclivity, the targeted victim would have no possibility of either giving informed consent or of refusing to give it.

The hypothetical test case is one in which a masochist with a paraphilic fantasy of stage-managing his own lust murder meets a sadist with a paraphilic fantasy of lust murdering. A minutely planned and flawlessly executed lust-death pact could succeed so well as to be undetectable. Soci-ety would not then be confronted with adjudicating the human right to make an erotic death pact.

It is only if the murderer succeeds, and is then detected, that he has to face the societal consequences of having wrongly predicated nondetection as the conclusion of the pact. He might then go on trial not for a sexual act, but for murder—just as a so-called mercy killer might go on trial not for an act of mercy, but for murder.

Society in this present era is savagely concerned with infringement of the right to sexual inviolacy, for which it has developed a new specialty, victimology, as a branch of criminology and criminal justice, and a new profession of social-science and social-work police. By accentuating sexual victimization, victimologists have concomitantly deaccentuated even lethal violence, coercion, and abuse, provided it is not sexual. In addition, by accentuating the victimization of women and children by men, they have deaccentuated the abusiveness of women who victimize children and men, and who covertly use victimology as a strategy of militancy against men. They have disregarded also the evidence that women victimize women, that men victimize men, and even that juveniles and underaged adolescents victimize adults.

Men are stereotyped as minotaurs of maniacal sexual brutality and importunity, and of coercion directed against women, and also against juveniles and adolescents of both sexes. The stereotype allows, however, no place for men who are themselves victims. Even when it is conceded that a male may be the victim of homosexual prison rape, the evidence is adduced as proof not of the vulnerability of the victim, but of the brutality of the attacker. The occurrence of rape in female prisons is an embarrassment to the antimasculine bias of victimology theory, and so is subject to professional neglect.

The gay community is well aware of the sexual victimization of males by other males whose inviolacy is abrogated in acts of paraphilic rape, paraphilic sadism, and paraphilic lust murder. Gay men are vulnerable also to nonparaphilic ambushment and lynching by marauding homophobes some of whom are living out their own malady, the exorcist syndrome (see Chapter 3, Section 9). Harassment and victimization affect lesbians as well as gay men, though probably less lethally.

6 PARAPHILIC COMPULSORINESS

A paraphilia that does not trespass upon or invade the inviolacy of the partner, but is one in which the two performers engage with mutual consent, does not necessarily meet with general approval or tolerance. All too often, the penalty of self-disclosure is stigmatization. Therefore, the paraphile avoids self-incrimination while awaiting evidence that, if he talks, he will not be stigmatized. He may be in psychotherapy for months, even years, and not disclose his secret until he has obtained evidence that the ears of his therapist can be trusted to hear it. In the letter that follows, the writer found the evidence he needed in quotations from an interview with me that was published in the science magazine *Omni* (Stein, 1986). It prompted him to renew, after an interval of two years, a medical correspondence that he had initiated six years earlier. He disclosed new information quoted with permission as follows.

> We corresponded some time ago, about my being an XYY male [cytogenetically confirmed], now on male hormone injections. And I have some of your books about mixed-up genes, interesting, but deep to understand.
>
> I am now 53 years old, divorced and live alone. Though lonely, I prefer to live alone and to enjoy my fetishes.
>
> Your article in *Omni* was most interesting to me, on two subjects, transvestophilia and men who wear diapers [autonepiophilia].
>
> I've had a fetish for wearing wet diapers and latex rubber panties, since being a bedwetter as a boy. I'm not sure when, but later in life,

found I also enjoyed dressing as a girl baby. But no interests in being T.V. [transvestite] or wanting to be a woman.

I am bisexual. Had first oral sex with an older boy at age eleven. But also dated and masturbated girls in high school.

I do have health problems. I'm on service-connected disability. I've had a prostate operation and now possible M.S. [multiple sclerosis] with bladder and bowel dysfunction. I'm on self-catheterization for the past three years.

Marriage was unhappy for me. I could not [permit myself to] enjoy wearing wet diapers at home, except for short time, in faking loss of bladder control.

Now divorced for the past fourteen years. Now enjoy corresponding with other men who love wet diapers too. Before AIDS, also very exciting to have diaper visitors, ending the visit with my having oral sex with them.

Over the years have been in seven adult diaper clubs and correspond with some 250 to 300 men, who love diapers, too.

Interesting to find other men, who love to dress as girl babies, also unhappily married. And equally unhappy in the gay world, as most gay men are turned-off to gay men who love diapers.

Though I now have some loss of erections and dry ejaculations [from prostatectomy], I still have very good orgasms, with masturbation. Of which I love wet diaper masturbation, or using my accu-jac, to suction me off. And at times, have fantastic catheter orgasms, too.

My next goal is to find another bisexual man who also has dry ejaculations, to fully enjoy AIDS-free sex, together, though no luck at present time.

I would very much like to hear from you again, when you have time to write.

The criterion of when to intervene and when to respect the moral right of nonconformity is not the sole criterion for the arbiter who must separate paraphilia as play from paraphilia as pathology. Another criterion is the personal and subjective discontent with having one's life dictated by the commands of a paraphilic lovemap. Personal discontent may be secondary to the imminence of arrest, or to having already faced charges. Alternatively, it may be discontent with the paraphilia itself, and its consequences that have no legal significance. A paraphilic infantilist (autonepiophile), for example, after losing a wife and three girlfriends, may reach a stage of being unable to cope with having to be dressed in diapers and having a mommy chastise him for being a bed-wetting infant so that he can then obtain an orgasm. Likewise, a paraphilic self-asphyxiator may hear about autoerotic deaths often enough to become ambivalent about secretly strangulating himself prior to achieving orgasm.

From self-referred paraphiles, one learns that a full-fledged paraphilia has nothing optional or elective about it. It is a usurper that takes over completely. Its injunctions are compulsory and must be obeyed, no matter what else they might interfere with. They may interfere during any waking hour, and as dreams or nightmares, during sleeping hours as well. They defy voluntary attempts at control, for the paraphilic attack, as aforesaid, brings on an altered state of consciousness as in a trance or fugue (see Section 2, this chapter).

The injunctions of a paraphilia are so pervasive that they may restrict a paraphile's career, or they may merge the whole career into the paraphilia. For example, J. M. Barrie was himself Peter Pan, the boy who never grew up. He led also a tortured life as a pedophile. As is typical in pedophilia, his sexuoerotic age did not mature with his chronological age but remained juvenile—as juvenile as the Davies brothers whose lives he ultimately ruined, and whose boyhoods he adored. For them he invented the game of the Lost Boys, Wendy, and Captain Hook, and photographed them playing it on the shores of the large, shallow pond at his summer estate. Then he turned the game into the written drama, *Peter Pan*, a pedophile's homage to boyhood (Birkin, 1979).

The compulsoriness of the injunctions of the paraphilia is matched in many paraphiles by compulsoriness in compiling lists and amassing things related to their paraphilia: all the words in the dictionary related to sex and strangulation, enough bathroom supplies to stock a supermarket, erotic publications depicting one's own lovemap, photographs of people conforming to the idealized lover of one's lovemap, lists of names and addresses of fellow paraphiles and meeting places, and so on. The lists, when seized by police, become the basis of a computerized, nationwide FBI catalogue of suspected sex offenders, classified by diagnostic type.

Compulsory orgasms are another paraphilic injunction, the sexual neurophysiology of which remains unknown. Whereas ordinary males cannot train themselves to be hyperorgasmic, having up to as many as ten orgasms every twenty-four hours, hyperorgasmic paraphilic males cannot train themselves to have fewer orgasms. The orgasms become less pleasant as the ejaculate becomes depleted and watery, before it is replenished during sleep. Paraphilic imagery is the prime stimulus. The ideal is to have a partner who has a reciprocally matching paraphilic lovemap and is therefore able to be genuinely aroused and responsive. Having an orgasm with a paraphilically nonresponsive partner is the equivalent of having it alone. Some paraphiles do have their orgasms not only alone, but with no stimulation of the genitals other than that evidenced by the mental replay of the paraphilic fantasy. In a paraphilic trance, their orgasms occur in clusters.

One paraphilic patient equated intercourse with his wife with masturbating in her vagina. In his paraphilic fantasy, she was a stage property, not a participant actor. Erotically excluded and lonely, such a partner complains, "You want me only for my body," and the couple drifts toward a breakup. Their lovemaps are reciprocally mismatched. Paraphilic mismatching of lovemaps applies to gay and lesbian as well as heterosexual couples.

7 PARAPHILIC ADDICTION AND OPPONENT-PROCESS

Compulsory and unyielding obedience to the injunctions and demands of a paraphilic lovemap is in the same category as obedience to that which, originally polarized as aversive, reverses polarity, and is repolarized as addictive. In paraphilia, it is not sex as a whole that is repolarized, but a very specific stimulus to arousal.

In psychology, the theory that is most on target to explain the reversal from aversion to addiction, and which is also compatible with concepts in neuroscience, is the opponent-process theory of Richard Solomon (1980a,b, 1982). Opponent-process theory is on target when applied to paraphilias, for it applies to the reconciliation of opposites whereby negative becomes positive, tragedy becomes triumph, and aversion becomes addiction, usually very rapidly and long-lastingly. The stratagem of a paraphilia converts tragedy to triumph and aversion into addiction. It does so by merging lust with a performance or ritual that not only negates love, but also evokes negative sanctions. After the merger, that which was once forbidden or repugnant becomes addictively sought after, despite the dangers, risks, and reprisals. If it is taken away or given up, various symptoms of withdrawal ensue, some physical, and some mental.

Paraphilic masochism exemplifies the conversion of eroticized humiliation and punishment into an addictive lust for humiliation and punishment, as in the following letter, quoted with the writer's permission and request to remain anonymous (Money, 1987a).

> I read with keen interest your recent interview in *Debonair* during your visit to India. Especially I read about the man who wanted his behind smacked for achieving orgasm. During my schoolhood in a Christian missionary Anglo-Indian Institute in Calcutta we were (all boys) often caned on our upturned, upraised buttocks by the headmaster (with his attractive wife sometimes looking on and passing humiliating, sarcastic comments). Needless to say this brutalized our love-maps and in certain cases brought about orgasms and a sickening addiction to the rod and a good whipping.
>
> I was nine when the canings began, and seventeen when I left school. For the others it may have started earlier, slightly. I got sexual feelings from around the age twelve, especially if she was watching. We usually collected five or six cuts of the cane, but once I got eighteen.
>
> This addiction has resulted in certain friends hiring Anglo-Indian prostitutes to spank them. One is going through a divorce because his wife can't stand an emotional, sexual cripple pervert, and leper (her words not mine)! I brooded on this problem for a long time and have hit upon a perfect solution—self-whipping! I feel the element of humiliation is totally separate from the physical or physiological pleasure of a good caning. It's just a mechanical or physical sensation. Even orgasms are different from the joys of the stinging, smarting bottom. The

human buttocks and prostate gland have to be stimulated powerfully for pleasure. So who better than oneself? There is nothing to be ashamed of as there is nothing effeminate, feminine, pansyish, homosexual, submissive or humiliating in pleasurizing your own self through violent sensations. In fact self-flagellation is self-reliantly masculine, macho. The medieval religious zealots and fanatics used to do it. The Russians and Swedes birch themselves in the steam-bath to open up their pores. It's purely a mechanical thing and not to be ashamed of any more than yoga, karate, or masturbation.

Opponent-process as applied to paraphilia is exemplified in this letter as follows: synchronous occurrence at an early age of genital exposure and being beaten with a cane, replacement of protective love and affection by the headmaster's personal paraphilic sadism manifested as disciplinary brutality and the collusional erotic humiliation and sarcasm of his wife, conversion of traumatic pain from tragedy into the triumph of erotic arousal and orgasmic pleasure, and transformation of aversion to the cane into long-term addiction to it.

In this example, the transformation from tragedy into triumph according to the principle of opponent-process entailed also the transformation of the cane as an instrument of aversion to an instrument of addiction. As an instrument of addiction, the cane usurped the role of a lover; the cane became the boy's mistress after he became pubertally mature. Eventually it fulfilled the role of mistress so well that it did not need to be handled by a sexual partner. The partner became superfluous and self-caning sufficed. Thus, this case illustrates well that the paraphile's partner not only feels superfluous, but also is superfluous. The exception occurs if the lovemap of the partner should be also paraphilic, in which case the two lovemaps are reciprocal matches of one another.

By the laws of chance, it may be extremely difficult for two people with reciprocal paraphilic lovemaps to find one another, for the specifications of each may be meticulously detailed and fastidious. Compromise is not satisfactory; nor is simulation, even in part, for the ultimate in sexuoerotic response is mutual. The correct sexuoerotic proposition is: everything that turns you on turns me on, and everything that turns me on turns you on, reciprocally, spontaneously, and without perfunctory adherence to a formula.

When two potential partners encounter one another, the closer their lovemaps approach the ideal of reciprocal matching, the greater the likelihood that the potential partnership will materialize. The principle of reciprocal matching applies not only to paraphilic lovemaps, but also to normophilic lovemaps equally, and to homosexual as well as heterosexual lovemaps. When reciprocal matching does occur, then the two partners may undergo that prodigy of human experience, falling in love or being love-smitten, which has only two parallels: being stricken with grief, and charismatic ecstasy.

When two homophilic or heterophilic people fall in love, they become limerent (Tennov, 1979). That is another way of saying that they become addicted to one another. Addiction to the lover provides the metaphorical glue of pairbonding. In the neurochemistries of the brain, it may well be the phyletic prototype from which all other human addictions are derived, or to which they are subsidiary. When addiction to the lover is symmetrically balanced in the reciprocity of love requited, it is construed as a proverbial bond forged in heaven. When the addiction is asymmetric, because the two lovemaps do not perfectly reciprocate one another, then sooner or later the more heavily addicted of the two people becomes lovesick from love unrequited.

Lovesickness of the most extreme and morbid degree is a foregone conclusion when the love affair is an autistic mirage projected onto a person of eminence so far removed from the importuning suitor by reason of social rank, wealth, fame, or career as to be unavailable and unresponsive as a lover. The film star, Jodie Foster, was the hapless recipient of John Hinckley's unwelcome importunacy. Her rebuffs intensified his lovesickness to its culmination in a final, national declaration of his desperation, demonstrated in a suicidal assassination attempt on the life of President Ronald Reagan on March 6, 1981. His farewell note was addressed to Jodie Foster and was dated 1:00 A.M., March 6, 1981. It read: "Goodbye! I love you six trillion times. Don't you like me just a little bit? (You must admit I'm different.) It would make all of this worthwhile. John Hinckley" (*Johns Hopkins Magazine*, Vol. 35, No. 1, pp. 44–45, February 1983).

Lovesickness of such unrelenting and, in this instance, lethal intensity was formerly termed erotomania. It is now known as the Clérambault–Kandinsky syndrome (Jordan and Howe, 1980). Existence of the syndrome is not widely known. It afflicts either heterosexual or homosexual lovers. It may pass unrecognize in suicides and homicides; for example, the assassination on December 8, 1980, of John Lennon by Mark David Chapman should be attributed to it.

Clérambault–Kandinsky lovesickness is typically resistant to known forms of treatment. Lovesickness of the more everyday variety, either homosexual or heterosexual, recedes quietly into spontaneous remission and around two years. Recovery is complete when the potential for a new love affair returns. Whether or not a new love affair eventuates will depend on the prevalence and availability of reciprocally matching lovemaps.

For a society to ensure equal availability of matching lovemaps for a population of men and women, the male–female ratio should be about 50 : 50, and the entire population should be either heterosexual only, or bisexual only with reciprocally equal attraction between men and women. In addition, there should be no lovemaps withdrawn from general circulation because of paraphilic embellishments and requirements.

Hypothetically, reciprocally equal availability of lovemaps would be guaranteed in a population of either men only or women only, if everyone in the population were homosexual and no lovemaps were withdrawn from the general circulation because of unmet paraphilic specifications.

The realities of the census are that, in most population zones or regions, people with lovemaps that match heterosexually, even though with no guarantee of perfect reciprocal matching, constitute the majority. Those whose lovemaps match homosexually only, with no bisexuality, constitute a minority. The more dispersed an exclusively homosexual minority, the fewer the chances of homosexual lovemap matching. The more concentrated the homosexual population, as in big metropolitan population zones, the greater the chances of not only homosexual lovemap matching, but also of finding a match for a homosexual lovemap that has an added paraphilic specification.

Homosexual men with even a minor paraphilic design incorporated into their lovemap are not guaranteed to find a partner with a reciprocal match, despite the availability of gay places where potential partners congregate and "cruise" in search of a partner. In a gay bar, the search may become a kind of "horizon sickness" that continues in vain until closing time. One compromise is to cruise in dark places. Then the visual fantasy of the lovemap can be projected onto a dark palpated shape, without risk of disillusionment. Homosexual men with paraphilic lovemaps that are fastidiously selective in their demands may circumvent the scarcity of reciprocal matching if they join a correspondence network or visit special locations or clubs where others of their own paraphilic type are known to meet and match—S&M clubs, for example, for sadomasochists, or a "foot fraternity" for foot fetishists.

Men with a paraphilic homosexual lovemap almost certainly have an advantage over those with a paraphilic heterosexual lovemap, insofar as paraphilias are more prevalent in males than in females. Thus it is more difficult for a heterosexual than a homosexual male to find, even for pay, a temporary partner with a nonsimulated paraphilic lovemap that genuinely reciprocates his own. Even if the heterosexual male does belong to a paraphilic network or support group, the proportion of women is probably too few.

The meeting and reciprocal matching of paraphilic lovemaps, although possible, may by the very nature of paraphilia condemn either a homosexual or a heterosexual relationship to failure over the long term. The stratagem of a paraphilia rescues lust from extinction by dissociating it from the saintliness of love. Thus the partner in lust who participates in performing the paraphilic stratagem may be precluded from becoming also the partner who participates in consensual and affectionate lust-free love. The partner of the malign Mr. or Ms. Hyde may not be the same person who is the partner of the benign Dr. Jekyll.

One possible resolution of this conflict would be to have only one partner: either a paraphilic partner for lust, or a nonparaphilic lust-free partner for affection and love. Another resolution would be to have two partners, as in the nineteenth-century Victorian gentleman's way of having a mistress for lust, and a wife for lust-free respectability and provision of progeny. A third resolution would be to search for a reconciliation of the incompatible: a partner in paraphilic lust who is concurrently a nonparaphilic partner in love. When this search fails, its pursuit is reiterated, over and over again. The demand of the paraphilic lovemap becomes insistently reiterative and compulsive, over and over again. Satisfying it becomes a paraphilic addiction.

Like all addictions, paraphilic addiction is always an addiction to something, alive or inanimate, and to performing something with it—for example, addiction to a cane and to being beaten with it, or to women's lingerie and wearing it, or to the stump of an amputee and caressing it, or to an enema syringe and using it, or to a urinary catheter and inserting it into the penis, or to baby diapers and wetting or soiling them, or to a juvenile's penis and sucking it, and so on.

Diagnostically, it has recently become fashionable to use the term sexual addiction diffusely and erroneously to mean addiction to anything and everything sexual (Carnes, 1983). The fashionable accompanying dogma is that sexual addiction is caused by sexual excess. This dogma has preliterate origins in the magic of semen conservation. It became incorporated into the very ancient teachings of Chinese and Indian (Ayurvedic) medicine. Subsequently, it entered into the teachings of prescientific European medicine in the eighteenth century as degeneracy theory (Money, 1985). Sexual degeneracy, it was falsely claimed, begins with concupiscent imaginations that, unless disciplined by the intellect and the will, find their outlet in wet dreams (grandly named the disease of spermatorrhea), in the secret vice (masturbation), and in the social vice (promiscuity). Degenerated by vice, it was also falsely claimed, the jaded imagination seeks ever stronger stimulation in the form of pornography and sexual depravity, with increasing frequency, insistence, and variety, until the end product is the sexual addict. The opposite of sexual addiction was defined as chastity, fidelity, and commitment, with no masturbation. Today's sexual addiction theory reiterates this prescientific logic of degeneracy theory.

The concept of addiction to sex is as absurd as the concepts of addiction to thirst (drinking), hunger (eating), inhaling, or injecting. Addiction always has not a participle, but a predicate. Thus one is addicted not to drinking, but to alcohol or some other fluid—including even water, in cases of water intoxication. The alcoholic's addiction is just as well satisfied by means of an alcoholic enema as by an alcoholic drink. Similarly one is addicted not to eating, but to chocolate, carbohydrate, or whatever else is ingested; not to inhaling, but to the substance inhaled; and not to injecting, but to the drug in the solution injected.

There is no such amorphous entity as sexual addiction. There is only addiction to someone or something in the context of sexual arousal. It may even be addiction to something that very few people recognize as sexual, like sexual addiction to pictures of amputees in beachwear, in the case of the apotemnophile who is addicted erotosexually to the stumps of amputees; or sexual addiction to murder movies on commercial television in the case of the lust-murder paraphile who is addicted to what is for him or her the surpassing and tender beauty of the fresh corpse. The object of the paraphilic addiction is highly specific. Over the course of time, the addiction ends as it began, unchanged. It may possibly unfold one scene at a time, but it does not degenerate and leap from one depravity to another. Sexual addictions are not socially contagious. They are not caught or copied from other people. Nor are they caught or copied from pornography, as is widely believed (see Section 12, this chapter).

8 PARAPHLIAS: LOVE MALADIES

As in all addiction, a defining characteristic of paraphilic addiction is that it exists as a state of being that always has a predicate, as exemplified in the following quotation from a teenaged college student: "His daddy is addicted to alcohol, and mine is addicted to women's clothes." In paraphilic addiction, lust is contingent not only on what the predicate specifies for its arousal and functionality, but also on the separation of this predicate from the predicate of love. Thus, the father in the quotation above lusted not after his wife but after women's clothes. He cared for his wife and provided for her, but there had been no falling in love to unite them in lust.

In paraphilic addiction, the cleavage between lust and love in the lovemap may be a chasm of such magnitude as to be virtually unbridgeable. Paradoxically, every paraphilic act of lust not only fails to build a bridge, but the more addictively it is repeated, the more unbridgeable the chasm becomes.

Paraphilia is conventionally classfied as a disorder of sex. More accurately, it is a disorder of love, and of falling in love, which is also known as limerence (see Section 7, this chapter). The paraphilic enactment usurps the place of falling in love, and competitively blockades its realization in mutually limerent pairbondedness. There is, as yet, no known specific intervention for unblocking the blockade and replacing the paraphilic lust stimulus with a limerent (falling-in-love) stimulus. Sometimes, however, the blockade does spontaneously lift, as in the course of combined hormonal and counseling treatment (see Section 13, this chapter; Money, 1970b).

The following excerpt from the *Diary of a Compulsive Cruiser*, intended for a gay publication, was written by a man whose paraphilic compulsion or addiction was cruising gay public places, anonymously, in search of the never-discoverable biggest penis. It is reproduced with permission. At the time of writing, he had not yet graduated from weekly combined hormonal/talking treatment on an elective basis.

This summer I fell in love with a man I courted for quite a while. We had a splendid if brief period of mutual bliss that for unexplained reasons was followed by the heartbreak of separation. It was my first experience of this kind, having previously kept a distance from men I was attracted to unless there was sufficient anonymity to insure I would not have a chance to get involved.

I sought quantity rather than quality and for me that meant taking dangerous risks: arrests, diseases, and violence were not unknown to me. Divorcing sex from love, I was left feeling like something was always missing in my life. Desperately repeating a pattern of behavior over which I had lost control brought on a sense of defeatism and depression. In what became a vicious cycle, I cruised compulsively, incapable of seeing that the reward I sought was part of a problem for me, and not the solution to anger, loneliness, frustration, neediness, or dissatisfaction with life.

Two years ago I reached a bottom and cried out for help. Surrender led me to counselors (sex-positive, gay-affirmative sexologists) and to convene a support group for gay men with similar experiences to mine. In that group each man was free to define for himself what was compulsive for him and what changes and goals he sought for himself. Each person, therefore, had both a freedom and a responsibility to examine his own pattern and to work out his own recovery plan. The group adopted a spiritual (not religious) program of twelve steps used by groups like Alcoholics Anonymous and Overeaters Anonymous as a method of recovery.

My own experience has been a frightening and painful one. A lot of the time I spent concentrating on what I was giving up. In withdrawal it was difficult to see what replacements were being presented to me and what gains I was making. Slowly I began to see that my life was changing dramatically. I discovered that my pattern had roots in early childhood trauma and was fed by deeply disturbing teenage experiences leaving me believing sex was dirty, I was no good, and love was too dangerous to seek or find. Witnessing sexual child abuse, being victimized by homophobia, and the loss of a parent damaged me. I retreated into an emotional shell from which I could not trust other people.

When I came out as a gay person, I still stayed in my emotional shell, where I was not able to merge my sexuality into my personality comfortably. I knew I could not let anyone in, so I sought sexual relief in the dark corners of the gay world. The lonelier I became and the more I became aware of what I was missing, the more I became fatalistic. Seeing no solution, I was driven to resignation. No amount of sex satisfied me, but I had become so dependent upon this security/ reward/pacifier/escape that I could not imagine giving it up.

Then I reached my bottom and surrendered. Fear of AIDS, fear of being caught in the web of escalating police repression, and fear of suicide out of despair (I'd tried it twice before) left me with no choice: I had to get help. Now, two years later, I feel like I have joined the human race and found a new freedom. The love I shared this summer was not the only reward I've received in my recovery, but it is the most significant because it shattered a misconception I carried around about myself for years, that I was not capable of being emotionally, erotically, and intellectually involved with someone who really knew me and loved me for who I was.

In my support group I have been able to share my secrets and fears, and I have learned I am not alone and not a bad person. I've grown to trust others and come out of my emotional shell. I've gained from listening to other men share their experiences, strength, and hope. Being agreeable to change, risking being open and vulnerable, getting through setbacks, has not been easy, but it has so far certainly been worthwhile. I owe some of this to the man I loved this summer, some of this to sensitive counselors and friends, some of this to my own willingness to participate in recovery, some of this to the Compulsive Cruisers Support Group, and most of this to my own concept of a higher power operating in my life today.

As here exemplified, limerence, the experience of being in love or love-smitten, is the same for gay men and lesbians as for straight men and women. In the early phase, being love-smitten is a fire that burns with high-leaping, searing flames. Later it glows with molten warmth.

The natural history of a love affair is that the duration of the leaping-flame stage is around two years, after which the molten glow takes over. For the reproduction of the species, this is time enough for the pairbonding of the love affair to have progressed to sexual intercourse, pregnancy, and delivery of the baby. Then, the pairbond of the love affair opens to make way for the baby to be included in a tribond. The baby is dependent on being bonded to someone, usually the mother, in order to be fed and to survive. If the mother and her consort remained still engrossed in the flame-out phase of being in love, the baby's existence would be imperiled, whereas the less tumultuous phase of the molten glow accommodates its existence.

Even though limerent pairbonding may have been decreed in sexological evolution as an antecedent of procreation and parent–child bonding, the natural history of the love affair is not dependent on successful procreation. Childless couples go through the same progression from hot flames to cooler glow as do childbearers. So also do same-sex couples, gay and lesbian, whose matching lovemaps are compatible with a long-term relationship. The love affairs of homosexual men and women are not, as one vulgar shibboleth claims, predestined to go up in the flames of promiscuity. The shibboleth of promiscuity is not based on a gay and lesbian census, but, on the contrary, on a complete lack of comparative statistics on the prevalence of long-lasting relationships, gay or straight, at different phases of the life span (see Section 10, this chapter). Among American heterosexuals, overall, 50 percent of marriages become unbonded and end in breakup and divorce.

Whereas limerence, when reciprocated, acts as a powerful pairbonding agent, if its reciprocation is in doubt, it becomes transformed into an agent of jealous possessiveness and self-sabotage. Jealousy flourishes when possessiveness is threatened by suspicion, even though evidence is lacking, that one's partner is or may become interested in someone else. Like limerence itself, jealousy is not rational, indeed, it is highly irrational. The way in which it is expressed is variable and, to a significant extent, conditioned by local custom, as in the so-called crime of passion in a jurisdiction in which the law finds in passion an extenuating circumstance. Thus a jealous husband is exonerated or lightly sentenced if, having caught his wife in the act of adultery, he murders his rival. If the woman herself is not murdered also, then her affection is alienated. So it is that jealousy creates a no-win situation. Even in its lesser, nonmurderous manifestations, jealousy destroys what it is supposed to possess. This dynamic of self-sabotage applies with equal effectiveness to homosexual and heterosexual relationships.

9 POLITICS OF GAY PARAPHILIA

A not uncommon difficulty encountered by a man like the writer of the foregoing diary excerpt is ostracism from gay activists for ostensibly playing into the hands of practitioners of the medical model. Their distrust of the medical model has historical roots in the diagnostic classification of homosexuality as a forensic and psychiatric disease, a perversion and a deviation. No one relishes being stigmatized as a pervert or a deviate, disqualified from being a human being.

Historically, the declassification of homosexuality as a disease was high on the agenda of the gay liberation movement. As in the women's liberation movement, the gay movement's first order of business was legal and political liberation and equal rights. Like the term gender, the term gay had entered into the universal English vocabulary by the 1960s. In the preceding decade, it had belonged in the vocabulary chiefly of the homosexual community. Its origin is obscure. It may have been adopted from the name of the historical era, the Gay Nineties, which were known not only for their frivolity in entertainment, but also for their partial sexual liberation from the dour Victorianism of the times. In its midtwentieth-century usage, gay fulfilled the need for a name by which the homosexual community could identify itself in the struggle for legal and political rights, without the erotic connotations of the suspect three-letter word, sex, and the even more suspect four-letter word, fuck, and its participle, fucking.

In the gay liberation movement, the struggle for legal and political rights being preeminent, homosexual became defined as gay on the criterion of a nonheterosexual life-style, not on the basis of past or present sexual practices. Coming out and being self-declared as gay was sufficient to be accepted as gay. A prior history of having been heterosexual or bisexual was no barrier. Rather it was an error en route to the discovery of a true self-identity as gay.

A prior or present history of paraphilic practices as a homosexual also was no barrier to having a bona fide gay identity. The only exception was the barrier raised in the 1970s against giving formal recognition to gay pedophile organizations. Otherwise, the informal assumption of gay organizations was that being paraphilic was of no more consequence to being homosexual than to being heterosexual.

A major political struggle of gay activists to have homosexuality upgraded from an illness to a social status required having it declassified from the *Diagnostic and Statistical Manual* of the APA. Since heterosexuality is not classified generically as an illness, but only as compatible with having a sexual illness, the terms of the struggle for equality had perforce to be that homosexuality also should not be classified as an illness, but only as compatible with having a sexual illness.

Inevitably, the old guard fought back. They were loath to relinquish their conviction that homosexuality is always a disease for the cure of which they provided a treatment (and earned an income). A compromise was reached: homosexuality per se is not a disease, but ego-dystonic homosexuality is one. The logic of this compromise demands that ego-dystonic heterosexuality and autosexuality (masturbation) also be classified as diseases. However, that logic was repudiated.

Its repudiation did not pass unnoticed, especially in the more militant faction of the gay community, which has retaliated by joining the ranks of those, psychiatrists included, who repudiate the medical model in favor of a moral and legal model. Without the constraints of the medical model, homosexuality could be forced to shed not only its old classification as an illness, but also its former qualification of being compatible with having an illness. Homosexuals, according to this viewpoint, are, in effect, disenfranchised from having an associated sexual illness, especially one classified as psychogenic. To classify them as having such an illness might imply ego-dystonic homosexuality, and would be stigmatizing in a way that heterosexuality is not stigmatizing because it cannot officially be ego-dystonic.

For the same reasons that some gay activists repudiate the medical model, they repudiate also biomedical research into the developmental origins of homosexuality and, as a consequence, into the origins of heterosexuality and bisexuality also. They are no less vociferous in repudiating social research, especially if it is designed to seek causes for homosexuality as psychogenic deviancy from the heterosexual norm.

The fallacy of censoring basic homosexological science is that ignorance as well as knowledge of the origin, cause, or genesis of anything, not only homosexuality that can be used politically in a manner that is either ethical or unethical. The political struggle should be for the ethical application of knowledge, not for the suppression of research.

It is true that society could use scientific knowledge to prevent the occurrence of homosexuality, if its cause were discovered. It is equally true that society could use the same knowledge to mass-produce homosexuality in a world not only overpopulated by breeding couples, but also in need of a new generation of creators of civilization like Leonardo and Michelangelo. Nature has her reasons for designing homosexuality into the potential of the human species, no matter how mysterious they may appear!

One consequence of repudiating the medical model, in nosology and in research, is that the gay movement has not yet been able to come to terms officially with the fact that having a homosexual lovemap without a paraphilia is not the same as having a homosexual lovemap with a paraphilia. Failure to make the distinction may have far-reaching political and personal consequences—and the same applies to heterosexual love-maps. Thus, a priest with a pedophilic or ephebophilic lovemap that attracts him to underage juveniles or adolescents is in the same paraphilic dilemma, personally, socially, and legally, regardless of whether his lovemap is homosexual of heterosexual. Likewise, anyone addicted to having anonymous sex with strangers is in the same personal and social dilemma, regardless of being male or female, gay or straight. The consequences of sexual anonymity in the new era of AIDS may be lethal. AIDS is a fact in the history of infectious disease for the occurrence of which, only four decades after the destructiveness of syphilis and gonorrhea had succumbed to the victory of antibiotics, no one was prepared.

10 GAY/LESBIAN PARAPHILIC RATIO

There is a widely held belief that compulsive promiscuity is more prevalent among homosexual than heterosexual men, but there are no statistics to substantiate it (see Section 9, this chapter). There are also no statistics on the prevalence of stable, pairbonded gay male relationships of the type reported by McWhirter and Mattison (1984). There is no a priori reason to differentiate homosexual from heterosexual males on the criterion of compulsive promiscuity. However, gay males who are compulsively promiscuous may have a greater chance than do compulsively promiscuous straight males of finding a partner with a reciprocally matched, compulsively promiscuous lovemap. More prevalently than straight men and women, gay men have a tradition of public meeting places in which to congregate. Some such places are known to cater to specific lovemaps—sadomasochistic (S & M) lovemaps, for example, or transvestophilic ones. By contrast, heterosexual women are likely to be more privately promiscuous than are the heterosexual men who have promiscuously matching lovemaps and who seek them as potential lovers. Lesbians also are likely to be more privately promiscuous than are gay men.

This difference between men and women makes it impossible to ascertain not only the relative prevalence of compulsive promiscuity in gays and straights, but also the relative frequency with which compulsive and promiscuous cruising conceals a paraphilic lovemap, as illustrated in the diary excerpt of Section 8, this chapter. There are no prevalence data to indicate whether paraphilias are proportionately or disproportionately distributed between heterosexual and homosexual men. All that can be said is that they are known to occur in both. It is not known to what degree, if any, the forty-odd paraphilias are differentially distributed between heterosexual and homosexual men. Consequently, there is, for example no support for the popular contention that pedophilia is more often homosexual than heterosexual. It may be equally prevalent, or heterosexual pedophilia could be disproportionately more prevalent than homosexual pedophilia, as arrest statistics would seem to indicate.

The statistical problems of ascertaining data on the relative prevalence of paraphilia in heterosexual and homosexual females are corresponding the same as for males. Paraphilia is known to occur in both lesbian and nonlesbian women, but its prevalence rate is not known. The prevalence rate of different types of paraphilia in lesbian and nonlesbian women is also not known.

It has long been an article of both popular and professional belief that women, including lesbians, are less prone to paraphilias than are their male counterparts. The evidence quoted in the media, popular and professional, is obtained from criminal and clinical statistics. These statistics may, however, be warped by the sexological platitude, still extant in our culture, that women are sexually inert or anerotic as compared with men. For example, a woman who sleeps in the same bed as her nearly pubertal son or daughter is not at much risk of being charged with sexual child abuse, whereas the father who does the same with either a daughter or a son would, if reported to the sexual child abuse squad of the police department, be instantly charged with incest and pedophilia. On the basis of the faulty victimological dogma that children never lie about sex, he would then be considered guilty until proven innocent.

Self-disclosure of information related to paraphilia is potentially self-incriminating. Therefore, the estimate of the prevalence of the various paraphilic stratagems in the lovemaps of women is no more accurate than it is for men. There is no statistic, but only an empirically based impression, that female paraphilic lovemaps differ from those of men in being less visual and more haptic or touchy-feely in ideation and imagery, and more likely to be characterized by themes of being erotically abducted and rendered erotically unresistant (Friday, 1973, 1975; Hite, 1976).

An example of a touchy-feely paraphilia (hyphephilia) in a female is one that, in a particular case, entailed the feel of babies or small dogs placed between the legs and rubbed against the genitals (Chapter 25 in Money, 1986a). This way of attaining orgasm surpassed that of ordinary sexual intercourse, which was so aversive that it was discontinued in the marriage. The paraphilic activity had its onset in a dismal history of illegitimacy and childhood neglect and traumatic abuse. In adolescence, there was a history of noncopulatory sexual activity with a middle-aged male relative.

In the manner typical for paraphilia, the feel of rubbing a small live creature between the legs was a stratagem for preserving lust as a commodity separate from love, which, in her life experiences, had always been either unattainable or warped. The moral struggle to be rid of the paraphilia was intense and not successful.

In dreams and in masturbation fantasies, an antipodal feature of the lovemap in this case was an alternative to molesting babies and dogs—namely, that of being molested and abducted by, or eloping with a stranger with "a big lovely penis."

Another example (unpublished) of the touchy-feely (hyphephilic) component of a paraphilia in a female belongs to a case of pedophilic sadism. In this case, the paraphilic stratagem was to gain access, for example as a babysitter, to a small child too young to explain what may have happened to her, and to fondle and lick the child's body, all over, especially in the genital area—rather as a mother cat might lick and groom her kitten. This activity was erotically stimulating, but not enough to bring the woman to the climax of orgasm, which could be released only by the shrieks and screams of traumatic injury. The injury was effected by means of a sharp instrument, or the hot end of a burned pencil, pushed into the child's vagina.

The woman had tried to rid herself of this paraphilic behavior by engaging in lesbian activities with age-appropriate partners toward whom she felt an erotic affinity, but these activities failed to suppress the paraphilia. She also made an abortive attempt at marriage. In desperation, she admitted herself to a state hospital where she lived for nearly four years until, caught on the wheel of enforced deinstitutionalization, she was released into the general population and lost to follow-up.

The origin of the prevalence of haptic as compared with visual imagery and ideation in female lovemaps, both normophilic and paraphilic, is open to unending debate as to whether it is phyletic, cultural, or a combination of both. There is no a priori reason to dismiss the idea of a phyletic difference between males and females with respect to the initiation of sexuoerotic arousal. There is such a difference in the four-legged mammalian species, in which the male is dependent on the sense of smell for him to become sexually attracted to a female, whereas she is not dependent on smell for mating. A bitch smells the male's urinary, pheromonal territorial markings, but her mating responses are initiated by the cyclic changes of her own internal hormonal secretions. At the time of ovulation, or being in heat, one of the functions of her hormones is to release from the vagina the odor, or pheromone, that attracts the male through his acutely sensitive nose.

In human beings, and to some degree in other primates also, not the nose but the eye is the organ of erotic turn-on. On the basis of contemporary evidence, it is more likely than not that the hypothesis of a phyletic difference between men and women is correct with respect to the primacy of vision in initiating erotic arousal—with men being more dependent on their eyes than women are. Hence the primacy of visual over haptic imagery and ideation in the wet dream, and in the development of the lovemap in boys. In girls, haptic ideation and imagery have primacy.

One paraphilic stratagem in the developing lovemap of girls disenfranchises the haptic experience of lust, so that it may not be positively initiated, but experienced only in a paraphilia of being a victim of marauding or predation. This paraphilic stratagem of victimization may be explicitly and brutally masochistic, as in the case (unpublished) of an American Jewish girl with an extremely traumatized childhood secondary to a birth defect of the sex organs. Her lovemap was bisexual. Heterosexually, it depicted her as the lover-victim of the blond and blue-eyed son of the commandant of a Nazi concentration camp. Such extreme paraphilic victimization in the lovemap is atypical. The more benign version of the stratagem of victimization is one of being taken, possessed, eloped with, carried away, seduced, or coerced into a romantic encounter that may or may not culminate in yielding to voluptuous genital-erotic activity. Although it is possible for a woman to stage-manage the actualization of such a paraphilic stratagem, the greater likelihood is that it will exist only in dream and fantasy, perhaps as a masturbation fantasy, and perhaps as a copulation fantasy. With a legitimate copulatory partner, it may be playacted, on an as-if basis.

In psychoanalytic and other doctrines of women's sexuality antedating the women's movement, victimization in the female lovemap was defined as masochism and as an inevitable and instinctual heritage of womankind. That doctrine still lingers on, incapable of either proof or disproof. It disregards the evidence of the omnipresent ideological heritage that continuously impinges on the developing lovemaps of growing girls, namely of the female as sexually and erotically submissive. All the verbs for sexual intercourse, vulgar or polite, are transitive verbs in which he does it to her.

The erotic stereotype of the female as the submissive recipient outlives efforts to change it if those efforts, albeit well intentioned, are ill-conceived. For example, victimologists (see Section 5, this chapter) have designed a campaign to protect children, especially girls, against submitting to sexual child abuse. Immunizing themselves against the terror evoked by the hype and overkill of alarming warnings, children of one Baltimore neighborhood have invented a new game, "The Rape Man." It is an update of games of escape, like "cops and robbers." The penalty for getting caught by the rape man is to be the play-victim of rape—to submit, and to be the recipient!

11 GENDER-CROSSCODED SATELLITE STRATAGEMS

In addition to the six paraphilic stratagems listed in Section 4 of this chapter, there is a satellite stratagem that may function within the orbit of any one of the other six. In the vocabulary of the theater, it is the strategem of the understudy, the one who, in case of emergency, is prepared to replace the leading actor, and play the actor's role.

In the course of growing up, children who have no direct experience of the theater know about taking the role of another, for it is an intrinsic aspect of childhood play. In addition, they hear stories of people who heroically substitute themselves and die to rescue another. They also become acquainted with this theme as a basic tenet of Christianity.

As a stratagem of paraphilia, the understudy or *subrogation stratagem* is one in which someone who represents saintly love is rescued from the defilement of lust by being replaced by an understudy or subrogate who becomes defiled instead. The understudy is oneself.

The subrogation/understudy stratagem has different manifestations. It applies to some highly specific cases of paraphilic adultery, for example, in which the adulterer saves his or her lust from extinction, but only on the condition of being a stand-in for the regular partner who would otherwise be lust-defiled instead. There are some highly specific cases of paraphilic incest in an adolescent girl, for example, in which the only condition whereby she is entitled to her own lust is that she become a stand-in for her mother, who would otherwise suffer unwanted defilement by the lust of the man, her father or stepfather, whose lust her mother has renounced. This same girl may, eventually, run away from home to become a prostitute. She may also become pairbonded as a lesbian, while earning her living by sexual service to men.

It may not be a daughter but a son who is the stand-in, saving his mother from the defilement of his father's lust by diverting it to himself instead, in a relationship that is both incestuous and homosexual. In that case the subrogation/understudy stratagem entails a degree of gender crosscoding or transposition in the son that may be full-fledged transexualism or gynemimesis at one extreme, or episodic transvestophilia, or at the other extreme entirely noneffeminated male–male bonding. Homosexual incest protects not only one female from the lust of a male, namely the homosexual son's mother from the lust of his father or stepfather. Insofar as the son becomes himself the recipient of the lust of other males, he diverts their lust away from other women. In addition, he himself does not defile the saintly love of a woman, because his own lust is homosexually male directed instead.

The combination of this understudy stratagem with gender crossing may occur as a subsidiary or satellite of other paraphilias (see Chapter 3, Section 9 and Section 6, this chapter). Gender crossing combined with a sacrificial/expiatory stratagem is exemplified in youths or men who are found wearing women's clothing, maybe the mother's, and dead from paraphilic self-asphyxiation by hanging—one type of autoerotic death.

These two stratagems were combined in the case of a young college student, a paraphilic patient in treatment, in whose lovemap the primary paraphilia was self-asphyxiation (asphyxiophilia) by strangulation or drowning (Chapter 24 in Money, 1986a). On the face side of the lovemap he became in person a substitute for those who, on the reverse side, were strangulated, though only in fantasy. On the face side, he was a femininely smooth gay boy who stood in front of a mirror clad only in bikini shorts, strangulating himself with a woman's white leotard tied as a noose around his neck while, synchronously, in fantasy, the strangulating hands were not his own but those of a homosexual lust murderer, an intruder, who would kill him. Exhausted and choking, at the last moment before blacking out and dying, he would release the noose and lie down.

Thereupon, the reverse side of the lovemap's mental tape would turn on. He would be no longer a gay boy, but a heterosexual man watching, with eidetic accuracy, a mental replay of a commercially produced murder mystery, for example a Hitchcock horror movie, in which the heroine was strangulated or drowned. With photographic recall, he had minutely coded in memory every detail of many prime-time televised or videotaped murder movies. The climax of his ejaculation and orgasm was contingent upon the climax of the death and beatific transfiguration of the heroine. As an image of paraphilic murder, the heroine was the equivalent of a medieval image of a saintly martyr, sacrificing her life for her faith. It is not uncommon for the images of religion and paraphilia to be shared, and perhaps to be derived from one another; with monotonous regularity, paraphiles have a religious history of relentlessly orthodox upbringings.

In some versions of the mental replay of murder movies, the asphyxiophiliac patient became an actor in the movie. In other versions he was a spectator only. He had no more cognitional control over which movie would mentally replay—or over whether he would be actor or spectator—than he did over the same show when it would replay mentally as a nightmare, and awaken him from sleep, masturbating.

Apart from when he was being an understudy for the role of a victim of asphyxiation, there were no other times, places, or fantasies when either his identity or role were homosexual. After initial trepidation, he began an elective period of weekly treatment with antiandrogenic hormonal injections with medroxyprogesterone acetate (Depo-Provera). The injections were given locally. Counseling treatment was unavailable locally, so it was provided by long-distance telephone, weekly or more often as needed. During two years of treatment, the patient has been free from self-asphyxiation, and does not have imagery of himself as a gay boy. The heterosexual, murder-movie imagery, though obsessional, fluctuates in frequency. It changes slowly, as is usually expected in the treatment of paraphilia (see also Section 12, this chapter).

A second example of gender crossing as a satellite of another paraphilia is that of a professor of architectural design engineering in whose lovemap the primary paraphilia was of becoming an amputee—apotemnophilia (Money, Jobaris, and Furth, 1977). He traced his obsession with becoming an amputee to a domestic accident at age two that had rendered him unable to walk for almost a year. He had capsized a pot of boiling oatmeal, and severely burned his left leg and foot. In his memory, he had heard someone excitedly yelling to cut it off, presumably referring to his clothing or shoe. There was no specific memory relating to gender crosscoding, only the nonspecific memory of continued and copious family psychopathology.

After long periods of psychotherapy over several years, this apotemnophile had given up on psychotherapists, as his paraphilic obsession had not been relieved. He had given up also on self-inflicted injury to his leg by drilling into the bone and then infecting the wound with excreta. Twice he had gone to the emergency room of a local major medical center where, to his chagrin, he had received antibiotic treatment that healed the infection and left his leg unamputated. He directed his quest for an elective amputation to the Johns Hopkins clinic for transexual sex reassignment, hoping in vain to be directed to a surgeon who would amputate his leg. Psychodynamically phrased, and reflecting his experience in psychotherapy, his letters contained the following statements.

> Since my thirteenth year, my conscious life has been absorbed, with varying intensity, in a bizarre and prepotent obsessive wish, need, desire to have my leg amputated above the knee; the image of myself as an amputee has as an erotic fantasy (each one different) accompanied EVERY sexual experience of my life: auto-, homo-, and heterosexual, since, and beginning with, puberty. . . .
>
> There are scattered occasions when I "feel like a woman," viscerally, in terms of body image, and in these situations I loathe myself—it makes me very apprehensive. Somehow this seems linked with the amputation fantasy. I would rather this [amputation] than lose the penis which would mean that I would be like a woman. . . . My entire erotic activity now consists of trying to make "real" the fantasy that I am an amputated homosexual adolescent, for in possessing my stump I can, concurrently, possess my penis. . . .
>
> Most of my emotional unrest accrues from the fact that I am acting out an overwhelming forbidden wish—like to be a girl—savagely forbidden. It is almost as if I will be establishing my male identity by means of the amputation. I could be trapped in a kind of surgical masochism . . . in trying to acquire characteristics more apt to secure my father's love or at least sympathy. Homosexuality at present is my retreat from overt masculine functioning. One of the anticipated "pleasures" (for me) of being an amputee is the possibility of a genuine experience of identification.

Hypothetically, it would appear from the foregoing that the patient's role as an understudy was to be enacted in relationship to his father. The alternative to sacrificing his penis and becoming his father's daughter was to sacrifice his leg instead of his penis and attain acceptance as his father's son.

There are some cases in which self-surgery related to gender crossing applies not to the limbs but to the genitals. In one of a trio of such cases (Money and DePriest, 1976), a man amputated his own penis but not his testicles. He had a firm belief that his rectum was a misplaced vagina, and that he should, therefore, have an ileostomy, so as to keep this vagina uncontaminated by feces. He had a delusion, based on a shared ancestral family name, that only by having his ostensible genital defect corrected would be he able to fulfill his destiny of saving the White House from a foreign plot.

In the second case, the man was an artist-fisherman, rugged in appearance and life-style. He had a well-researched and scholarly fixation on self-surgery to convert himself into a hermaphrodite, capable of copulating as both a male and female. He succeeded in creating an opening at the base of the underside of his penis, and was obsessed with enlarging it to be big enough to "accept a host penis" of adult size, instead of only a thin tube (Figure 4-1). Through this opening, he was able to confirm that he had rediscovered the alchemists' lost secret of the multiple male orgasm, in the bulbous urethra. To him it was more blissfully ecstatic than ordinary orgasm. He was convinced that, with this discovery, he was endowed with power to rescue the nation from the Russians, provided they did not get prior access to his secret and usurp the power of the urethral orgasm.

In the third case, there was no paranoia of becoming, through sexual renunciation, an understudy on the stage of international power, genitally prepared to be called into the role of self-sacrificial hero. This third case was of a man who, after many years of planning, emasculated himself by using a farmer's animal castration kit. His ideal was to be rid not of his penis but of his testicles only, so that he could forfeit his sexual role as a man and have the sexual life of feeling like a girl while he pleasured his wife with cunnilingus (see Chapter 3, Section 5). He had spent his entire life as an understudy for a girl, and at last was able to escape from what he construed, literally, to be the sin of defiling his wife with masculine, penile lust. His escape was augmented by the fantasy that his wife would marry his older, widowed brother who had carried a torch for her since she was an umarried teenager. That was not to be. His wife was too devoutly religious to become divorced.

12 PARAPHILIA AND PORNOGRAPHY

In the case of paraphilic amputeeism (see Section 11, this chapter), the patient found it erotically stimulating to watch amputees and their accomplishments in surmounting the handicap of the missing limb. His erotic fantasies would sometimes focus more on the achievement of a leg amputee walking with crutches than on the amputee as a partner in a sexual encounter. His visual aids during masturbation were photographs of amputees, either partly or fully dressed. Complete nudity with the genitals exposed was irrelevant, for the erotic focus of the photograph was the exposed stump. The stumps of male amputees, expecially teenaged, were erotically more stimulating than those of female amputees.

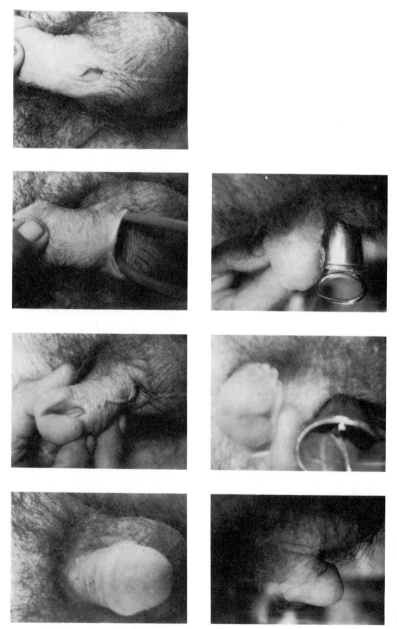

Figure 4-1. Self-made Polaroid photographs and an anatomical drawing supplied by the patient who produced an artificial hypospadias in himself.

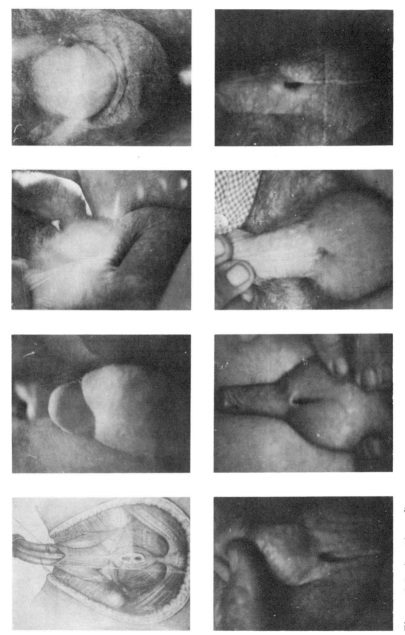

Figure 4-1. (continued)

163

Amputees and their stumps constitute the erotica or pornography of paraphilic amputeeism. In paraphilic asphyxia (see Section 11, this chapter), amputees and stumps have absolutely no erotic or pornographic value whatsoever. In the case of the paraphilic self-asphyxiator, pornography consisted of images of the dead bodies of women drowned or strangulated. It was not necessary for the genitalia to be exposed. The shapeliness of the clothed, or partly clothed female body sufficed. Access to this type of pornography was unrestricted, for it was available routinely on television and home videos in horror films and murder mysteries in scenes in which the heroine is drowned or strangled. The erotic significance of these scenes is made abundantly clear in a narrative written by the young man concerned, and here published with permission. He titled it "The Meese Commission on Pornography Missed Something."

> The Meese Commission on Pornography missed the drownings of girls on network televison. Whenever I see a drowning or strangling for that matter, I go crazy. I can go up to a maximum of six orgasms in one day over a period of several days, and it can be all wound up around seeing a girl drown on television. Now you might ask WHY?
>
> I don't know exactly what the cause is, but there is a name for my illness. It's called paraphilia (-philia meaning love, and para-meaning beyond normal, bizarre, or unacceptable), and there are lots of paraphilic disorders, but my exact one is called asphyxiophilia, which means I am obsessed and addicted to stranglings and drownings with orgasms in my fantasies—and before I was put onto medication, I would literally strangle myself with a woman's dance tights. Now you might ask WHY?
>
> I don't know exactly what the cause is, but I have had this problem of girls getting murdered by drownings and stranglings since I was very little, say age ten. And it's a bitch. I went through fifteen doctors before I found the right one who knew what I was talking about and knew what kind of medication to use. But I still have the nightmares, and I still have the orgasms, and I still lose control and have to watch a drowning on T.V., and I can't seem to get away from it. You might ask why I can't get away from it? Well, it goes like this, though I don't know the exact cause: When I see a girl getting drowned, I go crazy, and I have butterflies in my stomach, and I have pressure of some kind on my temples, and they seem to get hot, and I sometimes smell something burning, and I get really panic-like, and I feel some kind of feeling in my penis, and then my heart rate goes up to 120 per minute, and I sweat sometimes, and I get the runs, and I have to go all of the time, and then I masturbate over and over and over and over again six times a day over a period of days, and the fantasies are to the drowning that I saw, and I wish I could have videotaped it and watched it over and over and over again, and I have the head rush of that sweeping liquid-like feeling that goes through my brain when I see a drown-

ing, and the whole thing is crazy, and I breathe heavy, and I have asthma, and I have to use my inhaler to breath normal again, and I might not sleep for days on end, and I am in a constant state of fear and agitation, and I can't eat, and there are gases in my stomach, and I am always, always thirsty, but I do not drink liquor. My chest even hurts, and I ache all over, and it's all because of the drowning of the girl that I saw on T.V.

Now the last drowning that I saw (and I wish I hadn't) was on the harmless, new hit series "Matlock," which stars Andy Griffith. The series was fine until one day I saw a commercial advertising the next episode of "Matlock," and the narrator said that somebody puts a girl in a hot tub, and then they show this girl in the hot tub with the surging, circulating water, and somebody comes up from behind and grabs her by the shoulders and pushes her under. That commercial showed just a few seconds of that scene, and I freaked out. I was obsessed with "Matlock" coming Tuesday night, and the girl getting drowned, and the idea of course would be to tape it and watch it over and over. But I didn't set up for that. Oh no! I am not going to be tricked! I will not watch it! I mean I do have a will of my own, don't I?

Well, I was already masturbating to the commercial segment. My doctor lives a thousand miles away. He is one of the very few doctors in the world who know of my kind of problem, and there are none anywhere in my state. I have never seen him, only photos of him, and when he was on Donahue. All of the therapy has been done on the phone for the past two years, though I get my weekly shots locally. So I was unable to just fly to him. But I don't really need to see him, I said. I have a will of my own! Don't I?

I was able to fight off the temptation of the show and the commercial until the night before the show was to be on. I made the terrible mistake of taking a bath, and when I got up out of the tub and dried myself off, I was obsessed, and this was at 9:15p.m. Monday night. I sat in front of the television set, and there I waited and waited for the commercial to show the girl in the hot tub again. This was on the NBC network, and so there I sat, and finally they showed another commercial for "Matlock." It was a little different this time. They showed a still picture of the girl in the hot tub, and then the film started to roll, and the guy pushes her under. Then they showed a close-up of her hand trying to reach the rim of the tub, and that was it. I did not sleep all night. I was in agony. From the moment I got out of the tub, I was hit by all of those feelings, the butterflies, the hot, pressured temples, the gas, the asthma, the heart rate, that feeling in my penis, and then I knew that I had lost it. All day Tuesday while at school I was in misery. I go to college you see, big deal. And so an hour before the show "Matlock" starts, there I was masturbating right in front of the television, and I didn't get an orgasm until I was well into the "Moonlighting" show.

Then the show of "Matlock" comes on, and they show the killer pushing the girl into the hot tub, and her hand tries to grab hold of the rim. This is just the preview before the show even starts. So then they show some of the guest stars who are going to be on the show, and then a couple of seconds of the hot tub again, but this time of the camera in the water at the girl's foot end of the tub, and they show water splashing and swirling around because she was squirming and struggling. That was not shown in the commercial at all, and it was not even in the full-length final version of the murder during the show. Of course I'm pumping my penis like a madman, and then the girl comes into the bedroom, and she takes off her clothes, and then we see her underwear, and then in the next scene she is in the hot tub. She is wearing a black bikini. Then the killer comes up from behind her as she is leaning back in the hot tub relaxing, and the killer grabs her by the shoulders, and then he pushes her underwater. Then we see a camera shot from the killer's point of view, and we are looking down his arms while she is being held under the water, and you can just barely see her as the splashing, surging, circulating water of the hot tub makes it hard to see. Then you can see her black bra, and she reaches up and tries to grab the killer's arm, but she can't hang on. Then the camera goes to a different shot, and it is of him holding her under the water as before. Then we go to a close-up of her hand trying to hang onto the rim of the tub, and the water splashing around, and then she can't hang on to the rim of the tub. Then we go back to the killer's point of view, and then she is dead, and she floats away from the killer. She is found dead in the middle of the tub bobbing up and down from the surging, circulating water.

Now it never ceases to amaze me that drownings of girls are the longest murders that they do on T.V. A shooting of a girl isn't much, and neither is a stabbing (for me, psycho and slasher films don't count), but a drowning of a girl has more camera angles and lots more shots. It takes longer to drown a girl, and they have special music for the scene too, usually thrilling types of music that are supposed to be exciting, and maybe it is supposed to be scary, but I know one thing, that whole thing has fucked up my life for the past two weeks now. I keep seeing the vision of the murder over and over and over in my mind, over and over and over again. Orgasm after orgasm. For days and days. If only I could have taped it and watched it over and over again. In filming a girl drowning, a lot of the extra footage is not even used. I wish I could get a hold of that extra footage of her drowning.

Why didn't the Meese Commission do something about network programming? I thought "Matlock" was a good show! But now I think that all the suspects got a turn-on to the idea of the girl getting drowned in the hot tub. Even Matlock himself looked like he was getting an orgasm talking about it, especially when he knew who the killer was, and he said to him: "And that's when you closed your hands around her neck and held her head under the water." He said it so erotically. I can't stop watching these things. And when the show is rerun in the summer, I'm sure that I will tape it, so then I will have it. And have it and have it, and I will still be crazy and miserable over the whole thing. Let's face it, most murders on television can go from one second to five seconds at the most. Most of them are shootings, stabbings, poisonings, and so on and so forth. Sometimes the murder is never shown. It only shows them investigating the murder. But when they do a drowning, it can go from ten to thirty seconds for the drowning sequence alone. Parts where they show the girl in scenes before she gets drowned can go on for three minutes or more.

The whole thing is wrong. It is just wrong. Drownings are the most erotic way to kill a girl on television, and the Meese Commission did nothing about it. The sad fact about all of this is that this type of material of drownings and stranglings of girls is my pornography and no one else's. It makes me mad that no one else can get turned on to it. I'm alone. I'm all alone. The night that the show was on, I was at my apartment where I have no phone. It was at my parents' house that I had seen the commercial in the first place, and that is where the videotape recorder is also.

Paraphilia is a bitch. It's like epilepsy. Temporal lobe, I think they call it. There is something wrong with my brain. There has been since I was very little—since the day I was madly in love with Angela Cartwright on the show "Lost in Space," and she played Penny, and I was having a dream of her and me playing together in my bedroom. I had this dream when I was four years old. I wish I could get better. I wish I could get normal. At least my self-strangulation with leotards is under control with the medication. But not the networks.

The principle exemplified in the foregoing case examples is that erotica or pornography, to serve effectively as a person's erotic turn-on and aid to masturbation and copulation, must match the person's lovemap. Pornography is highly, if not uniquely personalized. It cannot be borrowed or lent, and be effective, unless the lovemaps of both borrower and lender closely resemble one another. Pornography cannot change a borrower's lovemap, no matter how intense, prolonged, or frequent the exposure. If it were otherwise, then horror and murder-mystery movies featuring strangulation and drowning would have converted the lovemaps of millions of American youth into asphyxiophilic lovemaps—which manifestly has not happened.

Pornography is not contagious. Anyone can test that statement using oneself as subject. For example, the eleven members of the Meese Commission on Pornography (1986) exposed themselves to vast amounts of pornography, but they have not confessed to having had their lovemaps changed thereby. None has admitted to having been turned into a marauding and predatory paraphilic practitioner of sexual violence, which, if the predictions of their report were correct, they should have been.

If pornography were contagious, then its contagion could easily be demonstrated by massively exposing heterosexuals to homosexual pornography, and changing them into homosexuals, or vice versa. It does not work. The effect of male homosexual pornography on heterosexual men is not to arouse them, but to make them bored, indifferent, or disgusted. Lesbian pornography, by contrast, may be highly arousing to those heterosexual men whose lovemap includes the image of having the simultaneous erotic attentions of two women.

Heterosexual women are predominantly not aroused by gay male pornography, in part no doubt because women's arousal is predominantly less visual than tactual. Lesbian women, unlike gay or straight men, for the most part are not strongly attracted to visual pornography. Not all women, however, are consistently indifferent to visual pornography, especially when they share viewing it with their partners.

If pornography were contagious, then heterosexual pornography in sufficient dosage would change homosexuals, gay or lesbian, into heterosexuals. It does not. Even if it were effective in only a few cases, there is no doubt that there would be a new therapeutic industry marketing the "pornography cure." It would be a variant of behavior modification, one of the methods claimed to be effective in changing homosexuals but effective, if at all, only with bisexuals who repudiate the homosexual component of their duality.

Because pornography is not contagious, it cannot cause sexual degeneracy in a descent from bad to worse to depraved. Sexually, it also cannot cause addiction, although obsessively amassing pornography may sometimes be pathognomonic of paraphilic addiction. Pornography is like money. No one has ever suggested that the minting of money by the state causes some of its citizens to become addicted to amassing material wealth, although amassing material wealth may indeed be an addiction, as also may be gambling it away. Analogously, the printing of postage stamps does not cause philatelic addiction, although some philatelists are addicted to collecting stamps.

A second principle, also exemplified in the foregoing case examples, is that there are some people whose visual erotica or pornography, insofar as it does not require explicit depiction of the genitalia and genitosexual activity, is mass-produced and distributed, and is freely available for trade and entertainment. It is not subject to censorship, does not qualify as lewd or obscene, and is therefore completely legal. This type of nongenital erotica and pornography may be innocuous, as in books and movies in which men impersonate women, or in which amputees heroically surmount their handicap, and which are erotic turn-ons and masturbation or copulation aids for, respectively, transvestophiles and apotemnophiles (or acrotomophiles). Conversely, nongenital erotica and pornography may be nocuous, as in newsclips and magazine pictures in which executions and battle dead are explicitly depicted, or in murder-mystery and horror movies and videos in which death by homicide is explicitly depicted. These uncensored, prime-time depictions are masturbation or copulation aids and erotic turn-ons for lust-murder paraphiles (erotophonophiles), and for those who paraphilically arrange their own assassination (autoassassinophiles).

Instead of being morally outraged, if society were authentically and scientifically concerned about eliminating the paraphilia of lust murder and preventing its headlining serial killings, then banning the legal brand of lust-murderer's pornography, namely murder and homicide in popular entertainment, would not be effective. Regardless of type, paraphilic pornography is not the cause of paraphilia in anybody. Rather, paraphilic pornography of each specific type is a mirror—a mirror specific to the paraphilia that it mirrors, and that already exists in the paraphile whom it arouses.

Banning pornography is not effective as a form of intervention to prevent paraphilia. The time for preventive interaction is not in adulthood, after a paraphilia already exists in a person, but long before, early in childhood development, when the lovemap has not yet been warped from a normophilic into a paraphilic shape by well-meaning parents and others who vandalize it by reason of their militant antisexual zeal.

Commercial pornography is a stimulus to erotic arousal, but only if it matches the user's own lovemap. It is not an aphrodisiac that generates erotic arousal, de novo, in any dormant system. It is not like the arrival of spring that indiscriminately arouses all hibernating creatures from hibernation. It enhances arousal selectively, and only in a person whose system is already prepared for it. Arousal expresses itself variably, alone in masturbation or together in copulation or other shared erotic activity. In paraphilias, arousal expresses itself in the performance of the paraphilic stratagem. According to traditional criminological doctrine, commercial pornography indiscriminately incites to performance, no matter what its context. Ostensibly, no one is exempt from its influence—except prosecutors, of course, and other law-enforcement officials. When apprehended, sex offenders themselves will fall back on this erroneous doctrine of influence, or rapidly learn to do so. They use it as an alibi to explain to themselves and their captors what otherwise is inexplicable, namely, why they sabotage themselves by reiterating their sex-offending paraphilic performance. The alibi gains them no leniency, but it does reinforce the judicial and public belief in the doctrine of commercial pornography as a cause of sex offenses.

There is no conclusive evidence, however, that commercial pornography has such power of causation. Its power is only that of a mirror that reflects a performance the staging of which has already been rehearsed in the lovemap deep within the paraphilic brain.

Far from being a cause, commercial pornography is an effect. The correct sequence, developmentally, in boys at puberty is from wet dream or masturbation fantasy, to homemade pornography, to commercial pornography. In most girls there is no precise equivalent of the wet dream that induces an orgasm while asleep. Homemade pornography mirrors the content of the wet dream. It may be improvised from cutouts in fashion magazines or mail-order catalogues (the underwear pages of the Sears, Roebuck catalogue have been a prime source of pornography for maturing boys for over 100 years), to which details are added. In one recent case a young male teenager with pedophilic lust-murder paraphilia collected photos and magazine pictures of boys aged six to eight. Over them he superimposed an acetate sheet on which, with felt-tip pens, he drew blood and murder wounds. Separated and stored separately, they had no paraphilic meaning to anyone except himself (pp. 127–130 in Money, 1986a).

This youth, raised in a conservative, religious home, had no access to commercial pornography. Should he have had access, he would have gravitated toward lust-murder pornography exclusively, and only if it depicted young boys as lover-victims. Whether or not he found commercial pornography to meet the specifications of his own lovemap would depend on supply and demand. Only people with a lovemap like his own would provide the demand. Without a large enough demand to be met, there would be no supply. Commercial producers and distributors of pornography operate businesses, not charities. The sales or rentals of their publications give a rough estimate of the proportionate size of not only the normophilic population, but also of the paraphilic population in each paraphilic category. Paraphiles buy or rent their own kind of pornography, and nonparaphiles do the same.

It is on this basis that commercial pornography for women traditionally has been predominantly narrative and not pictorial, and has had more focus on romantic exploits than explicitly genital ones. Commercial pornography for women is a mirror of their own eroticism. If women's demand for visual erotica and pornography changes, then the market will change. In fact, it has already begun to do so as women increasingly become producers and directors of videos of "Romantic Porn in the Boudoir" (*Time*, Vol. 129, No. 13, pp. 63–65, March 30, 1987).

Nonetheless, there continues to be a wide gulf between women's and men's commercial erotica and pornography. It represents a gulf of misunderstanding and acrimony between the sexes. Between mothers and their growing sons it is a misunderstanding that may have unforeseen and tragically paradoxical consequences, for it dictates that mothers, when they find that their sons have access to normophilic pornography or have acquired examples of it, become child abusers who, albeit inadvertently, destroy sexuoerotic normalcy in both heterosexual and homosexual boys. Joined by their antisexual male counterparts, women organized against pornography inadvertently and contrary to their avowed aim, destroy sexuoerotic normalcy and replace it with pathology on a national scale.

The national crusade against pornography, which is currently at the level of religious mania, is a response to a new cultural artifact in our midst, namely the videotape combined with not only the home video player but also the home video camera. Historically, the first crusade against pornography was precipitated by the mass production of sexually explicit stories made possible by the printing press. Inexpensive color printing, equated with "dirty French postcards," raised another furor a century ago, and soon was augmented by the technology of film, and the mass distribution of 8-mm movies. Today home video fuels the furor.

Antipornography crusading is favored by power-seeking politicians. In 1933, Hitler's first move against the Jews was cleverly disguised to obtain middle-class acquiescence by the burning of Magnus Hirschfeld's Institute of Sexology in Berlin, followed by the media declaration that all sexologists were pornographers, homosexuals, and Jews (Haeberle, 1978). In the United States today, the 1985 revision of the obscenity law in North Carolina makes all depictions of genital nudity a crime. There are no exemptions, not even for teaching in the state's medical schools. Thus the law paves the way for students to report their teachers, even in medical school, and for children to blackmail their own parents, or to have them arrested and imprisoned for possession of nude pictures. The great irony of North Carolina, and of today's fundamentalist crusade against pornography in the United States, is that antisexualism, including homophobia, is the one great issue in social policy on which American democracy and Russian communism are in complete totalitarian agreement (Money, 1979). Sexual democracy is not an article of religious, fundamentalist, and militant radical feminist faith in democracy.

13 PARAPHILIA, HYPOPHILIA, AND HYPERPHILIA

The stratagem of a paraphilic lovemap is to preserve lust from extinction by warping and distorting its expression, and creating a cleavage that separates lust from love. The stratagem of a hypophilic lovemap is, by contrast, not to preserve lust, but to reduce or eradicate it, while leaving love intact or expanded. The hyperphilic lovemap does the reverse: it reduces or eradicates love while leaving lust intact or expanded.

The paraphilic person typically may have a history of multiple casual partners in lust, and of one long-term, pairbonded partner in love who does not necessarily know of the multiple casual paraphilic lust encounters. The hypophilic person typically has a history of having no partner in lust, but only a single, long-term, pairbonded partner in love, with whom there is no difficulty in expressing affectionate hugging, cuddling, and kissing above the belt, but great difficulty in expressing lust below the belt because the sex organs fail to function properly. The hyperphilic person, by contrast, typically has a history of only transient and weakly bonded partners in love, inability to combine long-term pairbondedness with lust, and great facility with the sex organs in expressing lust with dozens, hundreds, or even thousands of casual partners, more or less indiscriminately, but without paraphilic kinkiness. Without boasting, one career women with a hyperphilic life-style estimated that by age fifty she had had more than 10,000 male sexual partners. Correspondingly, the estimate of a bisexual, mostly gay man, was more than 20,000 male partners.

By the logic of common sense, it might seem that two paraphiles with reciprocal lovemaps would be able to establish a long-term, pairbonded relationship of love combined with lust. In actual fact, it seldom works out that way. The stratagem of paraphilia is to separate defiling lust from purifying love. In consequence, if the lust partner should, by chance, fall in love with the paraphile, the relationship becomes not a resolution but an exacerbation of the irreconcilability of opposites. By the very nature of paraphilia, the paraphile is condemned to be unable to enter into a long-term pairbonded love relationship and a genital lust relationship with the same person (see Section 7, this chapter).

This hopeless incompatibility between love and lust is exemplified, at one extreme, by the paraphilia of lust murder (erotophonophilia), which precludes the possibility of long-term pairbond insofar as the occurrence of orgasm is synchronized with the death of the partner, or in the converse paraphilia (autassassinophilia), the death of the self.

A less extreme example is that of the incompatibility of love and lust in the juvenile partner of a pedophile, who becomes attached to the older person in a hero-worshipping, child–parent type of bond, but not in a reciprocated, long-term lover–lover bond. For the older person, the bond is one of lust combined with an unrealizable bond of long-term love—unrealizable because it self-destructs as soon as the juvenile partner matures and gets the hair growth and sweaty smells of puberty.

Another paraphilic example of the incompatibility of love and lust is epitomized in the case of male transvestophilia. At the outset of what will become a long-term attachment, the partner typically is unaware of either transvestophilia generally, or of its existence in this one particular person. Possibly, however, the female partner had a sixth sense of something feminine in her male partner, and was attracted toward it; or alternatively, being attracted and one-sidedly in love, grew into accommodating to the cross dressing once it was disclosed. Accommodating is not the same as being erotosexually turned on by having a partner in women's lingerie, however, and so the sex life of the couple becomes desultory and perfunctory. It is too much trouble. If the relationship is a heterosexual one, the woman loses interest, has inadequate vaginal lubrication, and has no orgasm. If the relationship is homosexual, the transvestophile's male partner becomes impotent, except if he is with another partner, or if he masturbates to the fantasy represented in his own lovemap. In either instance, the transvestophile in all likelihood becomes erotically apathetic toward the partner and genitally impotent, also, except maybe if he masturbates in female attire, perhaps before a mirror, or has a different and more responsive partner.

This transvestophilic example is prototypic of what happens between the paraphile and the long-term partner, in all the paraphilias. It explains why, when a presenting complaint in a sex therapy clinic is a hypophilic one, like erotic inertia (apathy, or so-called lack of sexual desire), impotence, or orgasm failure, one should always be alert to the possibility that behind a hypophilia, homosexual or heterosexual, there may lurk a hidden paraphilia.

The hypophilias are shared by men and women, homosexual, heterosexual, and bisexual (see Chapter 3, Section 9). In both sexes, they may be manifested as erotosexual inertia or apathy, as a phobia of genital penetration or entrapment, as numbness or diminution of feeling in the sex organs, as pain associated with intercourse, and as failure to reach the peak of orgasm. In men, there is also impotence and premature ejaculation; and, in women, vaginal dryness and vaginismus or premature muscular spasm closing the vagina. The common characteristic of the hypophilias is that the performance of the sex organs is below par.

Phyletically, if the lovemap has been vandalized and traumatized during the course of its development in childhood, one of the male/female differences may be a greater proneness for hypophilia in girls and paraphilia in boys. Court and clinic statistics currently do show a greater prevalence of paraphilias in males than females, but there is no guarantee that these statistics are fixed and eternal. The greater prevalence of orgasm failure (anorgasmia) in females than males, heterosexual perhaps more than lesbian, also is not destined to be eternal. It is very likely a product of erotosexual inhibition, which is culturally endemic in the rearing of girls in the major religious cultures of the world.

In the clinic it is not possible to get a sufficiently accurate and detailed account of factors that might be relevant to the treatment of hypophilic disorders of genital functioning without taking into account the patient's life-style as homosexual, bisexual, or heterosexual. That, in turn, absolutely entails that the person taking the history be a professional expert in nonjudgmentalism. People reveal intimate biographic information after becoming confident that it will not be used against them, and that they will not be chastised or disciplined.

It is popular today to classify hypophilic disorders in either homosexual or heterosexual partners as either organic or psychogenic in origin, and in some instances to make a hasty judgment on the basis of the history alone, or on the basis of the history and one or two tests. For example, it is still fashionable to believe that impotence is psychogenic if the nocturnal penile tumescence (NPT) test records that the penis became erect during the periods of rapid eye movement (REM) sleep. However, there are too many gradations between complete softness and complete rigidity of the penis for this one test to be conclusive.

The state of present-day knowledge makes it still impossible to pin down the cause of all cases of hypophilic dysfunction. The following is a list of possible contributing factors that may act alone or in combination.

- A birth defect of the internal and/or the external sex organs that affects their functioning.
- Impairment of the hormonal function in the brain, particularly in the region of the hypothalamus that governs releasing hormones, which in turn govern the pituitary gland and its hormones, which in turn govern the ovaries and testicles and their hormones. In some instances, hormonal deficiencies can be corrected with replacement therapy.
- Impairment of the response of target cells that utilize the sex-regulating hormones from the endocrine glands. The impairment may be irreversible.
- The toxic effect of drugs, either prescribed or obtained on the street, that block the function of nerves that govern the functioning of the sex organs. Prescription drugs well known for their sexual-blocking effect include antihypertensives for high blood pressure, and major tranquilizers or antipsychotics.
- Infections, especially local infections of the sex organs, that may leave an adverse aftereffect.
- Tumors that have a direct effect on the sex organs, or on the sexual nerves that connect the sex organs through the spinal cord and the autonomic nervous system with the sexual regions of the brain.
- Injuries, either from accidents or as an adverse side effect of surgery, that affect the sex organs either directly or by interfering with the nerve fibers or blood vessels that serve them.
- Vascular impairments that interfere with the flow of arterial blood into the sex organs, and the drainage of venous blood away from them. In some instances vascular impairments are secondary to another disease, of which one of the chief culprits is diabetes mellitus. In the male, when impotence is a major symptom of vascular impairment there are three approaches to treatment. One is by microsurgery to the blood vessels so as to increase the penile blood flow. Another is by the surgical implantation of flexible silastic stiffeners into the shaft of the penis; or by implanting a more complicated apparatus which has, in the scrotum, its own fluid reservoir and its own finger-press pump, used for inflating elongated balloons embedded in the shaft of the penis. The third approach is pharmacological and entails injecting a drug directly into the spongy bodies, the corpora cavernosa, of the penile shaft, where it has a direct effect on the tissues that regulate the flow of blood through the spongy tissues, and so creates an erection. The erection may last for two hours or more, and has been known to last much longer, which should be prevented by additional treatment (such as injection of sterile distilled water) to make the penis go soft before the tissues are permanently damaged. The erection-induc-

ing drug most used is papaverine, a nonaddictive derivative of the opium poppy. The use of penile injections is new, and dates from 1983 (Brindley, 1983; Virag et al., 1984). It is possible that these treatments are effective because of their interaction with one of a newly discovered and still expanding class of peptide hormones that are made not in specialized endocrine glands but in specialized cells scattered among different organs of the body, including the brain. In this instance, the hormone is vasoactive intestinal polypeptide (VIP), so named because it was first isolated from the gut. It is now known to be plentiful in the penis, and to be active in producing erection (Wagner and Sjostrand, 1988). Whatever the neurochemical mechanism proves to be whereby injected substances induce erection, these substances may justifiably be classified as belonging to one class of aphrodisiacs and, indeed, as the first predictively successful aphrodisiacs yet discovered (Money, Leal, and Gonzalez, 1987).

• Impairment of the function of the peripheral nerve supply to the genitalia and related pelvic organs from the lower spinal cord and the lower segment of the autonomic (sympathetic and parasympathetic) nervous system. These impairments may be secondary to another disease, or to injury, or tumor. Effective treatment is unlikely.

• Impairment of the brain's ability to regulate the functioning of the sex organs. This type of impairment is generally classified as psychogenic, especially if it is reversible in response to talking treatment or behavior modification treatment. It is classified as organic only if there is acceptable laboratory evidence of brain damage or dysfunction as, for example, temporal lobe epileptic seizures, a brain tumor, or radiographic evidence of brain deterioration. Organic does not necessarily imply irreversibile, for some organic conditions are treatable. There are many cases in which classification as either psychogenic or organogenic (organic) cannot be determined. There are also many cases of misclassification and, as a result, ineffectual treatment.

The hypophilic disorders in homosexual relationships were underreported and, for the most part, untreated in the era when homosexuality itself was classified as the disorder to be treated. It was then assumed that hypophilic complaints would dissipate with the advent of heterosexuality. Treatment is presently available for hypophilic disabilities in homosexual, as well as heterosexual or bisexual relationships. The availability of treatment for young people, especially unmarried adolescents, varies regionally. Overall it is not only in short supply, but deficient in guarantees of confidentiality and in health insurance coverage. Impediments to treatment on grounds of moral disapproval are greater for homosexual than for heterosexual adolescents, and for homosexual adults as well.

In the same way that a hypophilia may mask the existence of paraphilic imagery and ideation, if not paraphilic practice, so also may hyperphilia. In the case of compulsive cruising, for example (see Section 8, this chapter), it may not be readily apparent that the compulsive search is not simply hyperphilic but also paraphilic, such as in a paraphilia for fellating not only many strangers, but also those with the biggest penises. However, the hyperphilic compulsive and addictive characteristic of a paraphilia, rather than concealing or disguising it, puts it up front and on display more often than not. The paraphilias have a theatrical component that defies even the risk of self-incrimination.

It is not necessary to equate all hyperphilia with paraphilia. The hyperphilia that is a concomitant of some brain injuries is, for instance, an exception. Owing to the lack of detailed and systematic clinical studies of hyperphilia, there is not much that can be said about them. There are no data, for example, to help explain the hyperorgasmia—a rate that may be as high as five to ten orgasms daily—that is fairly consistently reported by paraphiles (see Sections 6 and 12, this chapter), and that people without hyperphilia cannot train themselves to attain. There are also no data regarding the relative distribution of hyperphilia among homosexuals, bisexuals, and heterosexuals.

14 PARAPHILIA: PREVENTION AND TREATMENT

The war currently being waged in the United States against pornography in general is directed specifically at the pornography of the sacrificial/expiatory and marauding/predatory paraphilias. These are the paraphilias that depict violence and activities that are classified by antipornographers as degrading women—but not men who engage in them! The aim of the war is to eradicate this paraphilic pornography from the commercial market. The rationale is that paraphilic pornography is contagious and infects and defiles the minds of those who use it, and so spreads an epidemic of violence and abuse of women and children. The grand strategy is to eradicate normophilic pornography also, because it ostensibly depraves and degenerates normal people and lowers their resistance to subsequent infection by paraphilically violent and degrading pornography.

The social contagion and degeneracy theories of pornography are wrong. Both are leftovers from the only theory of illness that medicine possessed before the discovery of germ theory in the 1870s, namely the degeneracy theory of Simon André Tissot (1728–1797) (Money, 1985). Degeneracy theory lingers on only in vulgarized sexual medicine, not in other branches of medicine that have become scientifically sophisticated.

The paradox of the war on pornography is that it will, in the long run, increase, not decrease an epidemic of paraphilic pornography, for it fails to

address the basic issue of the prevention of paraphilia in succeeding generations. As long as there are paraphiles with a thirst for paraphilic pornography, there will be a market to satisfy that thirst, even if it is a black market
operated illicitly by bootleggers and mobsters who pay no taxes, as in the
days of bathtub gin and prohibition.

Paraphilic prevention will not be accomplished by drying up the paraphilic pornography market. However, the market will dry up of its own
accord if society succeeds in preventing paraphilia from developing in today's infants. The accomplishment of preventing paraphilia will be by en-
suring healthy lovemap development in childhood. The sexual climate produced by a war on pornography is a sex-negative climate, and its
antisexualism permeates society. It is transmitted to young parents and
affects their childrearing with respect to their children's sexual learning and
their manifestations of normality, as in their juvenile sexual rehearsal play.
Sex-negative parents transmit sex negation to their children. Sex negation
at home is reinforced in the media, the community, the school, the religion,
and among peers.

Paraphilia, as well as other anomalies of sex and eroticism, flourish in an
environment of sex-negative rearing. Each sex-negative generation produces a larger proportion of sex-negative children, and a larger proportion
of paraphiles. Sex negation grows exponentially, and produces paraphiles
exponentially, generation by generation, in an ever-enlarging epidemic. It
is an epidemic the spread of which is measured not in days, weeks, or
months, but in years and generations. That makes it a difficult epidemic to
keep track of, and to account for—so difficult, in fact, that our present
generation has made the fallacious mistake of blaming it on the social
spread and contagion of pornography within its own lifetime—which is an
effect, not a cause. The blame should be correctly laid on the successive
failure of childrearing practices in each older generation to promote sexual
and erotic health in each new generation.

Sexuoerotic health is the only aspect of child development for which
there are no textbooks, and no chapters in textbooks of pediatrics, child
psychology, child psychiatry, or child development. Freud helped to guarantee these omissions by characterizing childhood as the latency period.
Piaget wrote about virtually every aspect of child development, but omitted
the development of sexological concepts. There is no specialty of pediatric
sexology, nor of ephebiatric (adolescent) sexology. There are no specialty
clinics to accept referrals of developmental lovemap disorders in childhood
and adolescence, and there are no resources for the better understanding
and promotion of healthy lovemaps, whether homosexual, bisexual, or
heterosexual. There is also no funding of research to advance the understanding of the etiology, diagnosis, treatment, and prognosis and prevention of paraphilic lovemaps.

The advancement of clinical research always goes hand in hand with the
provision of clinical service, for without clinical service, there are no patients. Because there are no pediatric or ephebiatric sexology clinics, there

are no concentrations of pediatric or adolescent sexology patients. Consequently there is an appalling ignorance of the possible variety of precursor manifestations, during childhood, of what later in life will be diagnosed as a paraphilia. There is a similar ignorance of the possible variety of factors that contribute to the etiology of a paraphilia, and of the relationship of such factors to the development of homosexuality, bisexuality, and heterosexuality, with or without a hypophilic or hyperphilic overlay. Knowledge of etiology is, of course, directly related to knowledge of prevention.

Where prevention has failed, amelioration or cure may succeed. In the case of paraphilia, there is no cure, in the sense of complete eradication or reversal of the cause. All treatments are therefore only ameliorative. A good analogy is the treatment of temporal lobe or psychomotor epilepsy. The seizure may be successfully controlled with medication, and the brain wave pattern normalized. After a given period of treatment, a test period without medication may be tried. In the case of a relapse, medication is resumed. With or without medication, the case is never considered closed, but maintained in continuous follow-up, with a checkup annually or more often.

The medication used in the treatment of paraphilia (see Chapter 3, Section 5, and Section 11, this chapter), in combination with talking treatment, is a hormone, medroxyprogesterone acetate (MPA), trade-named Depo-Provera. Its equivalent in Europe is cyproterone acetate, trade-named Androcur. MPA is a synthetic hormone. Its first use for treating paraphilia was by Money, Migeon, and Rivarola in 1966 (Money, 1970b). It is officially classified as a progestin or progestogen, and is related in biochemical structure to both progesterone and testosterone. Its biological action resembles that of progesterone, the hormone that in the body is the precursor of testosterone. It is competitive with testosterone in binding to receptor cells. Thus it is known as an antiandrogen. Unlike estrogen, also an antiandrogen, it is not feminizing.

MPA is taken up by those cells in the body that have a hunger for testosterone, where it usurps the place of testosterone. It puts the testosterone-producing cells of the testicles temporarily at rest, and therby lowers the blood level of testosterone to that of prepuberty. It is not the pharmacological equivalent of surgical castration, for it does not eliminate testosterone entirely, and above all, is reversible upon discontinuation of treatment.

A prepubertal level of testosterone in the bloodstream is translated into subjective apperception as a less insistent sex drive, a lessened feeling of tension and agitation, and greater calmness. Part of this effect is attributed not to diminished testosterone, but to a direct action of MPA in that zone of the brain in the forward part of the hypothalamus, the preoptic area, which in animals is known to be directly involved in the governance of mating behavior. The posterior hypothalamus in involved in the governance of pituitary-gonadal hormones of mating. In a study of adult male rhesus monkeys (Rees, Bonsall, and Michael, 1986), an intramuscular injection of radioactively labeled MPA was found in brain cells of the preoptic area as soon as 15 minutes after injection.

The protocol used to inform patients about the treatment, including dosage, so that they may give their informed consent, is reproduced in Money, 1987d.

MPA has a limited history as a treatment of paraphilia in women. In at least two cases, both of them involving the onset of paraphilic behavior following accidental brain injury, it proved beneficial. In brain injury cases, MPA combined with lithium treatment has also proved not only beneficial but, in some cases, more effective than MPA alone. This lithium effect may in the future lead to new understanding of the neurochemistries of paraphilic cyclicity and the cyclicity of other syndromes, notably manic-depressive cyclicity.

After a very long tradition of exclusively spiritual treatment for pedophiles and ephebophiles and other paraphiles who are members of religious orders or the clergy, the church has recently incorporated MPA into some of its treatment programs, for example, at St. Luke's Institute in Suitland, Maryland, and at the center of the Servants of the Paraclete in Jemez Springs, New Mexico. This adoption of a biomedical treatment is the thin edge of a wedge that may have far-reaching consequences on Vatican sexology (Money, 1987e). It gives official recognition to the proposition that sexual behavior is not attributable exclusively to the morality of good and evil, righteousness and sin. Repentance, prayer, and penance alone are not sufficient for the governance of paraphilic sexuality, even among those in holy orders. Nor are punishment and imprisonment.

15 ALPHABETIC LIST OF PARAPHILIAS

acrotomophilia (amputee partner)
adolescentilism (impersonating an adolescent)
andromimetophilia (male impersonator's partner)
apotemnophilia (self-amputee)
asphyxiophilia (asphyxiation)
autagonistophilia (live-show self-display)
autassassinophilia (self-staged own death)
autonepiophilia (infantilism, wearing diapers)
biastophilia (raptophilia)
catheterophilia (catheter)
chrematistophilia (blackmail payment)
chronophilia (age discrepancy)
coprophilia (feces)
ephebophilia (adolescent partner)
erotophonophilia (lust murder)
exhibitionism (indecent exposure)
fetishism (erotic token)
formicophilia (crawling things)
frotteurism (rubbing against a stranger)
gerontophilia (parent-aged partner)
gynemimetophilia (female-impersonator partner)
heterophilia (not a paraphilia)
homophilia (not a paraphilia)
hybristophilia (criminal or convict partner) [See p.180]

hyphephilia (tactile fetish)
hypoxyphilia (asphyxiophilia)
infantilism (impersonating a baby)
kleptophilia (stealing)
klismaphilia (enema)
masochism (being injured, humiliated)
mixophilia (scoptophilia)
morphophilia (physique discrepancy)
mysophilia (filth)
narratophilia (erotic storytelling)
necrophilia (corpse)
nepiophilia (infant partner, diaper-aged)
olfactophilia (smell fetish)
pedophilia (juvenile partner)
peodeiktophilia (penile exhibitionism)

pictophilia (erotic graphics or films)
raptophilia (rape, biastophilia)
sadism (injuring, humiliating)
scoptophilia (onlooker, mixophilia)
somnophilia (sleeping partner)
stigmatophilia (tattoo, piercing)
symphorophilia (disaster, conflagration)
telephonicophilia (lewd phone calling)
toucheurism (touching a stanger)
transvestophilia (cross dressing)
urophilia (urine)
voyeurism (illicit peeping)
zoophilia (animals)

16 EPILOGUE AND SYNOPSIS

Homosexuality has a long history of classification as a sexual deviancy or perversion. A sexual perversion in today's biomedical terminology is a paraphilia. Homosexuality, however, is not included in the current official classification of the paraphilias, for it has been declassified as a disease. Its medical status is like that of, for example, color blindness or left-handedness, which also once were classified as deviant, but now are considered simply as characteristics of a minority of the population who are functionally different from the majority.

Like heterosexuals, homosexuals fall in love and become limerently pair-bonded, and they suffer lovesickness when love is unrequited. Being able to fall in love only with someone whose body sex is different from one's own is the defining characteristic of heterosexuality. Likewise being able to fall in love only with someone whose body sex is the same as one's own is the defining characteristic of homosexuality.

Love is proverbially blind. People are said to fall in love. There is no application form. One does not arrange or choose intellectually to be in love. Those entrapped in the woeful misery of lovesickness would have arranged not to fall in love, or not to remain love-smitten, if only it were a matter of intellectual choice. John Hinckley, afflicted with lovesickness classified as the Clérambault–Kandinsky syndrome, would not have been driven to attempt to assassinate the President of the United States in order to convince the actress, Jodie Foster, of the seriousness of his plight had he been able to make a voluntary decision not to be lovesick.

Homosexuals do not make a voluntary or intellectual decision to be erotically attracted toward, and to fall in love with, someone of the same sex. The propensity to do so is something that reveals itself, in much the same way as a dream reveals itself. It may, indeed, be in a dream, perhaps a wet dream, that the propensity is first revealed.

Falling in love and becoming limerently pairbonded is neither masculine nor feminine, but shared equally by both sexes. Thus it is not atypical for a homosexual man or woman to have the experience. What is atypical, in the statistical sense, is that, among the homosexual minority of the population, the beloved is of the same sex as the self, whereas among the heterosexual majority, the beloved is of the other sex. In the homosexual lover–lover relationship the sex of the beloved is transposed from what it would be in a heterosexual relationship. Because of the transposition of the sex of the beloved from other sex to same sex, one says that there is a specific and limited limerent gender transposition. Homosexual lover–lover bonding is normophilic in the same ways that heterosexual lover–lover bonding is normophilic, except for society's ideology.

The logical symmetry of homosexual and heterosexual normophilia applies also to homosexual and heterosexual paraphilia. In the vernacular, the term for paraphilia is bizarre or kinky sex. In the law, it is deviation or perversion. Biomedically, it is defined as a pattern or template in the brain and the mind that governs and dictates ideologically rejected or unusual imagery, ideation, and practice that is essential for erotosexual arousal and attainment of orgasm. Until recently there was no name for the brain's erotosexual template, so I coined the term lovemap.

A lovemap may be either normophilic or paraphilic. It is defined as a personalized, developmental representation or template in the mind/brain that depicts the idealized program of what to participate in erotosexually with the idealized lover. The lovemap manifests itself in imagination, thinking, or actual erotosexual practice. It may express itself in a dream, a masturbatory fantasy, or a copulatory fantasy.

The tally of the paraphilias is not fixed, but the number is around forty. All of them may afflict either homosexuals or heterosexuals, with no special affinity for either. This is an important piece of information. The gay movement, because of its focus on the struggle for gay political rights, has not properly differentiated gay rights from paraphilic rights; nor has it recognized the potential hazards of the more dangerous paraphilias either to gay individuals or to the political reputation of the movement. Conversely, the enemies of the gay movement also have not differentiated gay rights from paraphilic rights, and have equated being homosexual as the first stage of a degenerative descent into paraphilia. For example, there is a heresy to the effect that homosexuals progress from same-aged partners, to teenagers, to juveniles, to infants, with increasing depravity that culminates in abduction and lust murder. There is no substantiating evidence for this heresy. It is based on total ignorance of paraphilia in general, and of the high degree of specificity of each paraphilia in particular.

Although healthy lovemap development in childhood ranks with all other aspects of child health in terms of its importance, it is virtually the only aspect of child health that is totally neglected. Its very existence, is indeed, denied. There is no specialty clinic anywhere in all of the Americas and Europe for pediatric sexual health, no textbook, and not even a chapter in a textbook of pediatric psychology, psychiatry, or child development. Juvenile erotosexual rehearsal play is widely viewed as an aberration, and a manifestation of original sin that evokes abusive punishment or, in some instances, exploitation. One consequence is that the developing lovemap becomes thwarted and warped so that erotosexual functioning in maturity will be hypophilic, hyperphilic, or paraphilic.

In hypophilia, the genitalia perform below par, as in impotence, premature ejaculation, deficient lubrication, vaginismus, and failure to achieve orgasm. In hyperphilia, there is an exaggerated and excessive focus on erotosexual activity, in a compulsive and unrelenting way. Hyperphilia is sometimes referred to as erotomania. In paraphilia, something sexuoerotically alien or kinky intrudes and becomes included in the lovemap. Or, the lovemap becomes skewed, so that something on the edges gets displaced into the center. Sadomasochistic bondage, discipline, and humiliation are an example of an inclusion. Exhibitionism/voyeurism is an example of a displacement, insofar as display and inspection of the genitalia, among primates, are preliminary to their use in copulation, but not the activity that surpasses the copulation and is prerequisite to orgasm.

Hypophilia, hyperphilia, and paraphilia occur in association with either homosexuality or heterosexuality. Hypophilia is more prevalent in women than men. Hyperphilia is joked about more than taken seriously, and so its prevalence is uncertain. Paraphilia is ascertained more often in men than in women. Women's paraphilias are more touchy-feely than visual, and vice versa for men; and women's paraphilias cast them in the role of being abducted or possessed more prevalently than do men's. There is a wider range of paraphilias recorded in men than women. In some instances, the symptoms of hypophilia mask a paraphilia; and conversely, the symptoms of hyperphilia may do the same.

The formula of a paraphilia is that it is a developmental stratagem for rescuing lust from total eradication from the lovemap, but at the cost of a cleavage between lust and love. Lust is for sinners, whores, and playboys. Love is for saints, madonnas, and providers. In a paraphilia, lust and love do not converge onto one person who is the ideal recipient of both.

There are six different paraphilic stratagems that ensure the paraphilic cleavage between lust and love. The stratagem of sacrifice and expiation requires that one of the partners make a sacrifice to expiate the guilt of lust, as exemplified in sadism/masochism. The extreme sacrifice is lust murder, either erotic homicide, or stage-managing one's own erotic assassination.

The stratagem of marauding and predation requires that the partner in lust be kidnaped, abducted, coerced, or violently assaulted, as no decent person would consent to be defiled by lust. The extreme example of this stratagem is rapistic violence and assault or raptophilia, of which the converse is self-arranged abduction or entrapment by an official decoy.

The mercantile and venal stratagem requires that the partner either pay for lust, or be paid for it, as no decent person would consent to the defilement of lust as an unpaid form of enjoyment. This stratagem commonly passes unrecognized behind the facade of commercial prostitution. It applies to male hustlers as well as female prostitutes and, conversely, to their customers. A person may set himself or herself up to be a victim of blackmail or robbery, or to blackmail or rob. Noncommercially, gifts or subsidies may be used instead of cash, or paying may be a game played with play money.

The fetish and talisman stratagem requires that the partner be saved from lust and that some token, the fetish or talisman, be the object of lust instead. There are two classes of fetishes: the smellies and the feelies. For the festishist the smell or feel of the fetish is, in each instance, associated with the human body—for example, the smell of shoes or jockstraps, or the feel of hair, fur, silk, rubber (from training pants), and so on.

The stigmatic and eligibilic stratagem requires that the partner have certain distinguishing marks or features (stigmas) that metaphorically identify that partner as an infidel eligible to be defiled by lust, not one of the chosen who must be redeemed by love alone. There are two classes of stigmas, morphophilic and chronophilic. In morphophilia, the partner is lust-eligible because of being different in body build, appearance, or racial stock. One somewhat extreme example is acrotomophilia, in which the partner must have an amputated stump to be caressed and fondled. The obverse is to become an amputee oneself (apotemnophilia), which may require a ruse, such as a self-arranged hunting accident. In chronophilia, the partner is lust-eligible only if disparate in age. The named chronophilias are infantophilia, pedophilia, and ephebophilia, all of which are legally classified as criminal, and gerontophilia, which is not criminal. For the ages between adolescence (ephebophilia) and advanced maturity (gerontophilia), there is a need for terms like twentiophilia and thirtiophilia, and so on. A twentiophilic relationship may fall apart when the twentiophile's partner's age advances from the twenties into the thirties or older. This paraphilia is a little known source of separation, divorce, and the breakup of long-term relationships, homosexual as well as heterosexual.

The stratagem of solicitation and allure requires that the partner be spared the defilement of lust by not progressing from the preliminaries of lovemaking to the stage of genital contact. In the vernacular, this is the stratagem of the cockteaser and the loving queen. It is also the stratagem manifested as a phobic aversion to genital contact so great that an unwary lover, male or female, who fails to recognize the phobia and retreat from it, is at risk of being accused of date rape or spouse rape. In the eyes of the law, the stratagem of solicitation and allure is exemplified in the genital exhibitionist whose maximum turn-on is by illicitly exposing the genitals to an unsuspecting stranger; and in the Peeping Tom (voyeur) whose maximum turn-on is by illicitly spying on the nudity or copulation of someone else. These actions must be illicit to be sexuoerotically effective. Licit nudity at a nudist resort has no arousal value for an exhibitionist or a voyeur.

There is a seventh stratagem that may ride piggyback on one of the other six. It is the stratagem of the understudy or subrogate who becomes a partner in the defilement of lust and so rescues someone else from that fate. It appears in some cases of adultery, and some of incest, for example, incest in which a son or daughter is a stand-in for the mother, rescuing her from the father's lust. For the son in this case, being a stand-in signifies some degree of gender crossing. In association with the subrogation stratagem, gender crossing has various guises. For example, a self-asphyxiating paraphile may cross dress in his mother's lingerie before embarking on his self-strangulation ritual. Only once does the ritual terminate as an unexplained, cross-dressed, autoerotic death.

The list of the more than forty paraphilias that have been named is not exhaustive, insofar as some paraphilias—for example, the fetishes—can be subclassified. The list is also not potentially infinite. Apparently there is a limited number of phylogenetically programed elements of human behavior, or phylisms, that can become rerouted from their primary service into the service of erotosexual arousal and orgasm.

Paraphilias are demanding, insistent and compulsory in their commands, and are not responsive to punishment or incarceration. They represent a special form of addiction. The addiction is not to sex in general, as has been falsely claimed, but very specifically it is an addiction to something or other, live or inanimate, that is sex associated. For example, in transvestophilia, the addiction is to women's clothes. Getting rid of them does not stop the addiction, but brings on withdrawal symptoms.

The theory or principle that most closely fits the phenomenon of paraphilic addiction is named opponent-process. According to this principle, the polarization of negative and positive becomes reversed. In paraphilia, the tragedy of lust threatened with extermination becomes the triumph of lust saved. That which was once aversive switches and becomes paraphilically addictive—even if the addiction is to a noose around one's own neck that may bring about autoerotic death.

Scientifically, it is too soon to specify whether all human beings are equally at risk for developing a paraphilic lovemap, other things being equal, or whether some are more vulnerable than others. The latter is more likely, although the cause of the vulnerability and the timing of its onset are unknown. It may be akin to the vulnerability that in some people produces temporal lobe, psychomotor epileptic attacks, which may be attributed to either prenatal or postnatal influences on the brain. Many paraphiles, when they carry out their paraphilic ritual, undergo an altered state of consciousness, termed a paraphilic fugue state, or a paraphilic attack. It is akin to the Dr. Jekyll and Mr. Hyde phenomenon of dual personality. There is already some preliminary indication that brain research with PET scanning will reveal the locus of the paraphilic fugue state in the brain.

Paraphilias are not socially contagious. They are not caught by associating with paraphiles, or by reading about them, or by looking at movies or videos of them engaged in paraphilic activity. They myth of social contagion, especially from exposure to visual depiction of paraphilias, underlies officialdom's current panicky fascination with pornography and with driving it underground. The truth is that paraphilic pornography does not defile normophilic lovemaps. It simply does not appeal to anyone except those whose lovemap already mirrors it. Suppression of pornography is a red herring that distracts society from its proper business, which should be to learn how to prevent the development of paraphilic lovemaps in each new generation of children in kindergarten and grade school. Without prevention, society will remain entrapped in an epidemic of paraphilia, the spread of which increases and is measured generation by generation, not month by month or year by year. Each generation produces more paraphilic children than did the generations before it.

If the two lovemaps of the two partners each reciprocally match one another, then a paraphilia, if playful and innocuous, as in mild bondage and discipline, will be mutually and socially acceptable. In the case of a mismatch, the partner who must fake a match finds the experience perfunctory, boring, or disgusting. It is an unsatisfactory experience for both. That is why paraphilia should properly be called a disorder not of sex, but of love. The more rare a paraphilia, the more rare the chance of finding a lover with a reciprocally matching lovemap.

The personal inconvenience of being paraphilically lonely and unable to find a matching partner brings some paraphilic people, homosexual as well as heterosexual, to the clinic for treatment. Others come because their paraphilia is dangerous, or it is self-offending and its expression is a crime. They are treated with the hormone medroxyprogesterone acetate (MPA), trade-named Depo-Provera. It has an antiandrogenic effect that lowers the level of male hormone circulating in the bloodstream to the level of prepuberty. It also has a direct, calming effect on brain cells that participate in the governance of mating behavior. The hormone is used in combination with counseling either singly or, preferably, with the partner included.

The question of individual right to treatment versus societal right to enforce treatment has vexed civil libertarians, including advocates of gay rights. A guideline that preserves both individual and societal rights is based on the criterion of personal inviolacy: no one has the right to infringe on someone else's personal sexual inviolacy by imposing his or her lovemap on a partner without the partner's informed consent. Informed consent presupposes that the terms of the contract are specified, and that the end is predicated by the beginning. No unexpected surprises are unilaterally imposed by one partner on the other. Homosexuals as well as heterosexuals are served equally well by this guideline. Its individual application saves gay as well as straight people from walking into paraphilic entrapments, sacrificing their own inviolacy, and in the case of the sacrificial/expiatory paraphilias, perhaps sacrificing their lives.

Glossary

acault (pronounced a·chow'): in Burma, the name given to a full-time female impersonator or gynemimetic. *See also* **hijra.**

acceptive phase: in a sexuoerotic relationship, the phase, following proception and preceding the possibility of conception, in which the genital organs become mutually involved in body contact, typically in genital union. *See also* **conceptive phase; proceptive phase.**

acrotomophilia: a paraphilia of the stigmatic/eligibilic type in which sexuoerotic arousal and facilitation or attainment of orgasm are responsive to and contingent on a partner who is an amputee (from Greek, *akron,* extremity + *tomé,* a cutting + -philia). An acrotomophile is erotically excited by the stump(s) of the amputee partner. The reciprocal paraphilic condition, namely self-amputation, is **apotemnophilia.**

Adam/Eve principle: in embryological development and subsequently, the principle that nature's primary template is that which differentiates a female, and that something must be added to induce the differentiation of a male.

addiction: a state or condition of existence characterized by habitually engaging in a highly specific and routine activity reiteratively and compulsively, irrespective of aversive or deadly consequences; the addiction is not to the activity, but to the object, substance, or person toward which the activity is directed. *See also* **sexual addiction.**

adolescence: the developmental period of maturation, predominantly during teenage, from puberty to young adulthood.

adolescent gynecomastia: in boys at puberty, the growth of glandular tissue and enlargement of the breasts in response to the hormones of puberty. Typically the enlargement is minimal and self-correcting, but in rare cases resembles that of a girl and requires corrective plastic surgery (mastectomy). The etiology, though obscure, is attributed either to an atypical utilization of the low level of estrogen normally produced by the testicles of the male, or to an atypical resistance to the counteracting effect of testosterone.

adolescentilism, paraphilic: impersonating an adolescent and being

treated as one by the partner—one of the stigmatic/eligibilic paraphilias. *See also* **ephebophilia; gerontalism; infantilism; juvenilism.**

adrenal cortex: the outer three layers of the adrenal gland, as contrasted
with the innermost part, the medulla. The cortex produces steroidal
hormones, among them the glucocorticoid, cortisol, and nonpotent
sex hormones. *See also* **adrenal gland; cortex.**

adrenal gland: an endocrine gland located immediately above the kidney. It
consists of two portions: a cortex and a medulla. The cortex produces
and secretes steroidal hormones, among them cortisol (a glucocorticoid), and weakly active sex hormones. The medulla produces
epinephrine (adrenaline), a catecholamine.

adrenocortex (*adj.* **adrenocortical**): *see* **adrenal cortex.**

adrenocortical hormone: one of the hormones, for example cortisol, secreted not from the internal medulla but from the external cortex of the
bilateral adrenocortical glands.

adrenogenital syndrome: *see* **CVAH.**

aegis: auspices, patronage, or sponsorship.

agenesis (*adj.* **agenetic**): partial or complete failure of an organ or part of
the body to form or develop.

agonistic: in opposition or opposed to; in pharmacology, a drug that com-
petes with a naturally occurring substance at cell receptors.

AIDS: acquired immune deficiency syndrome, caused by a retrovirus
(HIV-I, human immunodeficiency virus) infection, and lethal; no cure
has been discovered as of this writing.

allure: enticement; attractivity; seductiveness.

5α-reductase: a naturally occurring enzyme necessary for the conversion
of testosterone to dihydrotestosterone, the form of the hormone that
some androgen-dependent cells require for their activation.

Alzheimer's disease: cumulative degeneration of mental function in adulthood, associated with cortical atrophy characterized by degeneration
of brain cells into tangled spindles, and terminated by total dementia
and death.

ambiguous genitalia: a birth defect of the sex organs in which, from their
embryonically undifferentiated state, they have failed to become fully
differentiated as either male or female, but are unfinished. At birth the
baby's sex cannot be declared on the basis of visual inspection. Diagnostically, the term is hermaphroditism or intersexuality. Embryologically, it is not possible to develop a complete penis and scrotum together with a complete vagina and vulva.

ambisexuality (*adj.* **ambisexual**): having characteristics shared by both
sexes (from Greek, *ambi*, both + sex)—in human beings, for example,
nipples; pubic hair; birth-defective genitalia that look hermaphroditically ambiguous or intersexed; or mating behavior shared by both sexes.

ambitypic: as applied to sexual dimorphism of the genitalia, brain, or behavior, differentiation of both female and male anlagen together dur-

ing an initial phase, after which only one anlage, female or male, continues to develop and the other does not, as in the case of the müllerian (female) and wolffian (male) embryonic ducts. *Ant.* **unitypic.**

amenorrhea: absence or failure of the menstrual periods.

amygdala: a part of the brain situated in the temporal lobe. It belongs to the "old brain" or limbic system.

anabolic: having the effect of building tissue, especially muscle tissue.

Androcur: the trade name of the hormone, cyproterone acetate, manufactured by Schering A.G., West Berlin. The hormone resembles progestin and is antiandrogenic. It has various clinical applications, one of which is to help sex offenders gain personal governance of their sexuoerotic conduct. *See also* **Depo-Provera.**

androgen: male sex hormone (from Greek, *andros*, man), produced chiefly by the testis, but also by the adrenal cortex and, in small amounts, by the ovary. In biochemical structure, there are several different but related steroid hormones that qualify as androgens. They differ in biological strength and effectiveness.

androgen-induced hermaphroditism: a syndrome of hermaphroditic birth defect of the sex organs induced in the 46,XX gonadally female fetus by an excess of masculinizing hormone transmitted from the mother through the placenta. The syndrome may be experimentally induced in animals by injection of the hormone testosterone, whereas in human beings it is adventitious, the source of the hormone being a maternal (possibly placental) hormone-producing tumor.

androgen-insensitivity syndrome: a congential condition identified by a 46,XY chromosomal karyotype in girls or women who appear externally to be not sexually different from normal females, except in some cases for a swelling or lump in each groin, or for the absence or sparseness of pubic and axillary hair after puberty. The cells of the body are unable to respond to the male sex hormone, which is made in the testes in normal amounts for a male. They respond instead to the small amount of female sex hormone, estrogen, which is normally made in the testes. The effect before birth is that masculine internal development commences but is not completed. It goes far enough, however, to prevent internal female development. Externally, the genitalia differentiate as female, except for a blind vagina, which is usually not deep enough for satisfactory intercourse and needs either dilation or surgical lengthening in or after middle teenage. There is no menstruation and no fertility. Breasts develop normally. *Syn.* **testicular-feminizing syndrome.**

androgyne: a person who manifests a merging of the roles traditionally stereotyped as belonging to male and female, respectively (from Greek, *andros*, man + *gyne*, woman). Formery the term was also used as a synonym for male pseudohermaphrodite, along with gynandroid as a synonym for female pseudohermaphrodite.

androgynophilia: erotosexual pairing with a man and a woman serially or simultaneously by a member of either sex. It includes falling in love. *See also* **bisexuality.**

androgyny: the condition of showing some characteristics of both sexes in body, mind, or behavior.

andromimesis: a syndrome of male impersonation in a natal female who is able to relate sexuoerotically exclusively with women, and who may be hormonally, but not surgically sex-reassigned (from Greek, *andros*, man + *mimos*, mime. It is a syndrome of gender transposition, not paraphilia).

androphilia: love of a man by a woman (female androphilia) or by a man (male androphilia). It includes erotosexual bonding. *See also* **hetero-sexuality; homosexuality.**

androstenedione: an androgenic hormone, secreted by the adrenocortex, ovary, and testis, less potent than testosterone.

anerotic: not erotic; lacking eroticism.

anhedonia: lack of pleasure in doing or experiencing something, or doing it only as an obligation, duty, or drudgery.

anlage (*pl.* **anlagen**): in embryology, the initial element or structure that develops and differentiates into a more complex structure.

anorgasmia: a hypophilic condition or syndrome, variable in etiology, of being unable to attain orgasm with normally conducive modes of stimulation.

anovulatory: without ovulation, as when an estrous or menstrual cycle occurs without the release of an egg from the ovary. Anovulatory cycles are infertile cycles. Until ovulation resumes, a female is said to manifest anovulatory sterility.

antiandrogen: a hormone or other substance that replaces androgen within the nuclei of target cells, or excludes its entry. It inhibits the secretion of testosterone from the testis and is itself either biologically inert or functionally very weak.

antipode (*pl.* **antipodes;** *adj.* **antipodal**): the exact opposite or contrary of an idea, thing, or place (pronounce *sing.* to rhyme with ode; *pl.* an·tip'·od·eez').

anus: the opening at the end of the alimentary canal through which feces are discharged; used to receive the penis in anal intercourse, and the fist in "fisting."

apogee: the farthest or highest point; culmination; apex.

apophasis (*adv.* **apophasically**): to mention something in disclaiming the intention to mention it. *Ex.:* I dare not mention the abominable practice, the secret vice of masturbation.

apotemnophilia: a paraphilia of the stigmatic/eligibilic type in which sexuoerotic arousal and facilitation or attainment of orgasm are responsive to and contingent on being oneself an amputee (from Greek, *apo*, from + *temnein*, to cut + -philia). An apotemnophile becomes fixated on carrying out a self-contrived amputation, or obtaining one in a hospital. The reciprocal paraphilic condition in which the partner is an amputee is **acrotomophilia.**

apperceptive assimilation: informal learning on the basis of familiarity and experience.

asphyxiophilia: a paraphilia of the sacrificial/expiatory type in which sexuoerotic arousal and facilitation or attainment of orgasm are responsive to and contingent on self-strangulation and asphyxiation up to, but not including loss of consciousness (from Greek, *asphyxia*, no pulse + -philia). When the ritual is autoerotic, split-second failure to release the noose or gag at the onset of orgasm results in death. There is no technical term for the reciprocal paraphilic condition that is subsumed under the general category of **sadomasochism** with the dominant partner supervising or presiding over the ritual. *See also* **hypoxyphilia.**

assortative mating: the mating of individuals on the criteria of reciprocally matching features, behavior, or mental characteristics.

asymmetry: as applied to the brain, a proportional difference or discordance between the right and left hemispheres, particularly with respect to function.

atonement: an act of reparation or compensation to make amends for an offense or injury.

atresia (*adj.* **atresic**): congenital absence or closure of one of the openings or tubular organs of the body.

atrophy (*adj.* **atrophied, atrophic**): a defect or failure of cell nutrition manifested as decrease in size or healthiness of an organ or tissue. *See also* **dystrophy.**

autagonistophilia: a paraphilia of the solicitational/allurative type in which sexuoerotic arousal and facilitation or attainment of orgasm are responsive to and contingent on being observed or being on stage or on camera (from Greek, *autos*, self + agonistes, principal dramatic actor + -philia). The reciprocal paraphilic condition is **scoptophilia.**

autassassinophilia: a paraphilia of the sacrificial/expiatory type in which sexuoerotic arousal and facilitation of orgasm are responsive to and contingent on stage-managing the possibility of one's own masochistic death by murder (from Greek, *autos* self + assassin + -philia). The reciprocal paraphilic condition is **lust murder** or **erotophonophilia.**

autistic: self-preoccupied.

autoerotic death: death, typically from asphyxiation or electrocution, as an inadvertent culmination of a paraphilic sexuoerotic ritual involving self-strangulation or self-applied electric current.

autoeroticism (*adj.* **autoerotic**): self-directed erotosexual behavior [from Greek, *auto,* self + *erotikos,* erotic (Eros, the god of love)]. *Ant.* **alloeroticism.** *See also* **autophilia; autosexual.**

autonepiophilia: a paraphilia of the stigmatic/eligibilic type in which sexuoerotic arousal and facilitation or attainment of orgasm are responsive to and contingent on impersonating a baby in diapers and being treated as one by the partner (from Greek, *autos,* self + *nepon,* infant + -philia).

Autonepiophilia may be adjunctive to masochistic discipline and humiliation. The reciprocal paraphilic condition, namely having an infant as sexuoerotic partner, is **nepiophilia.** *Syn.* **paraphilic infantilism.**

autonomic nervous system: pertaining to that part of the nervous system that regulates involuntary reactions, especially those concerned with nutritive, vascular, glandular, and reproductive organs; and that traverses the body in large part outside the spinal cord, which encases the central nervous system below the brain.

autophilia (*adj.* **autophilic**): the condition in which love and lust are not attached to a partner but to the self (from Greek, *auto,* self + philia). *See also* **autoeroticism; autosexual.**

autosexual (*n.* **autosexuality**): characterized by self-sex contact, usually as a genital act (masturbation), with or without an accompanying erotic fantasy or ritual; or, rarely, as a long-term sexuoerotic status without a partner (from Greek, *auto,* self + sex). *See also* **autoeroticism; autophilia.**

axon: a threadlike structure on which impulses are transmitted away from the main body of a nerve cell (from Greek, *axon,* axle, axis). *See also* **dendrite; synapse.**

barbiturate: a salt or derivative of barbituric acid used medicinally as a sedative, sleeping pill, or anticonvulsant; and among street drugs used as a "downer."

berdache: the name given by early French explorers to American Indians whom they regarded as effeminate homosexuals but who had, according to tribal tradition, special spiritual status as shamans and healers and who took on a woman's role, including becoming a wife; contemporary berdaches continue the ancient customs.

biastophilia: a paraphilia of the sacrificial/expiatory type in which sexuoerotic arousal and facilitation or attainment of orgasm are responsive to and contingent on the surprise attack and continued violent assault of a nonconsenting, terrified, and struggling stranger (from Greek, *biastes,* rape or forced violation + -philia). Acquiescence on the part of the partner induces a fresh round of threat and violence from the biastophile. Biastophilia may be homosexual as well as heterosexual, but is predominantly the latter, whether the biastophile is male or female. There is no term for the reciprocal paraphilic condition, namely stage-managing one's own brutal rape by a stranger, which probably exists chiefly in attenuated form and rarely gets transmuted from fantasy into actuality. *Syn.* **raptophilia.**

bisexual (*n.* **bisexuality**): characterized by other-sex and same-sex contacts, either concurrently or sequentially in the course of development, either in genital acts or as a long-term sexuoerotic status (from Latin, *bi,* two + sex). The distribution of heterophilia and homophilia in bisexuality may be 50 : 50 or, more likely, in unequal proportions such as 60 : 40 or 20 : 80. Bisexuality is not a paraphilia, although paraphilias may exist in association with bisexuality. *Ant.* **monosexual.**

CAH: congenital adrenal hyperplasia. *Syn.* **CVAH.**

carnal: of the flesh, as opposed to the spirit; pertaining in a derogatory way to the use of the sexual organs as a manifestation of humanity's lower nature (from Latin, *carnis,* flesh).

catheterophilia: a paraphilia of the fetishistic/talismanic type in which sexuoerotic arousal and facilitation or attainment of orgasm are responsive to and contingent on having a catheter inserted up into the urethra (from Greek, *catheter,* catheter + -philia).

central nervous system (CNS): that part of the nervous system that includes the brain and the spinal cord, and their peripherl nerves, and that, as compared with the autonomic nervous system, governs voluntary muscular reactions.

cerebral cortex: the external gray layer of the brain, the neocortex. *See also* **limbic system.**

cervix: the neck of an organ; specifically the neck of the lower part of the uterus, or womb, where the vagina and uterus unite.

childhood: biomedically, the period of development between infancy and puberty; legally, in the United States, the period of development until the eighteenth birthday (Public Law 98-292, The Child Protection Act of 1984).

cholesterol: in biological chemistry, a white, fatlike, crystalline alcohol, synthesized chiefly in the liver and important as, among other things, a precursor of gonadal and other steroid hormones.

chordee: fixed curvature or tying down of the penis or hypertrophied clitoris as in the hypospadiac birth defect characteristic of various types of hermaphroditism.

chorionic gonadotropin: gonadotropic hormone of pregnancy secreted from the placenta, whereas pituitary gonadotropin is secreted from the anterior pituitary gland. *See also* **gonadotropin; FSH; LH.**

chrematistophilia: a paraphilia of the mercantile/venal type in which sexuoerotic arousal and facilitation or attainment of orgasm are responsive to and contingent on being charged or forced to pay, or being robbed by the sexual partner for sexual services (from Greek, *chremistes,* money dealer + -philia). There is no technical term for the reciprocal paraphilic condition of enforcing a charge or robbing.

chromosomal mosaicism: a chromosomal pattern in which some cells of the body have the standard number of chromosomes (46,XX or 46,XY), and others have more or less, as in 45,X/46,XY (a mosaic variety of Turner's syndrome); or 46,XY/47,XXY (a mosaic variety of Klinefelter's syndrome), and many others.

chromosome: one of twenty-six pairs of threadlike structures located within the nucleus of each of the body's cells, the function of which is to transmit genetic information to the cell that governs its growth and biological activity.

chronophilia: one of a group of paraphilias of the stigmatic/eligibilic type in which the paraphile's sexuoerotic age is discordant with his/her actual chronological age and is concordant with the age of the partner, as in, respectively, **infantilism** and **nepiophilia; juvenilism** and **pedophilia; adolescentilism** and **ephebophilia;** and **gerontalism** and **gerontophilia** (from Greek, *chronos*, time + -philia).

Clérambault–Kandinsky syndrome: a sexuoerotic pathology in which a male or female has a limerent fixation on someone unattainable, an unshakable and false conviction that his/her own life is totally under the control of the unattainable one, and that the unattainable one reciprocates his/her love, secretly if not openly.

clitoris (*pl.* **clitorides;** *adj.* **clitoral or clitoridean**): the small, hooded organ at the top of the cleft of the female vulva, which is the counterpart of the penis in the male (from Greek, *kleitoris*, clitoris).

clitoromegaly: extreme enlargement or hypertrophy of the clitoris.

clitoropenis: *see* **penoclitoris.**

coitus or **coition:** the sexual act, specifically the taking of the penis into the vagina, or the penetrating of the vagina with the penis; but more generally the complete interaction between two sexual partners. *See also* **copulate; intercourse.**

coming out: gay vernacular term to refer to the developmental experience of acknowledging to oneself and to others that one's sexuoerotic orientation is homosexual.

complementation (*v.* to **complementate**): the process, the converse of identification, of becoming and functioning differently than, and in reciprocation to someone else, by responding to that person's activities, behavior, and reactions. The term is applied especially to the differentiation of G-I/R (gender-identity/role). *See also* **identification.**

compulsive cruising: constantly reiterated searching, which is never satisfied, for an idealized sexual partner or sexual experience. *See also* **cruising; sexual addiction.**

conceptive phase: in a sexuoerotic relationship, the third and final phase which, if it occurs, is characterized by conception, pregnancy, and parenthood. *See also* **acceptive phase; proceptive phase.**

concupiscence: thoughts and imaginations characterized by ardent desire, especially as applied to sex or lust.

coprophilia: a paraphilia of the fetishistic/talismanic type in which sexuoerotic arousal and facilitation or attainment of orgasm are responsive to and contingent on being smeared with and/or ingesting feces (from Greek, *kopros*, dung + -philia). There is no technical term for the reciprocal paraphilic condition of defecating in the mouth or over the body of the partner. *Syn.* **coprolagnia.** *See also* **urophilia.**

copulate (*n.* **copulation**): to couple, join, or unite as in sexual interaction and genital union. *See also* **coitus; intercourse.**

copulation fantasy: a fantasy that precedes and/or accompanies loveplay and/or genital union. It may either include or exclude imagery of the actual partner. If the partner is included, fantasy may yield to the total immersion of both in their body sensations. In paraphilia, continuance of the fantasy is necessary for the paraphile, so as to distract attention away from the other partner, which alone ensures that orgasm does occur. *See also* **masturbation fantasy.**

core gender identity: a term introduced into contemporary psychoanalytic theory to refer to an infant's developing sense of self as a boy or girl in the second year of life, well in advance of the classic oedipal phase to which the origin of differences in the psychology of sex is attributed in traditional theory.

corpora cavernosa: the two cavernous or spongy bodies of the penis (or clitoris) that traverse the length of the shaft, one on each side, and that erect the organ when they become engorged with blood.

corpus luteum (*pl.* **corpora lutea**): "yellow body"; a yellow mass in the ovary formed from the graafian follicle after the egg is released. It produces progesterone, the pregnancy hormone, and grows and lasts for several months if the egg is fertilized and pregnancy occurs.

cortex (*pl.* **cortices**): literally, the bark or outer layer. In anatomy, the outer layer or section of an organ, as the cortex of the brain and the cortex of the adrenal gland. *See also* **adrenal cortex: cerebral cortex; neocortex.**

cortisol: in humans and other mammals the main glucocorticoid hormone produced by the adrenal cortices; also known as hydrocortisone. It is essential to the maintenance of life. It is available in synthetic form.

cortisone: one of the glucocorticoid hormones, a metabolite of cortisol. In synthetic form, it is used therapeutically, as in the treatment of CVAH, and converted in the body into the biologically more potent hormone, cortisol. Historically, the term cortisone has also been used generically to refer to all the synthetic glucocorticoids used therapeutically. *See also* **CVAH.**

courtship: sexually, the behavior of indicating attraction and of inviting or soliciting attention and a reciprocal response. *See also* **proceptive phase.**

critical period: a stage in the development of some aspect of an organism during which, for a limited period of time, the next stage of development is contingent upon incorporating a new input from the environment which, in turn, leaves a residual effect that is more or less immutable, and that cannot be induced either earlier or later in development. *Syn.* **crucial period; sensitive period.** *See also* **imprinting.**

crosscoded (*n.* **crosscodification**): as related to gender, discordance between various of those aspects of a person's genetic, hormonal, or social coding that are male and those that are female, somatically and/or mentally.

cross-complementation: as related to the developmental differentiation of G-I/R (gender-identity/role), concordance instead of discordance between the self and the complementation figure or model of the other sex, either male or female. *See also* **cross-identification.**

cross-identification: as related to the developmental differentiation of G-I/R (gender-identity/role), discordance instead of concordance between the self and the identification figure or model of the other sex, either male or female. *See also* **cross-complementation.**

cruising: vernacular term, especially among gay people, for the overt manifestations and responses of the proceptive sexuoerotic phase that indicate one's availability and attractedness toward a potential sexual partner. *See also* **compulsive cruising.**

cryptorchidism: the condition of having one testis (unilateral) or both (bilateral) undescended into the scrotum.

cunnilingus: erotic stimulation of the female external sex organs (from Latin, *cunnus,* vulva) with the tongue (from Latin, *lingere,* to lick), lips, and mouth of a partner of either sex, as a part of normal loveplay, and possibly inducing orgasm. *See also* **fellatio.**

cunnus: the Latin term for the female external genitals.

CVAH (congenital virilizing adrenal hyperplasia): a syndrome produced by a genetically transmitted enzymatic defect in the functioning of the adrenal cortices of males and females, which induces varying degrees of insufficiency of cortisol and aldosterone and excesses of adrenal androgen and pituitary adrenocorticotropin (ACTH). Abnormal function of the adrenal cortex starts in fetal life and, unless treated, continues chronically after birth. Females born with the syndrome have ambiguous genitalia and, if they survive without salt loss and dehydration, undergo severe virilization. Males are usually not recognized at birth, but if they survive, will prematurely develop pubertally during the early years of life. In the severe form of the disease, untreated, mortality rate is almost 100 percent for both sexes. Treatment with glucocorticoids and in some cases also with salt-retaining hormone is lifesaving and prevents untimely and, in girls, incongruous postnatal virilization. Plastic surgery is needed to feminize the genitalia. With appropriate therapy, prognosis for survival and good physical and mental health is excellent. *Syn.* **CAH.**

cyproterone: a synthetic, hormonal steroid substance, related to progesterone, which is potent as an antiandrogen. A variant form is cyproterone acetate (trade-named Androcur), which is more powerful in its antiandrogenic effect. *See also* **Androcur; Depo-Provera; medroxyprogesterone acetate.**

cytogenetic syndromes: those conditions of development marked by various physical and behavioral symptoms that stem from a deficiency, excess, or other gross defect in the number, size, or shape of the chromosomes in each of the body's cells. For example, in most girls with Turner's syndrome, one sex chromosome is missing (45,X); in most boys with Klinefelter's syndrome, the male's one X chromosome is duplicated (47,XXY); and in most boys with the supernumerary-Y syndrome, the male's Y chromosome is duplicated (47,XYY).

cytogenetics (*adj.* **cytogenetic**): that branch of the science of heredity that deals with the chromosomes and genes (carriers of the genetic code) within the cell nucleus.

defeminization: the developmental process in which feminization is inhibited or suppressed. In females the term applies chiefly to defeminization of the brain attributed to a hormonal anomaly in prenatal life.

demasculinization: the developmental process in which masculinization is inhibited or suppressed. In males, the term applies chiefly to to demasculinization of the brain attributed to a hormonal anomaly in prenatal life.

dendrite (*adj.* **dendritic**): a threadlike, branching extension from the main cell body of a nerve that establishes synaptic contact with other nerves (from Greek, *dendron*, tree). *See also* **axon; synapse.**

Depo-Provera: the trade name of the hormone, medroxyprogesterone acetate, manufactured by Upjohn in the United States. The hormone is progestinic and antiandrogenic. It has several clinical applications, one of which is to help sex offenders gain personal governance of their sexuoerotic conduct. *See also* **Androcur; cyproterone; medroxyprogesterone acetate.**

DES: diethylstilbestrol. A synthetic drug, not a steroid, that acts as a female sex hormone.

deviant: not in conformity with what is considered ideal, standard, or normal, according to a given criterion standard that may itself be deviantly radical, conventional, despotic, or arbitrary.

diagnosis: the procedure of identifying a disorder or disease and distinguishing it from other similar conditions.

didactic: taught with explicit rules and precepts.

diecious: denoting species in which male and female reproductive organs occur not in the same individual but in two different individuals (from Greek, *dis*, double + *oikos*, house). *Syn.* **dioecious.** *Ant.* **monecious.**

dihydrotestosterone: a powerful androgenic hormone formed from testosterone in peripheral target cells by the action of the enzyme, 5α-reductase.

dimorphism (*adj.* **dimorphic**): having two forms or manifestations, though of the same species, as in a juvenile and adult form, or a male and a female form. Though usually used to refer to physical form and appearance, the meaning of this term can be extended by analogy to apply to sex differences in behavior and language. *Ant.* **monomorphism.**

dissociate (*n.* **dissociation**): to separate or sunder that which is developing as a unity, or has become one, so that it becomes two or more unrelated or partially related entities. In mental life and its expression, these entities are experienced phenomenologically as trance states, alternative states of consciousness, fugue states, or multiple personalities.

dopamine: a neurotransmitter substance essential to brain functioning, the sexual function of which is to be an activator. *See also* **serotonin.**

drag queen: vernacular name for a male homosexual dressed in women's attire and impersonating a woman, often in an exaggerated way.

dualistic: paired or twofold; not monistic.

dual personality: *see* **multiple personality.**

dyspareunia: a hypophilic condition or syndrome of difficult or painful coitus, of variable etiology, in men and women (from Greek, *dyspareunos*, badly mated). The term is used chiefly in reference to women, but applies equally well to men.

dystrophy (adj. **dystrophic**):   partial atrophy of tissue or an organ as a result of imperfect cell nutrition. *See also* **atrophy.**

effeminate (*n.* **effeminacy**): a womanish or sissyish manner and bearing in a man or boy stigmatized as an unmanly homosexual.

ego dystonic: in psychiatry, the term used to apply to a proclivity, for example, toward homosexuality, in a person who seeks to repudiate it.

eidetic: characterized by vividly precise and accurate recall of objects, events, sounds or other imagery previously perceived.

ejaculation (*v.* **to ejaculate**): expulsion or spurting out, as of the semen at the time of sexual climax or orgasm.

elective mutism: failure to speak, or to be able to speak about certain topics, that is not necessarily permanent but is reversible under changed circumstances.

electrolysis: for cosmetic reasons, a method of removing hair by inserting a needle into the hair-growing follicle and killing it with a pulse of electric current.

eligibility: having the required qualification.

embryo: the unborn offspring from conception until, in the human species, the seventh or eighth week of gestation.

endocrine gland: one of the body's ductless glands from which a hormone is secreted directly into the bloodstream. *See also* **exocrine.**

endogenous: produced from within.

endometrium: the lining of the uterus or womb. Structurally, it is mucous membrane.

endorphin: the general term to refer to all of the body's own endogenous morphinelike substances. In chemical structure, they are neuropeptides. They are active as neurotransmitters and neuromodulators.

enkephalin: one of the endorphins, and the one that predominates in the brain. There are two basic types, methionine and leucine enkephalin. *See also* **endorphin.**

eonism: the term used by Havelock Ellis for the male cross-dressing syndromes now known as transvestophilia and transexualism (from Chevalier d'Eon, 1728–1810, French diplomatic and transvestic imposter at the court of Catherine the Great, in 1755; subsequently exiled to England).

ephebophilia: a paraphilia of the stigmatic/eligibilic type distinct from **nepiophilia** and **pedophilia** in that the age of the partner is postpubertal and adolescent (from Greek, *ephebos*, a postpubertal young person + -philia). The technical term for the reciprocal paraphilic condition in which an older person impersonates an adolescent is **paraphilic adolescentilism.** *See also* **gerontophilia; nepiophilia; pedophilia.** *Syn.* **hebephilia.;**

epicene: common to both sexes; neither one nor the other.

eponym (*adj.* **eponymous**): the name of someone so prominently connected with a time, place, group, or event as to become a figurative or symbolic designation for it.

erotic apathy: a hypophilic condition or syndrome, variable in etiology, of defective ability to experience sexuoerotic arousal under normally conducive circumstances; misnamed **lack of sexual desire.**

erotic inertia: a hypophilic condition or syndrome, variable in etiology, of inability to manifest sexuoerotic initiative or to maintain sexuoerotic activity under normally conducive circumstances.

erotic revulsion: a hypophilic condition or syndrome of variable etiology in which sexuoerotic activity, either in general or with a particular partner, is experienced as aversive and repulsive.

erotica: depictions of ideas and images in the literary and visual arts that have sexual and erotic appeal and, for at least a selected audience, sexual arousal value, without being condemned as pornographic.

eroticism (*adj.* **erotic**): the personal experience and manifest expression of one's genital arousal and functioning as male or female, either alone or with a partner, and particularly with reference to the ideation, imagery, and sensory stimuli of arousal (from Greek, *eros*, love). *Syn.* **erotism.** *See also* **sexuality.**

erotography: graphic or written material of an erotic nature, not stigmatized as pornography. *See also* **pornography.**

erotomania: morbid exaggeration of, or preoccupation with sexuoerotic imagery and activity (from Greek, *eros*, love + -*mania*, madness). *See also* **Clérambault–Kandinsky syndrome.**

erotophonophilia: a paraphilia of the sacrificial/expiatory type in which sexuoerotic arousal and facilitation or attainment of orgasm are responsive to and contingent on stage-managing and carrying out the murder of an unsuspecting sexual partner (from Greek, *eros*, love + *phonein*, to murder + -philia). The erotophonophile's orgasm coincides with the expiration of the partner. The reciprocal paraphilic condition is **autassassinophilia.** *Syn.* **lust murder.**

erotosexual: the erotic and the sexual experienced as a unity, with more emphasis on erotic imagery and ideation than sexual behavior. It is possible to be erotic without being sexual in the sense of copulation, fertility, or reproduction. Conversely, it is possible, as in donor insemination, to be sexual without being erotic.

estradiol: the most biologically potent of the naturally occurring estrogens. It is produced chiefly by the ovary and in small amount by the testis. Commercially, it is prepared in various compounds, such as estradiol benzoate and ethinyl estradiol.

estrogen: female sex hormone, produced chiefly by the ovary, but also in a small amount by the adrenal cortex and the testis, and named for its role in lower animals inducing heat or estrus (from Greek, *oistros*, gadfly; from Latin, *oestrus*, vehement desire, that which drives one mad). *See also* **estrus.**

estrus (*adj.* **estrous**): phenomenon of being sexually receptive, or in heat, as manifested at the ovulatory phase of the sexual cycle of the female, especially in subprimate species.

ethnography (adj. **ethnographic**): the branch of anthropology that studies the artifacts, customs, and life-styles of ethnic groups and tribes with different cultural histories.

etiology: the theory of the factors in the genesis, origin, or cause of a disorder or disease.

eunuchoid (*n.* **eunuch**): having the developmental sexual characteristics and appearance resembling those of a person who, like a castrate, has failed to mature pubertally.

exemplar: a person who becomes a pattern or model for oneself.

exhibitionism: a paraphilia of the solicitational/allurative type in which sexuoerotic arousal and facilitation or attainment of orgasm are responsive to and contingent on evoking surprise, dismay, shock, or panic from a stranger by illicitly exhibiting an erotic part of the body, including the genitals (from Latin, *exhibere,* to exhibit). The reciprocal paraphilic condition is **voyeurism,** also known as being a "Peeping Tom." *See also* **peodeiktophilia.**

exigency theory: in psychology, the theory that, regardless of its determinants, human responsivity is contingent upon five universal exigencies of existence (see Chapter 3, Section 11).

exocrine: pertaining to a gland with a duct through which its secretion, for example, tears or saliva, passes. *See also* **endocrine gland.**

exogenous: produced from without.

exorcise: to expel or drive off an evil spirit with a special ritual; to deliver a person from being possessed by a demon.

exorcist syndrome: a sexual condition of repeatedly assaulting, stigmatizing, or punishing people who manifest symptoms or behavior that threaten to occur in oneself.

expiation: atonement; penance.

exteroceptive: pertaining to a sensory organ that registers information from outside the body. *Ant.* **interoceptive.**

falling in love: the personal experience and manifest expression of becoming intensely, and possibly suddenly, attached or bonded to another person. It may be reciprocal and a source of great ecstasy, or one-sided and a source of great agony. Usually it is erotosexual. *See also* **limerence.**

fallopian tubes: the left and right tubes of the uterus that connect the uppermost part of the uterine cavity bilaterally with the ovaries. They are so positioned as to be able to transport the egg released from the ovary to the uterine cavity for implanting. They are named for the Italian anatomist Gabriello Fallopius (1523–1562). *Syn.* **oviducts.**

fantasy (*v.* **to fantasy**): in imagination, a series of mental representations connected by a story line or dramatic plot that may possibly be translated into actuality. *See also* **copulation fantasy; masturbation fantasy.**

fantasize: colloquial modification of the verb, **to fantasy.**

fellatio: erotic stimulation by sucking (from Latin, *fellare*) of the penis with the lips, mouth, tongue, and throat, by a partner of either sex, as a part of normal loveplay, and possibly inducing orgasm.

feminine (*n.* **femininity**): characteristic of, or attributed to the female sex.

fetish: an object of special devotion to which mystical power may be attributed.

fetishism: a paraphilia of the fetishistic/talismanic type in which sexuo-erotic arousal and facilitation or attainment of orgasm are responsive to and contingent on a particular talisman or fetish object, substance, or part of the body belonging to the partner. There is no technical term for the reciprocal paraphilic condition in which the fetish (e.g., a uniform) must belong to the self.

fetus: the unborn offspring from the end of the embryonic period of development until birth, which in the human species extends from 7–8 weeks until delivery at 36 weeks.

fibroblast: a connective tissue cell.

fictive image: an image in the mind that is not perceived through the senses, but construed in the imagination on the basis of past perceptions retrieved from memory and reconstituted. *See also* **perceptual image.**

fisting: a vernacular term for the sexuoerotic practice of inserting the hand and forearm into the rectum or vagina, also known, respectively, as brachiorectal and brachiovaginal insertion.

flagellant: a person who undergoes whipping or scourging, especially as a religious penitent, or as a sexual masochist.

follicle: a small cavity, sac, or gland, such as a hair follicle or ovarian follicle. The latter secretes hormones, estrogen and progestin, that regulate the menstrual cycle. *See also* **graafian follicle.**

forensic: pertaining to or applied in legal proceedings.

foreplay: the traditional term for erotosexual activity during the proceptive phase in which manual, oral, and other skin and body contact ensure erection of the penis, lubrication of the vagina, and an urgency of being ready for orgasm, usually penovaginally induced.

formicophilia: a specialized variety of **zoophilia** in which sexuoerotic arousal and facilitation or attainment of orgasm are responsive to and contingent on the sensations produced by small creatures like snails, frogs, ants, or other insects creeping, crawling, or nibbling the genitalia and perianal area, and the nipples (from Latin, *formica*, ant + -philia).

45,X/46,XY syndrome: a chromosomal variant of **Turner's** (typically 45,X) **syndrome** evident neonatally by reason of a birth defect of the sex organs, which look hermaphroditically ambiguous. The gonads are neither ovarian nor testicular, but malformed or dysgenic streaks. Short stature is characteristic. At the age of puberty and thereafter, sex hormone treatment is necessary. Some babies with this condition are assigned, reared, and clinically habilitated as boys, some as girls, the latter being more satisfactory.

frigidity: in sex, the failure to become sexually aroused or passionate. Traditionally, it has been applied chiefly to women but now is considered too imprecise.

frotteurism: a paraphilia of the solicitational/allurative type in which sexuoerotic arousal and facilitation or attainment of orgasm are responsive to and contingent on rubbing expecially the genital area against the body of a stranger in a densely packed crowd (from French, *frotter*, to rub). There is no technical name for the reciprocal paraphilic condition, namely being sexuoerotically dependent on being rubbed by a stranger. *Syn.* **frottage.** *See also* **toucheurism.**

FSH (follicle-stimulating hormone): a gonadotropin secreted by the anterior lobe of the pituitary gland that stimulates sperm formation in the testis, and the formation of the graafian follicle and the secretion of estrogen from the ovary.

fuck (*n., v.*): the Anglo-Saxon synonym for sexual intercourse, coition, or copulation (all Latin-derived). To copulate and to fuck are the only one-word verbs for mutual genital intercourse. The former is too stilted for vernacular use. The latter, being tabooed as dirty, is often replaced by euphemisms like to screw or to ball.

fugue: an altered state of consciousness in which what is happening now is unrelated to, or dissociated from what had happened then, in the preceding phase of existence; as for example in the alternating manifestations of dual or multiple personality (from Latin, *fuga*, a flight). *See also* **multiple personality; schizophrenia.**

gay: vernacular term for a male with a homoerotic status and life-style.

gender: one's personal, social, and legal status as male or female, or mixed, on the basis of somatic and behavioral criteria more inclusive than the genital criterion and/or erotic criterion alone. *See also* **gender-identity/role.**

gender coding: combined genetic coding, hormonal coding, and social coding of a person's characteristics of body, mind, and/or behavior as either exclusively male, exclusively female, or nonexclusively androgynous, relative to a given, and in some instances arbitrary criterion standard. *See also* **gender crosscoding.**

gender crosscoding: gender coding in which there is discordance between the natal anatomical sex and one or more of, in particular, the behavioral variables of male and female. *See also* **gender coding.**

gender dysphoria: the state, as subjectively experienced, of incongruity between the genital anatomy and the gender-identity/role (G-I/R), particularly in the syndromes of transexualism and transvestism. *See also* **gender crosscoding; gender transposition.**

gender-identity/role (G-I/R): gender identity is the private experience of gender role, and gender role is public manifestation of gender identity. Both are like two sides of the same coin, and constitute the unity of G-I/R. Gender identity is the sameness, unity, and persistence of one's individuality as male, female, or androgynous, in greater or lesser degree, especially as it is experienced in self-awareness and behavior. Gender role is everything that a person says and does to indicate to others or to the self the degree that one is either male or female or androgynous; it includes but is not restricted to sexual and erotic arousal and response (which should never be excluded from the definition).

gender role: *see* **gender-identity/role.**

gender transposition: the switching or crossing over of attributes, expectancies, or stereotypes, of gender-identity/role (G-I/R) from male to female, or vice versa, either serially or simultaneously, temporarily or persistently, in small or large degree, and with either insignificant or significant repercussions and consequences. *See also* **gender cross-coding; gender dysphoria.**

gene: a unit of genetic material that belongs on a chromosome, and to which belongs a segment of the double-helix molecule of DNA.

genital: having to do with the sex organs. *See also* **eroticism; sex.**

genital penetration phobia: *see* **penetration phobia.**

genitalia: the sex organs, internal and external. The word is often used to refer to the external organs only. *Syn.* **genitals.**

genitoerotic: erotic feeling and activity specifically involving the genitals in imagery and/or practice.

genotype: the genetic constitution that characterizes an individual, or the species or subtype to which he/she belongs. *See also* **phenotype.**

gerontalism, paraphilic: impersonating an older person and being treated as one by a partner—one of the stigmatic/eligibilic paraphilias. *See also* **adolescentilism; gerontophilia; infantilism; juvenilism.**

gerontophilia: a paraphilia of the stigmatic/eligibilic type in which the partner must be parental or grandparental in age (from Greek, *geras,* old age + -philia). The technical term for the reciprocal paraphilic condition in which a younger person must impersonate a parent or grandparent is **paraphilic gerontalism.** *See also* **ephebophilia; nepiophilia; pedophilia.**

gestagen: a synthetic type of progesterone. *Syn.* **progestin; progestogen.**

gestation: the period of bearing a pregnancy from fertilization to delivery.

G-I/R: *see* **gender-identity/role.** *See* page 231.

glucocorticoids: generic name for hormones secreted by the adrenocortical glands that are not mineralocorticoids. The glucocorticoids are typified by cortisol or cortisone and are deficient in the syndrome of CVAH.

GnRH: gonadotropin-releasing hormone. *See* **LHRH.**

gonad: a sex gland, either an ovary or a testis.

gonadectomy: surgical removal of a gonad, either an ovary or a testis, on one side or both; castration.

gonadotropin: a hormone that stimulates the gonads (ovaries or testicles) to secrete their own hormones, namely, progesterone, testosterone, and estrogen. *Syn.* **gonadotrophin.** *See also* **FSH; LH.**

graafian follicle: the follicle on the ovary in which the egg grows. After the egg is released, the graafian follicle becomes the corpus luteum. Named for Regner de Graaf, Dutch anatomist (1641–1673).

Grafenberg spot: a zone of erotically sensitive glandular tissue, palpable at finger depth through the frontal wall of the vagina during sexual arousal, that corresponds to the prostate gland in the male, and that may release fluid through the urethra at the climax of orgasm (named for Ernest Grafenberg, 1881–1957). *Syn.* **G-spot.** *See also* **paraurethral glands.**

grand mal seizure: an epileptic seizure with convulsing and unconsciousness. *See also* **petit mal seizure.**

growth hormone: a growth-promoting peptide hormone secreted from the anterior lobe of the pituitary gland, also known as **somatotropin** and, in human beings, **hGH** (human growth hormone).

gynandromorphy: a term of Greek etymology meaning woman-man-shape. Thus, literally, the term means having some of the body morphology and measurements of an average woman and some of an average man, or being at neither extreme.

gynecomastia: the development of breasts on a male, spontaneously or as a result of hormonal treatment.

gynemimesis: a syndrome of female impersonation in a natal male who is able to relate sexuoerotically exclusively with men, and who may be hormonally but not surgically sex-reassigned (from Greek, *gyne,* woman + *mimos,* **mime**). It is a syndrome of gender transposition, not a paraphilia.

gynemimetophile: a person whose primary sexuoerotic attraction is toward a gynemimetic "lady with a penis."

gynemimetophilia: a paraphilia of the stigmatic/eligibilic type in which sexual attraction is predominantly or exclusively toward a gynemimetic or, usually preoperatively, a male-to-female transexual (from Greek, *gyne,* woman + *mimos,* mime + -philia).

gynephilia: love of a woman by a man (male gynephilia) or by a woman (female gynephilia). It includes erotosexual bonding. *See also* **heterosexuality; homosexuality; lesbian.**

haptic: having to do with touch and the sense of touch.

hebephilia: *see* **ephebophilia**

hemisphere: as applied to the brain, either its left or its right half.

hermaphroditism: having genital attributes of both sexes (from Greek, *Hermes* and *Aphrodite,* god and goddess of love). Some invertebrates are simultaneous hermaphrodites, and some fish are sequential hermaphrodites that change from male to female, or vice versa, once or more often in the course of a lifetime. In the human species, hermaphroditism is a form of birth defect, also known as intersexuality. It is defined as male or female hermaphroditism, if only testes or ovaries are present, respectively; as true hermaphroditism if both tissues are found as in ovotestes, and as gonadally dysgenic when neither tissue is clearly differentiated. Human hermaphrodites do not have the complete sex organs of both sexes. *See also* **pseudohermaphroditism.**

heterogeneous: dissimilar in type, and having different or opposing characteristics.

heterophilia (*adj.* **heterophilic**): the condition in which love and lust are attached to those of the other sex (from Greek, *heteros*, other + *philia*, love). *Syn.* **heteroerotic.**

heterophobia (*adj.* **heterophobic**): the condition in which those whose love and lust are attached to persons of the other sex are dreaded or feared (from Greek, *heteros*, other + *phobos*, fear or fright). *See also* **homophobia.**

heterosexual (*n.* **heterosexuality**): characterizied by other-sex contact, either as a genital act or as a long-term sexuoerotic status (from Greek, *heteros*, other + sex). It is analogous to right-handedness in being in conformity with the norm and therefore is not pathological in itself, though subject to other pathology. A heterosexual person is able to fall in love with, and become the pairbonded sexuoerotic partner of only a person of the other morphologic sex. Paraphilias occur predominantly in association with heterosexual pairing.

hijra: in India, the name given to a full-time female impersonator or gynemimetic, in some cases also a eunuch with partial surgical sex reassignment, who is a member of a traditional social organization, part cult and part caste, of hijras whose worship is of the goddess, Bahuchara Mata, and whose sexuoerotic role is as women with men. *See also* **acault.**

hirsutism: hairiness, especially excessive hairiness.

homicidophilia: *see* **erotophonophilia.**

homogeneous: of the same type, or having the same characteristics.

homophilia (*adj.* **homophilic**): the condition in which love and lust are attached to those of the same sex (from Greek, *homos* , same + -philia). *Syn.* **homoerotic.**

homophobia (*adj.* **homophobic**):   the condition in which those whose love and lust are attached to others of the same sex are dreaded or feared (from Greek, *homos,* same + *phobos,* fear or fright). *See also* **heterophobia.**

homosexual (*n.* **homosexuality**): characterized by same-sex contact, either as a genital act or as a long-term sexuoerotic status (from Greek, *homos,* same + sex). It is analogous to left-handedness in being not pathological in itself, though not conforming to the statistical nor the ideological norm, and not being exempt from other pathology. A homosexual person is able to fall in love with, and become the pairbonded sexuoerotic partner of only a person of the same morphologic sex. Homosexuality is not a paraphilia but a gender transposition, variable in extent and degree. Paraphilias may occur in association with either homosexual or heterosexual pairing.

homosexology: sexological science as applied to homosexuality and its relationship to heterosexuality and bisexuality. *Ant.* **heterosexology.**

hormonal cyclicity: regularly recurrent changes in the level of one or more hormones secreted into the bloodstream, for example, the changes in pituitary and ovarian hormones in synchrony with the menstrual cycle in women.

hormonalize (*n.* **hormonalization**): to change or shape by means of a hormone the outcome of development, for example as masculine or feminine, as manifested somatically or behaviorally.

hormone: a chemical messenger secreted into the bloodstream from specialized glandular cells, including those of the endocrine glands, of the brain and neuroendocrine systems, and of some visceral tissues. It carries information to other cells and organs of the body. *See also* **pheromone.**

hormonodynamics: hormonal changes that take place in synchrony with changes in other processes manifested within or by a living organism, and that are presumed to have a governing or determining effect.

hustler: a person who works with energy and persistence, especially in marketing. As applied to sex, it is a vernacular term especially for males who earn money by servicing women or other men of a more effeminate disposition than their own.

H-Y antigen: Y-chromosome-induced histocompatibility antigen. It is believed to adhere to the surface of all male mammalian cells, including the Y-bearing sperm of fertilization. In the course of normal embryogenesis, it is held responsible for programing the cells of the undifferentiated gonadal anlage into a testis.

hybristophilia: a paraphilia of the marauding/predatory type in which sexuoerotic arousal and facilitation and attainment of orgasm are responsive to and contingent on being with a partner known to have committed an outrage or crime, such as rape, murder, or armed robbery (from Greek, *hybridzein,* to commit an outrage against someone + -philia). The partner may have served a prison sentence as a convicted criminal, or may be instigated by the hybristophile to commit a crime and so be convicted and sent to prison.

hyperorgasmia: the phenomenon of having an inordinate number of orgasms within a given period, as compared with a given criterion standard.

hyperphilia: a condition or syndrome, variable in etiology and diagnosis, of being sexuoerotically above standard or inordinate, particularly with respect to some aspect of genital functioning prior to and at the acceptive phase.

hyphephilia: one of a group of paraphilias of the fetishistic/talismanic type in which the sexuoerotic stimulus is associated with the touching, rubbing, or the feel of skin, hair, leather, fur, and fabric, especially if worn in proximity to erotically significant parts of the body (from Greek, *hyphe,* web + -philia).

hypophilia: a condition or syndrome, variable in etiology and diagnosis, of being sexuoerotically substandard or deficient, particularly with respect to some aspect of genital functioning at the acceptive phase.

hypospadias (*adj.* **hypospadiac**): a birth defect in the positioning of the urinary opening on the penis. In mild hypospadias, the opening is only slightly displaced from the tip of the penis. In severe hypospadias, the opening is in the female position, and the penis has an open gutter on its underside, instead of a covered urinary canal. A hypospadiac penis may be normal sized or small. *See* **micropenis.** A small penis with a severe degree of hypospadias is identical in appearance with an enlarged clitoris below which is a single opening or urogenital sinus leading to both the urethra and the vagina. *See* **hermaphroditism.** Artificial hypospadias may occur as a sequel to an injury, as in a circumcision accident, or be self-inflicted.

hypothalamus: a structure of the diencephalic part of the brain of special importance in governing vital functions, including sex, by releasing neurohumoral substances from nerve cells which, in turn, govern the hormones of the nearby pituitary gland, and also the behavior of mating.

hypoxyphilia: asphyxiophilia (from Latin, *hypoxia*, oxygen deprivation + -philia).

hysterectomy: surgical removal of the uterus or womb (from Greek, *hystera*, womb + *ektome*, excision).

IAG: idiopathic adolescent gynecomastia. *See also* **adolescent gynecomastia; idiopathic.**

ideation: in mental life, the collective representation of thoughts and ideas presently recognized, recalled from memory, or projected into the future, singly or in combination.

identification: the process of becoming like someone as a sequel to assimilating or copying that person's activities, behavior, and reactions. The term is applied especially to the differentiation of G-I/R (gender-identity/role). *See also* **complementation.**

ideological norm: the standard of what is normal as defined by those who, even though in a minority, exercise their authority to impose their own ideology and values on others whom they overpower.

ideology (*adj.* **ideological**): a set of ideas, beliefs, or principles to which a person or group adheres, lives by, and possibly dies for.

idiopathic: of unexplained origin, as in the development of a symptom or syndrome that is apparently spontaneously generated.

imagery: in mental life, the collective representation of mental images or depictions of anything either perceived (perceptual imagery) or, if not actually present as a sensory stimulus, recognized in memory (memory imagery), or in dream, confabulation, or fantasy (fictive imagery).

immutable: long-lasting and unchangeable.

impersonator: an actor or person who assumes the personality and plays the role of being somebody else.

impotence: a hypophilic condition or syndrome, of variable etiology, in which erection of the penis is lacking or defective under normally conducive conditions.

impregnation: the process of being rendered pregnant by the intromission of sperm into the uterus and the union of egg and sperm.

imprimatur: sanction; approval.

imprinting: developmental learning of a type first brought to scientific attention in studies of animal behavior by ethologists. Imprinting takes place in a given species when behavior phyletically programed into the nervous system of that species requires a matching socio-environmental stimulus to release it, when the matching must take place during a critical or sensitive developmental period (not before or after), and when, having occurred, the resultant behavior pattern is unusually resistant to extinction. In human beings, native language learning is a manifestation of imprinting. *See also* **critical period.**

incest: sexual contact customarily or legally forbidden on the criterion of the close kinship of the two people, variably defined on the basis of genealogical or totemic descent, or by reason of marriage or adoption (from Latin, *incestus*, unchaste).

infancy: babyhood; the period of development between birth and the beginning of early childhood between the ages of 2 and 3 years.

infantilism, paraphilic: impersonating an infant and being treated as one by the partner—one of the stigmatic/eligibilic paraphilias. *Syn.* **autonepiophilia.** *See also* **adolescentilism; gerontalism; juvenilism; nepiophilia.**

infatuation: foolish and extravagant passion, especially as applied to a love affair that does not meet with family or local community or religious approval, and does not conform to customary criteria of a well-arranged marriage.

inframasculinize: to masculinize insufficiently. *Syn.* **hypomasculinize.** *Ant.* **supramasculinize.**

inguinal: pertaining to the *inguen* or groin, the region or crease between the abdomen and the thigh.

intercourse: connection or interaction between people. In sexual intercourse, the connection is usually defined as being between two people. It is erroneously restricted to putting the penis into the vagina (or anus) or the vagina (or anus) onto the penis (penovaginal or penoanal intercourse, respectively). The entire sexual interaction between the partners constitutes sexual intercourse. *See also* **coitus; copulate.**

intersexuality: an alternative term for hermaphroditism. In past usage, a genetic etiology was sometimes assumed for intersexuality, and a hormonal etiology for hermaphroditism, but the distinction is now known to be untenable.

intromission: the insertion of one part into another; in sexual intercourse, the insertion of the penis into the vagina.

inviolacy: the right to be free from behing harmed, harassed, or encroached upon.

in vitro fertilization: the combining of an egg and a sperm into a fertile cell (zygote) in a glass dish; used especially when the normal process of fertilization within the body fails (from Latin, *in vitro,* in glass).

Jekyll and Hyde: a character with dual personality, the law-abiding Dr. Jekyll, and the monstrous Mr. Hyde, created by the author, Robert Louis Stevenson.

juvenilism, paraphilic: impersonating a juvenile and being treated as one by the partner—one of the stigmatic/eligibilic paraphilias. *See also* **adolescentilism; gerontalism; infantilism; pedophilia.**

Kallmann's syndrome: a condition characterized by pubertal failure, inactive testicles (or ovaries), failure of the pituitary gland to secrete gonadotropic hormones, and failure of the hypothalamus to stimulate the pituitary gland, in association with absence of the sense of smell secondary to defective olfactory function in the brain.

kinesis: body movement and activity.

kleptophilia: a paraphilia of the marauding/predatory type in which sexuoerotic arousal and facilitation or attainment of orgasm are responsive to and contingent on illicitly entering and stealing from the dwelling of a stranger or potential partner (from Greek, *kleptein,* to steal + -philia). A kleptophile may or may not also forcefully demand or steal sexual intercourse. There is no technical term for the reciprocal paraphilic condition of setting onself up as the recipient of kleptophilic robbery by a stranger or an acquaintance. *Syn.* **kleptolagnia.**

Klinefelter's syndrome: a condition identified by a chromosomal anomaly in morphologic males with the pathognomonic symptoms of a small penis, small testes, sterility, and in some cases gynecomastia. The basic genetic defect is an extra sex chromosome with a total count of 47,XXY. Variants of the syndrome are characterized by more than one extra X chromosome, e.g., 48,XXXY. The secondary sex characteristics are usually weakly developed and do not respond well to treatment with male sex hormone.

klismaphilia: a paraphilia of the fetishistic/talismanic type in which sexuoerotic arousal and facilitation or attainment of orgasm are responsive to and contingent on being given an enema by the partner (from Greek, *klusma,* enema + -philia). There is no technical term for the reciprocal paraphilic condition, namely of being the enema giver. Klismaphilia may be adjunctive to rubber fetishism or to bondage and discipline.

labia (*sing.* **labium**): in the female sex organs the outside lips (**labia majora**) and the inside lips (**labia minora**) that converge to cover the clitoris with the clitoral hood.

labioscrotal (*n.* **labioscrotum**): formed and looking like female labia that, instead of being completely separated, are partially fused to resemble a scrotum; or are like a divided scrotum that resembles labia.

lactation: the secretion of milk from the breasts; the period of suckling the young until weaning.

laparotomy: a surgical incision through the flank or loin or, less precisely, the abdominal wall, as for the purpose of exploring the morphology of the internal reproductive organs.

lesbian (*adj.* **lesbian**): female homosexual, named after the Aegian island, Lesbos, whence came the homosexual woman poet, Sappho, of ancient Greece. There is no corresponding eponym for a homosexual or gay male.

Leydig cells: in the testes, the hormone-producing cells that are packed in like bunches of grapes between the seminiferous tubules in which sperms are produced.

LH (luteinizing hormone): a gonadotropin secreted by the anterior lobe of the pituitary gland that stimulates testosterone secretion from the testis, in the male, and the formation of the corpus luteum and the secretion of progesterone from the ovary, in the female.

LHRH (luteinizing hormone-releasing hormone): from the hypothalamus, a hormone that triggers the release of the pituitary gonadotropins, LH and FSH. LH frees the ovum and changes its graafian follicle into the corpus luteum. LHRH, LRH, LRF (F = factor), and GnRH (gonadotropin-releasing hormone) are synonymous.

libido: sexual drive, subjectively experienced and reported. Hypothetically, in psychoanalytic doctrine, it also means the positive life force of Eros as compared with Thanatos, the death force.

limbic system: the old cortex or paleocortex, as contrasted with the neocortex, of the brain. Its functions pertain to those aspects of the human mind and behavior that are shared by lower, especially mammalian species.

limerence (*adj.* **limerent**): a recently coined name (Tennov, 1979) for the experience of having fallen in love and being irrationally and fixatedly love-smitten, irrespective of the degree to which one's love is requited or unrequited.

lordosis: in four-legged animals, the crouching, saddle-back, mating posture of the female presenting her hind end to the male for copulation (from Greek, *lordosis*).

love: the personal experience and manifest expression of being attached or bonded to another person. There is sacred and profane love, and affectional and erotic love. The word is also used in the vernacular as a synonym for like. *See also* **falling in love.**

loveblot: a person (or image) who sufficiently resembles the image depicted in someone else's lovemap as to become the recipient onto whom the lovemap is projected in a limerent love affair, regardless of whether the response is one of love requited or, being unrequited, induces a pathological reaction of lovesickness.

lovemap: a developmental representation or template in the mind and in the brain depicting the idealized lover, the idealized love affair, and the idealized program of sexuoerotic activity projected in imagery or actually engaged in with that lover.

lovemap displacement: an intrinsic element that, developmentally dislocated from its regular place, becomes respositioned in a lovemap, changing it from a normophilic lovemap into a paraphilic one of the displacement type—for example, genital display in paraphilic exhibitionism.

lovemap inclusion: an extraneous element that becomes developmentally incorporated into a lovemap, changing it from a normophilic lovemap into a paraphilic one of the inclusion type—for example, paraphilic fetishism.

lovesickness: the personal experience and manifest expression of agony when the partner with whom one has fallen in love is a total mismatch whose response is indifference, or a partial mismatch whose reciprocity is incomplete, deficient, anomalous, or otherwise unsatisfactory.

lust: longing, eagerness, inclination, or sensuous desire; normal sexual desire, or sexual desire stigmatized as degrading passion.

male hermaphroditism: a generic term applied to several different syndromes of birth-defective ambiguity of the sex organs occurring in the 46,XY gonadal male. The defect is induced in fetal life by a deficiency of hormonal masculinization secondary to either the quantity or type of male hormone available, or to insensitivity of the tissues to male hormone. *Syn.* **male pseudohermaphroditism.**

manic-depressive cyclicity: in manic-depressive illness, the repeated sequence of a period of being high (manic) followed by one of being low (depressive).

marauding: raiding; taking by force.

masculinacy: the quality or state of being masculine. *Ant.* **effeminacy.**

masculine (*n.* **masculinity**): characteristic of, or attributed to the male sex.

masculinate (*n.* **masculinacy**): adjective describing a mannish or virilistic manner and bearing in a woman or girl stigmatized as an unwomanish lesbian.

masculinization: the developmental process of differentiating and/or assimilating masculine features and characteristics.

masochism: a paraphilia of the sacrifical/expiatory type in which sexuoerotic arousal and facilitation or attainment of orgasm are responsive to and contingent on being the recipient of abuse, torture, punishment, discipline, humiliation, obedience, and servitude, variously mixed (named after Leopold von Sacher-Masoch, 1836–1895, Austrian author and masochist). The reciprocal paraphilic condition is **sadism.**

masturbation: sexuoerotic self-stimulation, usually though not necessarily climaxing in orgasm (from Latin, *manus,* hand + *stuprare,* to deflower, ravish, fornicate, or to engage in adultery, incest, or rape). From its Latin derivation, the literal meaning of masturbation is to use the genitalia to ravish or rape the hand. *See also* **secret vice.**

masturbation fantasy: cognitional rehearsal of erotically stimulating activity that accompanies, and may precede, an episode of masturbation. To the extent that the content of its imagery and ideation, like that of a sleeping dream, has a high degree of autonomy and individual specificity in its power to stimulate genital arousal, it is not voluntarily chosen or preferred. *See also* **copulation fantasy.**

Mayer-Rokitansky-Kuester syndrome: a sexual birth defect characterized by impaired differentiation of the müllerian ducts so that the uterus is rudimentary and cordlike. The deep part of the vagina is absent and the outer part is shallow or in the form of a dimple. The fallopian tubes may be defective, and there may be other sporadic congenital anomalies. The ovaries are normal and induce normal femininizing puberty, except for lack of menstruation secondary to the defective uterus. Psychosexual differentiation is as a female.

meatus: an opening or passageway in the body, such as the urinary meatus.

mechanism: the arrangement or association of the elements or parts of anything in relation to the effect they generate; the combination of mental processes by which an effect is generated.

medroxyprogesterone acetate (MPA): the generic name of **Depo-Provera.** It has many of the physiological properties of progesterone, and so is known as a synthetic progestin, although in chemical structure it is actually an androgen, like testosterone, which is closely related to progesterone. Therapeutically, MPA has varied uses: to suppress ovulation (in the birth control pill); to prevent spermatogenesis (as a male contraceptive); and as an antiandrogen to suppress androgen release and sexuoeroticism, reversibly, in male sex offenders. *See also* **Androcur; cyproterone.**

menopause: in a female, the so-called change of life marked by the cessation of menstrual functioning. It does not preordain cessation of sex life.

menstruation: in women, the periodic (monthly) bloody discharge from the uterus and vagina approximately two weeks after ovulation.

mercantile: commercial; obtained by purchase.

metabolite: in the body, a substance that is produced by the body's own chemistries.

metamorphosis: a striking change in appearance, form, or substance.

micropenis: a birth defect in which the penis is extremely small. The maximum stretched length is not greater than 2.5 standard deviation units (SDU) below the mean for age, and possibly as small as 5.0 SDU below. The diameter is correspondingly small, with extreme hypoplasia of the corpora cavernosa. As compared with a micropenis, the average adult penis's stretched length is 6.6 inches (16.7 cm), with a standard deviation of 0.77 inches (1.95 cm) (Money, Lehne, and Pierre-Jerome, 1984).

minotaur: in Greek mythology, a monster, half man and half bull, confined in the labyrinth built by Daedalus for Minos, where it devoured the periodic tribute of seven youths and seven maidens sent by Athens, until it was slain by Theseus.

mixophilia: *see* **scoptophilia.**

mixoscopia: *see* **scoptophilia.**

monecious: denoting species in which male and female reproductive organs occur not in two different individuals but in the same individual (from Greek, *monos,* single + *oikos,* house). *Syn.* **monoecious.** *Anto.* **diecious.**

monistic: single or whole; not dualistic or pluralistic.

monomorphism (*adj.* **monomorphic**): having not male and female, but only one sexual form or manifestation in a species as, for example, in those species of lizard that reproduce by parthenogenesis. *Ant.* **dimorphism.**

monosexual (*n.* **monosexuality**): characterized by either exclusively heterosexual or exclusively homosexual contacts either in genital acts or as a long-term sexuoerotic status (from Greek, *mono,* single + sex). *Ant.* **bisexual**

morphophilia: one of a group of paraphilias of the stigmatic/eligibilic type in which sexuoerotic arousal and facilitation or attainment of orgasm are responsive to and contingent on a partner whose body characteristics are selectively particularized, prominent, or different from one's own (from Greek, *morphe,* form + -philia).

motivation theory: in psychology, the theory that internal forces and purposes determine human responsivity.

mount: together with thrusting, the penovaginal part of sexual intercourse. In human beings, either sex may get in position to mount the other, whereas in most other animals, the female presents, and the male mounts. *See also* **coitus; copulation; intercourse.**

müllerian duct structures: the structures in the fetus that will, in the female, develop into the uterus and fallopian tubes; named for Johannes P. Müller, German physiologist (1801–1848). *See also* **wolffian duct structures.**

müllerian-inhibiting hormone: a hormone produced by the fetal testis. Its function is to vestigiate the primordial müllerian ducts, thus preventing the development of a uterus and fallopian tubes in the male.

multiple personality: split personality; a mental condition in which a person experiences him/herself as two or more different people, differently named, and with major extremes in behavior and life-style, each dissociated from the other, with variable degrees of overlap and shared memory or mutual amnesia. Paraphilic sex crimes are commonly committed in a fuguelike, or dual-personality state. Transvestophiles have a male and a female personality. *See also* **dissociate; fugue; personality; schizophrenia.**

multivariate: having more than one variable, or caused by more than one determinant.

Munchausen's syndrome: a factitious or sham illness or condition in which the symptoms mimic those of another illness but are clandestinely produced by the patient in himself or herself; or, by proxy, by a parent in his/her child [named for Baron von Münchhausen (1720–1797), author of fantastic and confabulatory tales].

mutable: transient and able to be changed.

mysophilia: a paraphilia of the fetishistic/talismanic type in which sexuoerotic arousal and facilitation or attainment of orgasm are responsive to and contingent on self-defilement by smelling, chewing, or otherwise utilizing sweaty or soiled clothing or articles of menstrual hygiene (from Greek, *mysos,* uncleanness + -philia). There is overlap between **mysophilia, coprophilia, and urophilia.** There is no technical term for the reciprocal paraphilic condition, namely of being the provider of the mysophilic materials.

narratophilia: a paraphilia of the solicitational/allurative type in which sexuoerotic arousal and facilitation or attainment of orgasm are responsive to and contingent on using words and telling stories commonly classified as dirty, pornographic, or obscene, in the presence of the sexual partner (from Latin, *narrare,* to narrate + -philia). The same term is used for the reciprocal paraphilic condition, namely of being dependent on reading or listening to such material for sexual arousal. *See also* **pictophilia.**

natal sex: the sex of a baby at birth.

native lovemap: by analogy with native language, the lovemap that is assimilated as one's own personal, inalienable possession, regardless of how many of its attributes are shared, or not shared by others.

natural law: according to theological doctrine, divine law as revealed in nature. The doctrine of natural sexual law is that the divine purpose is procreation, and that sexual passion is sinful and immoral.

necrophilia: a paraphilia of the stigmatic/eligibilic type in which sexuoerotic arousal and facilitation or attainment of orgasm are responsive to and contingent on not a live partner, but a corpse (from Greek, *nekros,* dead + -philia). There is no reciprocal paraphilic condition except in the make-believe of being dead and copulating in a coffin in preparation for burial—for which there is no technical term.

neocortex: the outermost layer or cortex of the brain, which in the evolutionary sense is new and is most highly developed in humans. It is contrasted with the paleocortex (the old cortex or limbic system) that it encapsulates.

nepiophilia: a paraphilia of the stigmatic/eligibilic type like **pedophilia** except that the age range is restricted to infancy (from Greek, *nepon,* infant + -philia). The reciprocal paraphilic condition is **autonepiophilia,** or **paraphilic infantilism,** impersonating a baby. *See also* **ephebophilia; gerontophilia; pedophilia.**

neuroanatomy: the branch of neurology and anatomy that is concerned with nerve cells and the nervous system, including the brain.

neurobiology: biology of the nervous system and its functional responsivity in the organism.

neurohormone: *see* **neurotransmitter.**

neuromodulator: a neurochemical substance that is not classified as either a neurotransmitter or a neurohormone, but which influences or modulates the actions of either or both.

neuropeptide: a class of biochemical substances, related to peptide hormones, that are active in the brain and nervous system, for example, as neurotransmitters. *See also* **endorphin; neurotransmitter; peptide hormones.**

neuroscience: the science of how the brain and the nervous system work at the cellular level.

neurotransmitter: one of many different body chemicals released by brain and nerve cells, that carry messages from cell to cell across neuronal junctions. Some neurotransmitters are classified as neurohormones.

nihilism: a principle or doctrine that nothing can be proved, and that nothing matters or is worth doing (from latin, *nihil*, nothing).

nocturnal penile tumescence (NPT): spontaneous erection of the penis during sleep occurring initially within the womb and from birth to advanced old age, typically in three episodes a night for a total of 2–3 hours. It is associated with the rapid eye movement (REM) phase of sleep and with erotosexual dreams. It is measured by harnessing the penis into an expandable ring. Less is known about the corresponding phenomenon in females as there is no fully satisfactory technique for measuring vasocongestion of the female genitals.

nonjudgmentalism: in the practice of sexual medicine, the constant maintenance of an alliance between the professional and the patient against the syndrome, so as to avoid any hint of blaming the patient and of implicitly accusing him/her of being responsible for the illness.

normophilia (*adj.* **normophilic**): a condition of being erotosexually in conformity with the standard as dictated by customary, religious, or legal authority (from Latin, *normo-* + -philia). *See also* **paraphilia.**

nosocomial: belonging to or associated with a hospital, clinic, or other location of the practice of any branch of medicine, surgery, radiology, psychiatry, or pediatrics.

nosology: the science or system of classification of disease (from Greek, *nosos*, disease + -*logy*, science or study of).

nucleus: in neuroanatomy, a general term used to designate a group of nerve cells that connect with a particular nerve; also the innermost part of a cell.

nymph: in Greek and Roman mythology, one of the minor nature goddesses personified as a beautiful maiden of river, mountain, or woodland habitat.

nymphomania: in psychiatry, a term, loosely applied to females believed to have an insatiable sexual appetite. *See also* **nymph; satyriasis.**

object-relations theory: a branch of psychoanalytic theory, first proposed by W. R. D. Fairbairn, in which particular attention is given to relations with people or things in the course of development.

obscenity: actions or utterances, predominantly sexual, that are traditionally classified as forbidden, disgusting, or offensive to chastity and modesty; pornography.

oedipal: in Freudian theory, pertaining to the Oedipus complex.

olfaction (*adj.* **olfactory**): the function of smelling.

olfactophilia: one of a group of paraphilias of the fetishistic/talismanic type in which the sexuoerotic stimulus is associated with smell and odors emanating from parts of the body, especially the sexual and adjacent parts (from Latin, *olfacere,* to smell + -philia).

ontogenetic (*n.* **ontogeny**): belonging to the developmental history covering the life span of a single individual or organism, as compared with the phylogenetic history of the development of the species (from Greek, *onta,* things that exist + -*geny,* generation or development). *See also* **phylogenetic.**

opioid: a peptide, naturally occurring in the brain and elsewhere in the body, the effect of which resembles that of opium or a morphinelike synthetic opiate.

opponent-process theory: a theory, recently proposed by Richard Solomon, to augment traditional stimulus–response learning theory, according to which powerful aversion or attraction to a particular activity or experience undergoes reversal, as for example, pain reversing into pleasure, tragedy into triumph, terror into euphoria, or the proscribed into the prescribed.

organogenic (*n.* **organicity**): in psychological and psychiatric theory, the principle that some mental symptoms or syndromes attributed to the mind actually have a somatic or organic basis, for example, in the brain. *Syn.* **organic.**

orgasm (*adj.* **orgasmic**): the high peak or climax of erotosexual feeling that is accompanied by spasmodic muscular contractions in the sex organs and, in the male, usually but not invariably by discharge of semen.

osteomyelitis: inflammation of bone induced by infection.

ovariectomy: surgical removal of the ovaries; female castration.

ovary: in the female, one of the two sex glands, left and right, in the abdominal cavity, where ova or eggs are formed, and from which female sex hormones, estrogen and progesterone, are secreted.

oviducts: *see* **fallopian tubes.**

ovulation: the process by which an egg is ejected from its follicle on the surface of the ovary, ready to enter the fallopian tube and, in the presence of sperms, become fertilized.

pairbond: a strong and lasting closeness between two human beings or other creatures, such as exists between parent and child or two lovers.

paradigm: a model or pattern (from Greek, *paradeigma,* shown or set up as an example).

paranoid (*n.* **paranoia**): characterized by thinking that is delusional and sometimes hallucinatory. It is incorrectly used as a synonym for suspicious.

paraphile: *see* **paraphiliac.**

paraphilia: a condition occurring in men and women of being compulsively responsive to and obligatively dependent on an unusual and personally or socially unacceptable stimulus, perceived or in the ideation and imagery of fantasy, for optimal initiation and maintenance of erotosexual arousal and the facilitation or attainment of orgasm (from Greek, *para-*, altered + -philia). Paraphilic imagery may be replayed in fantasy during solo masturbation or intercourse with a partner. In legal terminology, a paraphilia is a perversion or deviancy; and in the vernacular it is kinky or bizarre sex. *Ant.* **normophilia.**

paraphiliac: a person with a paraphilia. *Syn.* **paraphile.**

parasympathetic nervous system: *see* **autonomic nervous system; sympathetic nervous system.**

paraurethral glands: in females, a zone of glandular tissue located around the canal of the urethra that, in some cases, releases a fluid which escapes from the urethral opening at the time of orgasm. The male counterpart is the prostate gland.

parthenogenesis: development of an egg into a newborn without fertilization by a sperm. Parthenogenic species are monochoric, that is, all members of the species are of the same gonadal type; for example, some species of whiptail lizard.

partialism: fetishism of the type in which the fetishistic attachment is not to an object but to a part of the partner's body, for example the hair or, in the case of acrotomophilia, the stump of an amputated limb.

pathognomonic: pertaining to a distinctive sign, symptom, or characteristics of a disease on which a diagnosis can be made.

pederasty: literally, boy love. *See* **pedophilia.** Pederasty is usually used in the restricted sense to refer to anal intercourse performed by an older youth or man on a prepubertal or early pubertal boy. It is not conventionally applied to the relationship between an older woman and a boy.

pedophilia: a paraphilia of the stigmatic/eligibilic type in which sexuoerotic arousal and the facilitation or attainment of orgasm in a postpubertal adolescent or adult male or female are responsive to and contingent on having a juvenile partner of prepubertal or peripubertal developmental status (from Greek, *paidos*, child + -philia). Pedophile relationships may be heterosexual or homosexual or, more rarely, bisexual. They may take place in imagery or actuality, or both. The technical term for the reciprocal paraphilic condition in which an older person impersonates a juvenile is **paraphilic juvenilism.** The age and developmental status of the partner distinguishes pedophilia from **nepiophilia** and **ephebophilia.** *See also* **gerontophilia.**

penetration phobia: a hypophilic condition or syndrome, variable in etiology, of irrational panic and disabling fear that prevents having the vagina (or anus, or mouth) entered by something, particularly the penis, or the penis enveloped in something, particularly the vagina (or anus, or mouth). *Syn.* **aninsertia.**

penis: the male urinary and copulatory organ, comprising a root, shaft, and at the extremity, glans penis and foreskin (from Latin, *penis*). The shaft or body of the penis consists of two parallel cylindrical bodies, the **corpora cavernosa,** and beneath them, surrounding the urethra, the **corpus spongiosum.** The penis in the male is the homologue of the clitoris in the female.

penoclitoris: in cases of birth defect of the sex organs, a protuberant structure that could be either a small and deformed penis that lacks a urinary tube, or an enlarged clitoris. *Syn.* **clitoropenis.**

peodeiktophilia: a paraphilia of the solicitational/allurative type in which sexuoerotic arousal and facilitation or attainment of orgasm are responsive to and contingent on evoking surprise, dismay, shock, or panic from a stranger by illicitly exhibiting the penis, either flaccid or erect, with orgasm induced or postponed (from Greek, *peos,* penis + *deiknunain,* to show + -philia). There is no technical term for the reciprocal paraphilic condition, namely staring at the penis, which is subsumed under the broader concept of **voyeurism.** There is also no technical term for paraphilic exhibitionism of the female genitalia. *See also* **exhibitionism.**

peptide hormones: a class of hormones biochemically constructed of the same components of which proteins are made. They include neurohormones that govern the hormones secreted by the pituitary gland, e.g., gonadotropin-releasing hormone (GnRH).

perceptual image: an image in the mind as presently being perceived through one or more of the senses. *See also* **fictive image.**

perineum (*adj.* **perineal**): the region between the thighs, bounded by the anus and the scrotum or the vulva in, respectively, males and females.

personality: the uniqueness that characterizes an individual as a person as compared with, and in response to others, with respect to consistency or inconsistency of behavior and life-style (from Latin, *persona,* a mask, as worn by actors).

perversion: the pejorative and also the legal term for paraphilia.

PET scan: in nuclear medicine, an advanced technique of positron emission tomography (PET) for visualizing or scanning details of soft internal organs, for example, the brain, that do not show up on an X-ray film.

petit mal seizure: an epileptic seizure characterized by lapse of attention and awareness, and failure of subsequent recall, but without convulsing or unconsciousness. *See also* **grand mal seizure.**

phalloplasty: in plastic surgery, the procedures for attempted construction or reconstruction of a penis in cases of birth defect, of female-to-male transexualism, and of accidental or surgical amputation of the penis.

phallus: a synonym for penis, which is also used to refer to the enlarged clitoris or penislike structure of a female hermaphrodite.

phenotype: the observable traits that characterize the morphology, function, or behavior of individual members of a genotype. The phenotype may be many steps removed from the genotype. *See also* **genotype.**

pheromone: an odorous substance or smell that acts as a chemical messenger between members of the same or different species and serves as a foe repellant, boundary marker, child–parent bonding agent, or lover–lover, mating attractant. *See also* **hormone.**

-phile: a word ending, grammatically transformed from **-philia,** for noun usage. *Ex.:* one person, a **paraphile.** *Syn.* **-philiac,** as in one person, a **paraphiliac.**

-philia: a word ending meaning love, or erotic and sexual love of a person, thing, or activity (from Greek, *philos,* loving, dear). *See also* **normophilia; paraphilia.**

-philiac: a word ending, grammatically transformed from **-philia,** for noun and adjectival usage. *Ex.:* one person, a **paraphiliac** (*n.*); one **paraphiliac** person (*adj.*). *See also* **-phile; -philic.**

-philic: a word ending, grammatically transformed from **-philia,** for adjectival usage. *Ex.:* a **paraphilic** syndrome. *Syn.* **-philiac,** as in a **paraphiliac** syndrome.

phimosis: constriction of the foreskin so that it does not pull back, retracted over the glans of the penis.

phobia (*adj.* **phobic**): morbid and persistent dread or fear (from Greek, *phobos,* fear).

phocomelia: a birth defect of a limb, likened in everyday speech to a seal flipper, the hand or foot being attached to the trunk of the body by a single, small, deformed bone without, respectively, an elbow or knee (from Greek, *phoke,* seal + *melos,* limb).

phyletic: of or pertaining to a race. Phyletic components or aspects of behavior in human beings are those shared by all members of the human race, as compared with behavior that is individual and biographically or ontogenetically idiosyncratic (from Greek, *phylon,* tribe or race). Phyletic behavior is the product of both prenatal and postnatal determinants, as is personal biographic behavior. Each is the end product of both innate and experiential determinants.

phylism: a newly coined term (Money, 1983) used to refer to an element or unit of response or behavior of an organism that belongs to an individual through its phylogenetic heritage as a member of its species (from Greek, *phylon,* tribe or race). *See also* **phyletic; phylogenetic.**

phylogenetic (*n.* **phylogeny**): belonging to the developmental history of an animal or vegetable species, which is the genealogical history shared by all members of the species (from Greek, *phylon,* tribe, race, or genetically related group + *-geny,* generation or development). *See also* **ontogenetic.**

pictophilia: a paraphilia of the solicitational/allurative type in which sexuoerotic arousal and facilitation or attainment of orgasm are not only responsive to, but also contingent on viewing pictures, movies, or video cassettes of activities commonly classified as dirty, pornographic, or obscene, alone or in the presence of the sexual partner (from Latin, *pictus,* painted + -philia). The same term is used for the reciprocal paraphilic condition, namely of having sexuoerotic arousal contingent on showing visual erotica to the partner. *See also* **narratophilia.**

pituitary gland: an endocrine gland situated deep in the brain in the midline behind the eyes, and directly associated with the hypothalamus. The hormones of the anterior pituitary regulate many functions of the other endocrine glands of the body. The pituitary is also known as the hypophysis.

placenta: the thick plaque of tissue that forms when an embryo attaches itself to the inner wall of the womb, and which is joined to the baby by the umbilical cord (from Latin, *placenta,* flat cake).

polemicist: a person skilled in polemics, that is, in the art of controversy and disputation.

pornography: explicit erotic writings and especially graphic depictions of a sexuoerotic nature that are legally or by custom classified as forbidden. *See also* **erotography.**

praxic: requiring visuomotor coordination and characterized by action and doing something rather than talking about it (from greek, *praxis,* practice doing something

praxon: a unit of action or behavior that, by analogy, corresponds to a word or word-group in a sentence. (from Greek, *praxis,* practice, doing something).

precocious puberty: *see* **premature puberty.** *Syn.* **pubertas precox.**

predation: plunder; pillage; taking without permission.

predicate: to know or proclaim the nature or outcome of something from a knowledge of its beginnings.

prednisone: the generic name of one of the synthetic glucocorticoid hormones, used therapeutically as a substitute for cortisol from the adrenal cortices.

premature ejaculation: a hypophilic condition or syndrome, variable in etiology, of being unable to sustain the preorgasmic period of sexuoerotic stimulation, so that ejaculation occurs too soon relative to a self-defined, or partner-defined criterion, for example, at the moment of intromission. The partner of the premature ejaculator has the reverse condition of not climaxing soon enough.

premature puberty: puberty that begins before the normally appointed time and is completed by 9 years of age or earlier in girls, and 11 or earlier in boys. It may be an error of timing only, or may be associated with a brain lesion that affects the biological clock of puberty in the brain. *Syn.* **precocious puberty.** *See also* **pubertal delay.**

prenatal masculinization: in embryonic and fetal life, the masculinizing effect on the sexual anatomy and/or the sexual pathways of the brain that is induced by testosterone, estradiol, or other androgenizing sex hormones. The male fetus produces its own androgenic hormones.

The female fetus does not need to produce feminizing hormones in order not to masculinize, as nature's basic design is to differentiate a female. Masculinizing is not synonymous with defeminizing. Thus some masculinization and some feminization of the brain and behavior may coexist.

preoptic: situated anterior to the left/right crossover of the optic nerves at the optic chiasm in the hypothalamic region of the brain, behind the bridge of the nose.

preoptic nucleus: a group of nerve cells in the anterior or frontal region of the hypothalamus.

prepuce (*adj.* **prepucial**): the foreskin of the penis; or the hood of the clitoris.

present (*pronounce* pree·zent'): in animal mating, the position assumed by the female to allow the male to mount and thrust. For the penovaginal part of human sexual intercourse, either sex may present to the other. *See also* **copulation; intercourse.**

priapism: persistent abnormal and painful erection of the penis, usually without sexual desire. The cause is often unknown. Untreated, it almost always results in destruction of the spongy tissues of the penis as a result of coagulation of blood in them, with resultant irreversible impotence.

Priapus: in Greek and Roman mythology, the male god of generation, often represented with an erect penis.

primatologist: a scientist whose specialty is the study of apes and monkeys, i.e., the subhuman primates.

proceptive phase: in a sexuoerotic relationship, the initial phase of reciprocal signaling and responding to attraction and solicitation, in a ritual of wooing or courtship prerequisite to the acceptive (copulatory) phase. Proceptive rituals are species specific, and the signals are variably odors, visual displays,movements, sounds, or mixed. In human beings proceptive rituals are known to be represented in imagery as well as carried out in behavior. *See also* **acceptive phase; conceptive phase.**

progesterone: pregnancy hormone, one of the two sex hormones chiefly characteristic of the female. It is produced by the ovary in the corpus luteum, following ovulation, and also by the placenta during pregnancy. The metabolic pathway of hormone production in the body leads from progesterone to androgen to estrogen.

progestin: a synthetic type of progesterone. *Syn.* **gestagen; progestogen.**

progestin-induced hermaphroditism: a syndrome of hermaphroditic birth defect of the sex organs induced in the 46,XX gonadally female fetus by synthetic hormones, derivatives of progesterone and 19-nortestosterone, formerly used in cases of threatened miscarriage in the untried belief, subsequently proved erroneous, that they would preserve the pregnancy. After crossing the placenta,in a small percentage of cases the hormone given to the mother had a masculinizing effect on the external genitalia of the daughter fetus.

prognosis: a forecasting of the probable course and termination of a disease.

prolactin: the milk-stimulating hormone secreted from the pituitary gland.

prosthesis: an artificial substitute for a missing organ or limb of the body.

prosthetics: the field of knowledge relating to prostheses.

prurient (*n.* **prurience**): itching, longing, or having a desire, in particular a desire that meets with moral disapproval because of the quality of the lasciviousness or lewdness attributed to it.

pseudohermaphroditism: hermaphroditism. The prefix was once used to denote the fact that the gonads were not hermaphroditically mixed (ovarian plus testicular tissue) as in true hermaphroditism, but were either testicular (male pseudohermaphroditism) or ovarian (female pseudohermaphroditism). In modern usage, the preferred terms are male, female, and true hermaphroditism. Agonadal hermaphroditism is a fourth form.

psychiatric (*n.* **psychiatry**): pertaining to the medical specialty that deals with mental disorder.

psychic: pertaining to the mind and its ideas and images.

psychodynamics: changes in recognition, recall, imagery, ideation, or other mental processes that take place in synchrony with other processes manifested within or via the behavior of a living organism, and that are presumed to have a governing or determining effect.

psychoendocrinology: the branch of knowledge that deals with the two-way relationship between mental functioning and endocrine or hormonal functioning.

psychogenic (*n.* **psychogenesis**): in psychological and psychiatric theory, the principle that some mental symptoms or syndromes can be explained mentally, i.e., psychologically without reference to the brain, the nervous system, or any other functional system of the body such as the endocrine system, immune system, or genetic code.

psychohormonal: pertaining to the two-way relationship between mental life and hormones. *Syn.* **psychoendocrine.**

psychological (*n.* **psychology**): pertaining to mental life as manifested through language and behavior.

psychopathological (*n.* **psychopathology**): pertaining to the origin and nature of mental disorder.

pubertal delay: failure of puberty to begin until after the normally appointed upper limit of the age for its completion, namely 13 years in girls and 15 in boys. It may be an error of timing only, or it may be associated with a permanent hormonal deficit in the functioning of the gonads, the pituitary gland, or the hypothalamus in the brain. *See also* **premature puberty.**

puberty: the period between childhood and adolescence when the secondary sexual characteristics have the onset of their development, culminating in procreative maturity. *See also* **precocious puberty; premature puberty; pubertal delay.**

pudendum (*pl.* **pudenda**) in human beings, especially females, the external genitals.

pulsatile (*n.* **pulsatility**): occurring not continuously but in bursts or pulses that may be either regular or sporadic in frequency.

purdah: a screen or veil (from Persian, *pardah*, veil); among women in Islamic cultures, the custom of veiling the face in public in the presence of men.

radioimmunoassay (RIA): a procedure for assaying or quantifying minute amounts of target substances such as hormones, neurotransmitters, or drugs in blood or other tissue fluid. It is based on the action of the target substance to bind onto another substance, an antibody, for which it is known to have a special affinity. A measured amount of the target substance is labeled with a radioactive label. It is then mixed with the unlabeled target substance that circulates in unknown quantity in a sample of blood or other fluid, and a measured amount of the antibody is added. The amount of unlabeled target substance present can then be quantified, because it varies according to how much of its radioactive rival becomes antibody bound, and the latter can be measured with a radioactivity counter. This is the classical method of antigen competition.

rape: to seize and take away by force; to plunder; to have carnal knowledge of a woman without the legal consent of her father, husband, or herself; (in contemporary usage) to be coercive sexually after a female partner has said no. Rape is not synonymous with raptophilia, the paraphilic syndrome. *See also* **biastophilia; raptophilia.**

raptophilia: *see* **biastophilia** (from Latin, *rapere*, to seize + -philia).

reciprocation: the mutual process of adaptation, one to the other, as when the behavior of a person of one sex adapts itself to the behavior of the other. *Syn.* **complementation.**

reductionism: the theoretically incorrect practice of reducing causality that is complex and multivariate to a single or univariate cause.

RH: releasing hormone, also known as releasing factor. One of the newly discovered peptide hormones secreted by cells in the hypothalamus of the brain. They release other hormones, especially from the nearby pituitary gland.

Rokitansky syndrome: *see* **Mayer-Rokitansky-Kuester syndrome.**

romantic (*n.* **romance**): having a wondrous or storybook quality, visionary and idealized. Romantic love belongs to the proceptive phase of a relationship, especially at its onset. Historically, in the songs of the troubadours of the twelfth and thirteenth centuries, romantic love stopped short of the acceptive phase of sexual intercourse and marriage, but today there is no strict dividing line.

sacrifice: an offering to propitiate, obtain forgiveness, make amends, or gain favor.

sadism: a paraphilia of the sacrificial/expiatory type in which sexuoerotic arousal and facilitation or attainment of orgasm are responsive to and

contingent on being the authority who variously imposes abuse, torture, punishment, discipline, humiliation, obedience, and servitude
(named after the Marquis de Sade, 1740–1814, French author and sadist). The reciprocal paraphilic condition is **masochism.**

sadomasochistic sacrifice: a paraphilic ritual in which sexuoerotic fulfillment requires sadistic dominance in reciprocal interaction with masochistic victimization, and/or vice versa, with or without mutual consent.

satyr: in Greek mythology, a woodland deity, usually depicted as having
the hind end of a hairy, hoofed goat and the head end of a horned
man, an attendant of Bacchus, fond of merriment and lechery.

satyriasis: in psychiatry, a term loosely applied to a male believed to have
an insatiable sexual appetite. *See also* **satyr; nymphomania.**

schema (pl. schemas or schemata): a plan, outline, or arrangement, which
may be mental as well as physical (from Greek, *schema*, form, shape).

schizophrenia: a major mental illness or psychosis characterized primarily,
though not exclusively, by disordered thinking, ideation, and logic
(from Greek, *schizein*, to divide + *phren*, mind). Etymologically it means
divided mentation. Colloquially it is erroneously used to mean split
personality or dual personality. *See also* **fugue; multiple personality.**

scoptophilia: a paraphilia of the solicitational/allurative type in which sexuoerotic arousal and facilitation or attainment of orgasm are responsive
to and contingent on watching others engaging in sexual activity, including sexual intercourse (from Greek, *skopein*, to view + -philia).
The reciprocal paraphilic condition is sometimes also referred to as
scoptophilia: or by its own name, **autagonistophilia.** *Syn.* **mixophilia;
mixoscopia; scopophilia.**

scrotum (*adj.* **scrotal):** the bag or sac that hangs below the penis and
houses the testicles or balls.

secret vice: masturbation. *Syn.* **self-abuse; self-pollution; solitary vice.**
Ant. **social vice.**

serendipitous: discovered or recognized by chance, often in the course of
another undertaking, and not as a result of organized planning.

serotonin: a neurotransmitter substance essential to brain functioning, the
sexual function of which is to be an inhibitor. *See also* **dopamine.**

sex (*n.*): one's personal and reproductive status as male or female, or uncertain, as declared on the basis of the external genitalia. Also, a vernacular synonym for genital interaction, as in the expression, to have sex.

sex adjunctive: characteristic of male/female differences that are tertiary or
subsidiary to sex-derivative, secondary differences, and are only peripherally related to sex-hormonal differences with respect to the division of labor between the sexes.

sex adventitious: characteristic of male/female differences that are quater-
nary or subsidiary to sex-adjunctive, tertiary differences, and are more
or less fortuitously a product of cultural history with respect to the
division of power between the sexes.

sex chromatin: a spot that shows up when stained on the nucleus of cells taken from mammalian females, but not males, and is attributed to the inactivated second X chromosome; it is also called the Barr body (named after Murray L. Barr, 1908–   ).

sex derivative: characteristic of male/female differences that are secondary or subsidiary to sex-irreducible, primary differences, and are for the most part under the influence of sex hormones.

sex irreducible: characteristic of male/female differences that are primary and nontransferable between male and female, namely, male impregnation and female ovulation, menstruation, gestation, and lactation.

sex roles: specifically, patterns of behavior and thought that are related to the sex organs and procreation; generally, behavior and thought that is traditionally or stereotypically classified or coded as typical of, or especially suited to, either one sex or the other. *See also* **gender-identity/role.**

Sexaholics Anonymous: analogous to Alcoholics Anonymous, a network of self-help therapy groups for people with a particular sexual compulsion or addiction.

sexing-stealing-lying syndrome: a syndrome in which a forbidden or illicit sexual activity coexists with kleptomanic stealing, as in shoplifting, which is not per se erotic, and with confabulatory deception or pseudologia fantastica (fantastic or fictitious logic).

sexology: the body of knowledge that comprises the science of sex, or, more precisely, the science of the differentiation and dimorphism of sex and of the erotic/sexual pairbonding of partners. Its primary data are behavioropsychological and somatic, and its primary organs are the genitalia, the skin, and the brain. The scientific subdivisions of sexology are genetic, morphologic, hormonal, neurohormonal, neuroanatomical, neurochemical, pharmacological, behavioral, sociocultural, conceptive-contraceptive, gestational-parturitional, and parental sexology. The life-span subdivisions of sexology are embryonal-fetal, infantile, child, pubertal, adolescent, adult, and gerontal sexology. *See also* **sexosophy.**

sexophobia (*adj.* **sexophobic**): dread or fear of the sex organs and of whatever pertains to them (from sex + Greek, *phobos*, fear or fright).

sexosophy: the body of knowledge that compromises the philosophy, principles, and knowledge that people have about their own personally experienced eroticism and sexuality and that of other people, singly and collectively. It includes values, personal and shared, and it encompasses culturally transmitted value systems. Its subdivisions are historical, regional, ethnic, religious, and developmental or life span. *See also* **sexology.**

sexual (*n.* **sexuality**): pertaining to sex or, more particularly, the stimulation, responsiveness, and functions of the sex organs either alone or with one or more partners. *See also* **erotic.**

sexual addiction: compulsively frequent reiteration of highly ritualized usage of the sex organs, under conditions of extreme specificity. The addiction is not to sex, generically, but to a particular animate or inanimate sexuoerotic stimulus, or type of stimulus, that is incorporated into the ritual activity. The activity itself may or may not qualify as paraphilic. The analogue of sexual addiction to a given stimulus is drinking addiction to alcohol, from which the concept derives.

sexual drive: the personal and subjective desire or feeling of readiness to have an erotosexual experience. It cannot be measured directly.

sexually dimorphic nucleus: in the preoptic area (SDN/POA) or region of the hypothalamus, a group of cells so named (by Roger Gorski) because it is smaller in females than males.

sexual rehearsal play: motions and positions observable in infantile and juvenile play, such as pelvic thrusting and presenting, and coital positioning, that are components of, and prerequisite to healthy sexuoerotic maturity in human and other primates.

sexuoerotic: the sexual and the erotic experienced as a unity, with more emphasis on sexual behavior than erotic ideation and imagery. *See also* **erotic; erotosexual; sexual.**

shaman (*adj.* **shamanistic**): a priestly healer and mediating agent of the spirit world.

sissy boy: a vernacular term applied to a boy whose developmental differentiation of gender-identity/role (G-I/R) is in variable degree discordant with the evidence of his genital morphology. *See also* **tomboy.**

social vice: promiscuous sex, chiefly with prostitutes or hustlers. *Ant.* **secret vice.**

solicitation: invitation; incitement.

solipsism: a princple or doctrine that the self knows only its own experiences (from Latin, *solus,* alone + *ipse,* self).

somatic: pertaining to the cells and structures of the body, and their function.

somnophilia: the sleeping princess syndrome, a paraphilia of the marauding/predatory type in which erotic arousal and facilitation or attainment of orgasm are responsive to and contingent on intruding on and awakeneing a sleeping stranger with erotic caresses, including oral sex, not involving force or violence (from Latin, *somnus,* sleep + -philia). There is no technical term for the reciprocal paraphilic condition of being the recipient, which occurs more readily in fantasy than in actuality.

spermatorrhea: the term for ejacualtion while asleep and having an erotosexual dream, medically used in the era when this normal occurrence was falsely classified as pathology. *Syn.* **wet dream.**

statistical norm: the standard of what is normal as defined by what the middle 50 percent of a community represent in what they are, and in what they say and/or do.

statistics (*adj.* **statistical**): systematic collection, classification, and mathematical compilation of evidnece or information with respect to its amount, range, frequency, or prevalence.

statutory rape: sexual intercourse with someone who, by legal statute, is defined as unqualified to give consent, usually because of being under-age; the law applies even if the accused partner, a boy, is the younger of the pair, and was actually seduced by the girl.

STD: sexually transmitted disease, including but not limited to contagious genital infections.

steroid hormones: a class of hormone biochemically constructed of the same components of which fats (lipids) are made. They include the hormones of the testis, ovary, and adrenal cortex. *See also* **peptide hormones.**

steroids (*sing.* **steroid**): the general or generic name for physiological compounds comprising, among others, sex hormones and adrenocortical hormones.

stigmata (*sing.* **stigma**): signs, marks, or features that indicate special fitness or suitability. *Syn.* **stigmas.**

stigmatophilia: a paraphilia of the stigmatic/eligibilic type in which sexuoerotic arousal and facilitation or attainment of orgasm are responsive to and contingent on a partner who has been tattooed, scarified, or pierced for the wearing of gold jewelry (bars or rings), especially in the genital region (from Greek, *stigma*, mark + -philia). The same term applies to the reciprocal paraphilic condition in which the self is similarly decorated.

stimulus–response theory: in psychology, the theory that human responsivity is determined by contingencies of reward and punishment in the external environment.

Stockholm syndrome: the name for the bond of attraction that sometimes develops between abuser and abused, molester and molested, captor and captive, and in particular between terrorist and hostage. The term stems from the recent case of a woman held hostage at a bank in Stockholm, Sweden, who became so pairbondedly attached to one of the robbers that she broke her engagement to her prehostage lover and remained faithful to her captor during his prison term.

stratagem: a strategy or plan that is circuitous and deceptive on the basis of an artifice or ruse.

subcutaneous: below the skin.

subrogation: occupying the place of another; substitution.

supramasculinize: to masculinize in excess. *Syn.* **supermasculinize.** *Ant.* **inframasculinize.**

symbiosis(*adj.* **symbiotic**): the dependence on one another's existence of two dissimlar organisms that live in close proximity and interaction.

sympathetic nervous system: pertaining to that part of the autonomic nervous system the functions of which contrast with or reciprocate those of the parasympathetic system. *See also* **autonomic.**

symphorophilia: a paraphilia of the sacrificial/expiatory type in which sexuoerotic arousal and facilitation or attainment of orgasm are responsive to and contingent on stage-managing the possibility of a disaster, such as a conflagration or traffic accident, and watching for it to happen (from Greek, *symphora*, disaster + -philia). The same term is applied to the reciprocal paraphilic condition in which the person arranges to be at risk as a potential victim of arranged disaster.

synapse: in the nervous system, the place where the fibers of neurons meet (from Greek, *synapsis*, a conjunction or connection).

syndrome: an unhealthy condition or disease typified by a characteristic set of signs and symptoms (from Greek, *syn-*, with + *dramein*, to run); also, a regular and orderly concurrence of characteristics or practices.

taboo also **tabu,** and in Polynesia, **tapu,** (sacred and forbidden): prohibited by tradition or social usage or other authority. A taboo generates fear, shame, and guilt in those who disobey it, thus enabling those in authority to wield power over those under them.

tactile: pertaining to the sense of touch.

talisman: a token or charm that has special power or magic.

teleology: in philosophy, the doctrine that nature or natural processes are shaped by a purpose and directed toward an end or goal by a driving force or power. *Ant.* **mechanism.**

telephonicophilia: a paraphilia of the solicitational/allurative type in which sexuorotic arousal and facilitation or attainment of orgasm are responsive to and contingent on deception and ruse in luring or threatening a telephone respondent, known or unknown, into listening to, and making personally explicit conversation in the sexuoerotic vernacular (from telephone + -philia). Typically, the caller is not dangerous, only a nuisance. There is no technical term for the reciprocal paraphilic condition of inviting and possibly charging for such telephone calls. *Syn.* **telephone scatophilia** (from Greek, *skato,* dung).

template: a pattern or mold that regulates the shape or appearance of a construction or idea.

temporal lobe: in the brain, the part of each cerebral hemisphere that is named for its location internal to the temple.

temporal lobe trauma: injury to the temporal lobe of the brain, of either external or internal origin, with which is associated an increased risk of temporal lobe epileptic seizures and, rarely, associated paraphilic attacks.

territorial marking: in some animals, the marking of the boundary of the home territory with an odorous substance or pheromone secreted from a specialized, testosterone-responsive marking gland, typically near the chin or rump, or secreted in the urine.

testicular-feminizing syndrome: *see* **androgen-insensitivity syndrome.**

testis: in the male, one of the two egg-shaped bodies, the sex glands, left and right, in the scrotum, where sperms are made (in the tubules) and from which the male sex hormone, testosterone, is secreted (from the Leydig cells). *Syn.* **testicle.**

testosterone: the biologically most potent of the naturally occurring androgens, measurable in blood plasma and urine. It is produced chiefly by the testis from its precursor hormone, progesterone. In females testosterone is the precursor of estrogen in the ovaries. *See also* **progesterone.**

thalidomide: a sedative and hypnotic drug first marketed in the 1950s before it was known to cause pregnant women to give birth to babies with either missing limbs (amelia) or phocomelia (seal-flipper deformity of arms and/or legs).

threshold: the point, stage, or degree of intensity at which an effect begins to be produced. The lower the threshold, the sooner and more easily does the effect begin.

tomboy: a vernacular term applied to a girl whose developmental differentiation of gender-identity/role (G-I/R) as stereotypically defined is in variable degree discordant with the evidence of her genital morphology. *See also* **sissy boy.**

toucheurism: a paraphilia of the solicitational/allurative type in which sexuoerotic arousal and the facilitation or attainment of orgasm are responsive to and contingent on surreptitiously touching a stranger on an erotic part of the body, particularly the breast, buttocks, or genital area (from French, *toucher*, to touch). There is no technical name for the reciprocal paraphilic condition, namely being sexuoerotically dependent on being touched by a stranger. *See also* **frotteurism.**

transexual: a person manifesting the phenomenon of transexualism.

transexualism: the condition of crossing over to live full-time in the role of the other sex, with hormonal and surgical sex reassignment (from Latin, *trans*, across + sexual). The term signifies a method of treatment and rehabilitation rather than a diagnostic entity. There are different biographic antecedents to sex reassignment, one of which may be paraphilic transvestism (transvestophilia). Transexualism itself is not a paraphilia. *See also* **gynemimesis, gynemimetophilia, transvestophilia.**

transpositions: in G-I/R, the interchange of masculine and feminine expectancies and stereotypes mentally and in behavior and appearance.

transsexual: transexual.

transvest: to cross dress.

transvestism: cross dressing (from Latin, *trans*, across + *vestis*, garment).

transvestophilia: a paraphilia of the fetishistic/talismanic type in which sexuoerotic arousal and facilitation or attainment of orgasm are responsive to and contingent on wearing clothing, especially underwear, of the other sex (from Latin, *trans*, across + *vestis*, garment + -philia). *See also* **transvestism.**

trauma: a wound or injury, whether physical or psychic.

Turner's syndrome: a condition marked by a chromosomal anomaly in phenotypic females with the chief pathognomonic symptoms of absence of ovaries (gonadal agenesis or dysgenesis) and short stature. The basic genetic defect is a missing sex chromosome, so that the total count is 45,X. There are several variants of this syndrome. For example, the second X may, though present, be partially deleted. In one variant of the so-called mosaics, some cells of the body are 45,X and some 46,XX. Treatment includes giving female sex hormone at the age of puberty to induce adult appearance and menses. Girls with Turner's syndrome are almost invariably sterile.

understudy: one who rehearses and is prepared to act another's part.

unitypic: as applied to sexual dimorphism of the genitalia, brain, or behavior, differentiation of homologous female and male forms from the same original beginnings or anlagen, as in the case of the clitoris and penis, each of which differentiates from the primitive genital tubercle. *Ant.* **ambitypic.**

univariate: accounted for or explained as having been determined, produced, or caused by only one variable.

urethra: the canal through which urine is discharged, extending from the neck of the urinary bladder to the external opening or meatus.

urogenital: pertaining to both the urinary and genital structures; genitourinary.

urophilia: a paraphilia of the fetishistic/talismanic type in which sexuoerotic arousal and facilitation or attainment of orgasm are responsive to and contingent on being urinated on and/or swallowing urine (from Greek, *ouron,* urine + -philia). There is no special technical term for the reciprocal condition of urinating on or in the mouth of the partner. *Syn.* **urolagnia.** *See also* **coprophilia.**

uterus: the womb; at its lower end is the vagina, and at its upper end, the left and right fallopian tubes and ovaries.

vagina: in female mammals, the canal that opens into the vulva and, internally, connects with the cervix or mouth of the womb. It encloses the penis in sexual intercourse. *See also* **vulva.**

vaginal dryness: insufficient lubrication of the vagina, or its premature loss of lubrication, during the proceptive or acceptive phase of an erotosexual episode.

vaginismus: recurrent premature contraction of the musculature of the vagina before or at the acceptive phase of an erotosexual episode, so that it is too tight and too dry to receive the penis.

vaginoplasty: in plastic surgery, the operative procedures for construction or reconstruction of a vagina, in cases of birth defect, of male-to-female transexualism, and of accidental or surgical trauma to the vagina.

vascular: supplied with or pertaining to vessels or ducts that convey fluids, especially blood.

venal: bargained for; marketed, possibly corruptly.

ventromedial nucleus of the hypothalamus: bilaterally, in the ventral (frontal) part of the middle (tuberal) region of the hypothalamus, a group of nerve cells associated with several vital functions such as food intake and sexual behavior.

VIP: vasoactive intestinal polypeptide: a peptide hormone first isolated from the small intestine and subsequently found to have many physiological roles, one of which pertains to arousal of the sex organs, including erection of the penis.

voyeurism: a paraphilia of the solicitational/allurative type in which sexuo-erotic arousal and facilitation or attainment of orgasm are responsive to and contingent on the risk of being discovered while covertly or illicitly watching a stranger disrobing or engaging in sexual activity (from French, *voir*, to look at). The reciprocal paraphilic condition is **exhibitionism.** *See also* **peodeiktophilia.**

vulva (*adj.* **vulvar**): the external female genitalia. *See also* **vagina.**

wet dream: a dream with erotosexual content that ends in sexual orgasm. It occurs with greatest frequency in pubertal and adolescent boys. In some instances, the content of the dream is lost or fails to exist, and the ejaculate is the sole sign of the occurrence. *See also* **spermatorrhea.**

wolffian duct structures: the embryonic structures that develop into the internal reproductive anatomy of the male, attached to the testicles; named for Kaspar F. Wolff, German embryologist (1733–1794). *See also* **müllerian duct structures.**

womb: in female mammals, the organ in which the young live and grow before birth. *Syn.* **uterus.**

xanith (pronounced han·eeth): in Arabic, the term usually translated as male homosexual, but applied only to men who partially impersonate women in clothing, manner, and life-style, and in their sexuoerotic role with other men.

X-linked recessive: in genetics, a defect that is carried on the X chromosome, and that can express itself only if both X chromosomes in an individual carry the defect (in females) or if the X chromosome carrying the defect is paired with a Y chromosome (in males). These defects are much more commonly expressed in males than in females.

XO syndrome: *see* **Turner's syndrome.**

XXY syndrome: *see* **Klinefelter's syndrome.**

XYY syndrome: a condition identified by a supernumerary Y-chromosomal anomaly in morphologic males who are typically over 6 feet (183 cm) in height, and are likely to have one or more of a varied assortment of congenital physical anomalies, including sterility in some cases. The basic genetic defect is an extra sex chromosome with a total count of 47,XYY, although other variants also occur, e.g. 48XXYY; 48,XYYY. In behavioral development, there is an increased risk of impulsiveness, including antisocial and lawbreaking impulsiveness.

youth: the period of development between puberty and maturity; adolescence.

zenith: the summit; the highest peak.

zoophilia: a paraphilia of the stigmatic/eligibilic type in which sexuoerotic arousal and facilitation or attainment of orgasm are responsive to and contingent on engaging in cross-species sexual activities, that is, with an animal (from Greek, *zoon*, animal + -philia). There is no technical term for the cross-species reciprocal paraphilic condition in which an animal mates with a member of the human or other species, although the phenomenon does exist.

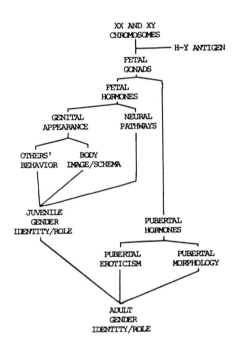

Developmental sequence and differentiation
of gender identity/role (G I/R)

APPENDIX

Treatment and Guidelines for Informed Consent for Combined Antiandrogen and Counseling Therapy of Paraphilic Sex Offenders

RATIONALE FOR DEPO-PROVERA® TREATMENT OF SEX OFFENDERS (PARAPHILES)

Studies begun by the author in 1966 have shown that paraphiles, including those in trouble with the law as sex offenders (for example, paraphilic raptophiles [rapists], pedophiles or exhibitionists), treated with the anti-androgenic hormone, Depo-Provera®, plus counseling have gained in self-regulation of sexual behavior. Depo-Provera® lowers the level of male sex hormone in the bloodstream so that it becomes the same as before puberty. It functions not as female hormone, as it is sometimes wrongly said to do, but as a precursor of male hormone. It fools the cells of the body into absorbing it as if it were a male hormone. Biologically, it is inert as compared with male hormone. It suppresses or lessens the frequency of erection and ejaculation and also lessens the feeling of sexual drive and the mental imagery of sexual arousal. To illustrate: for the pedophile there will be a decreased erotic attraction to children. This medication can be thought of as a suppressant of the feeling of sex drive, intended to make self-governance easier, usually with the help of individual or couple counseling as well.

ANTIANDROGENIC EFFECT OF DEPO-PROVERA®

Depo-Provera®, a long-acting, injectable form of medroxyprogesterone acetate manufactured by Upjohn, is a synthetic progestin which is classified

232

pharmacologically as an antiandrogen. Antiandrogen inhibits the release of testosterone, the predominantly male hormone, from the testicles. Some progestinic hormone is normally present in the male body but at a very low level. Increasing the level allows progestin to compete with androgen and take control. Androgen is an erotic activator, whereas progestin is erotically inert. It therefore induces a period of sexual quiescence in which the feeling of sex drive is at rest. The patient "has a vacation" from his or her sex drive.

MODE OF ENDOCRINE ACTION

In terms used by endocrinologists, Depo-Provera®, through its effect upon neural pathways in the brain, inhibits the release of luteinizing hormone (LH) from the pituitary gland. LH is the chemical messenger which normally stimulates the testicles to produce androgen. Hence, the ultimate effect of Depo-Provera® is to reduce the level of androgen, especially testosterone, in the bloodstream. Typically, in the adult male, Depo-Provera® reduces the blood level of testosterone to that of a normal prepubertal boy (from approximately 575 nanograms/100 millileters to 125 nanograms/100 millileters or less).

BRAIN EFFECTS

In addition to lowering the level of testosterone, Depo-Provera®, like all progestinic hormones, acts directly on brain cells in the hypothalamus. In the dosage used in the treatment of paraphilias, the influence on sexual pathways in the brain, though mild, has the great advantage of being sexually calming or tranquilizing. The patient feels relief from an urge that was formerly insistently commanding, distressing, and not subject to voluntary control.

PERIPHERAL PHYSIOLOGICAL EFFECTS

Depo-Provera®, through decreasing the testosterone level, temporarily decreases penile erection and ejaculation, and the production of sperm (spermatogenesis). This means that a man probably could not father a child while taking the medication. The medicine is not feminizing (men do not grow breasts). In addition, the sexual accessory organs, the prostate and seminal vesicles, temporarily shrink. Increased frequency of drowsiness and weight gain, as well as increased blood pressure, can occur. Other possible side effects have been noted but are so infrequent that they cannot be attributed directly to Depo-Provera® alone.

REVERSIBILITY OF CHANGES

The changes attributed to the medication are reversible upon cessation of treatment; within seven to ten days erectile and ejaculatory capacity begin to return, along with the subjective experience of more sexual drive. Return of fertility is slower, taking from three to six months. As the use of this medication is still relatively new for paraphilia (its first use was in 1966), the possibility of side effects from very long term treatment cannot be completely excluded. However, the duration of treatment, in most instances, is not excessively prolonged beyond two or three years. Then the patient is weaned off treatment for a trial period. If a relapse threatens, treatment can be resumed.

DOSAGE LEVEL

Depo-Provera® is marketed in two concentrations, 100 mg/ml and 400 mg/ml. Because the more concentrated form is thicker, some patients experience pain at the injection site for several hours despite the smaller volume of the injection. It is injected intramuscularly, usually in the buttock. Larger doses (for example, 5 cc at the 100 mg/ml conncentration) are divided for injection, half into each buttock. The beginning dosage is 500 mg (milligrams) every seven days, or more for larger, heavier patients. After four or more weeks the dosage may be progressively lowered in 50 mg increments. The size of the maintenance dosage is judged on the basis of the patient's subjective report of how well the paraphilic imagery and ideation is under control, together with the blood level of testosterone. Tailored to individual need, the maintenance dose has ranged from 150 mg to 800 mg per week.

PILL FORM OF PROVERA®

Provera® is the non-Depo, noninjectable form of the hormone, marketed in pill form. It is not well absorbed from the gut, and is not satisfactory for the treatment of paraphilia.

HORMONE MONITORING

Hormonal measures of testosterone and LH initially can be monitored periodically to gauge the effectiveness of the dosage. Usually an interval of six months to a year is sufficient, though perhaps more often in the earliest phase of treatment. The recent application of radioimmunological techniques to the assay of testosterone and LH has made such endocrine monitoring precise, reliable, rapid, and relatively inexpensive, as compared with prior methods.

NO INCREASED TOLERANCE

Most patients do not require a progressively increasing dosage because there is no build-up of tolerance to Depo-Provera®. However, for some patients, the initial dosage is too low and needs to be increased.

COMPARISON WITH SURGICAL CASTRATION

Prior to the discovery, manufacture, and medical use of antiandrogen, the method of reducing the level of testosterone in men was surgical castration. Used in many societies throughout history, castration is disfavored in contemporary American legal-medical management of sex offenders. Obviously, surgical castration is irreversible. It is also less effective than hormonal antiandrogenic therapy because it does not replace testosterone in brain cells with another more calming hormone. Castration also increases levels of LH from the pituitary gland, whereas medication lowers these levels and directly affects sex-regulating brain cells in the hypothalamus.

BEHAVIORAL OUTCOME OF DEPO-PROVERA® TREATMENT

In some cases, patients may be weaned off Depo-Provera® completely. Since weaning is the step-by-step lowering of the hormone dosage, it is possible for the patient to discover how completely he has become relieved of the tendency to engage in the paraphilic behavior, in both actuality and imagination. In some cases, there is long-lasting remission, so that the patient is no longer compelled to commit paraphilic sexual acts, but is able to have a sex life with a socially suitable consenting partner instead. Those patients who establish a strongly pair-bonded, falling-in-love relationship with a permanent partner appear to be additionally guaranteed against relapse. The counseling component of treatment facilitates this achievement and is essential. Even though married, paraphiles typically have never had a genuine love affair; paraphilia is really a love disorder, not a sex disorder.

COMPLIANCE

Some patients, as in all specialties of medicine, are more faithful than others in adhering to medication schedules. Some overly confident patients drift into noncompliance. Other patients neglect specific instructions about their medication schedule. For this reason, it is advisable that as a condition of probation or parole, supervision be legally required so as to ensure strict compliance in adhering to the treatment schedule.

FOLLOW-UP

Paraphilic sex offenders treated with Depo-Provera® should be kept in long-term follow-up on at least a half-yearly basis, so that if a relapse should threaten, it can be controlled immediately. Paraphilic sex-offending is one of the few medical conditions in which a relapse is defined by the law as recidivism and is punished instead of treated. In an early study of twenty patients maintained in follow-up between five months and fifteen years, seventeen proved able to self-regulate their sexual behavior while receiving the medication, and three had relapses (J. Money & R.G. Bennett, *Int. J. Ment. Health*, 10:122–133, 1981). Almost all who stopped medication against medical advice subsequently relapsed. Some patients elect to remain on hormonal treatment indefinitely. Others try a supervised test period of no hormonal treatment and begin taking Depo-Provera® again if threatened with a relapse.

COUNSELING THERAPY

Counseling sessions are provided weekly at first, and then may be tailored to individual needs. These sessions are intended to help the patient establish a new life style and to cope with problems that have developed as a consequence of his or her prior life style. Therapy may be either individual or in a group.

TREATMENT CENTERS

There are a few major medical centers in the United States and Canada that have a special clinic for the Depo-Provera® treatment of paraphilias of both the sex-offending and non-offending variety. There are also many general practitioners and family doctors who, though they do not specialize in treating paraphilias, take on individual cases for injections of Depo-Provera®, provided the patient is under the care of a specialist in psychological and sexological health care. In Europe, Depo-Provera® is used in some countries where an alternative hormone, Androcur® (cyproterone acetate, Schering A-G) is also available. Androcur has not yet been cleared by the FDA for use in the United States, but it is used in Canada.

INFORMED CONSENT

Having been read, discussed, and understood by the patient, this document may be signed by the patient as evidence of informed consent, and co-signed by the doctor or other responsible professional as a witness. In addition, the patient may dictate a tape-recorded statement explaining in his or her own words what he or she is consenting to.

. . . . (patient's signature)

. . . . (witness's signature)

Date . . . .

Bibliography

Abramovich, D.R., Davidson, I.A., Longstaff, A., and Pearson, C.R. Sexual differentiation of the human midtrimester brain. *European Journal of Obstetrics, Gynecology, and Reproductive Biology,* 25:7–14, 1987.

Allen, L.S., Hines, M., Shryne, J.E., and Gorski, R.A. Two sexually dimorphic cells groups in the human brain. *Endocrinology* (Suppl.), 118:633, 1986. (Abstract)

Arnold, A.P., and Gorski, R.A. Gonadal steroid induction of structural sex differences in the central nervous system. *Annual Review of Neuroscience,* 7:413–442, 1984.

Barsky, L. Holy hormones . . . . male pregnancy? *Chatelaine,* 59(8):62–63, 123–124, 1986.

Baum, M.J. Differentiation of coital behavior in mammals: A comparative analysis. *Neuroscience and Biobehavioral Reviews,* 3:265–284, 1979.

Baum, M.J. Role for estrogen in neuro-psychosexual differentiation of male mammals. *International Academy of Sex Research Twelfth Annual Meeting: Abstracts,* Amsterdam, p. 5, 1986. (Abstract)

Baum, M.J., Gallagher, C.A., Martin, J.T., and Damassa, D.A. Effects of testosterone, dihydrotestosterone, or estradiol administered neonatally on sexual behavior of female ferrets. *Endocrinology,* 111:773–780, 1982.

Bauman, R. *The Gentleman from Maryland: The Conscience of a Gay Conservative.* New York, Arbor House, 1986.

Beach, F.A. Hormonal modification of sexually dimorphic behavior. *Psychoneuroendocrinology,* 1:3–23, 1975.

Bell, A.P., Weinberg, M.S., and Hammersmith, S.K. *Sexual Preference: Its Development in Men and Women.* Bloomington, Indiana University Press, 1981.

Benjamin, H. *The Transsexual Phenomenon.* New York, Julian Press, 1966.

Birkin, A. *J.M. Barrie and the Lost Boys: The Love Story That Gave Birth to Peter Pan.* New York, Clarkson N. Potter, 1979.

Bleier, R., Byne, W., and Siggelkow, I. Cytoarchitectonic sexual dimorphisms of the medial preoptic and anterior hypothalamic areas in guinea pig, rat, hamster, and mouse. *Journal of Comparative Neurology,* 212:118–130, 1982.

Bloch, I. *Strange Sexual Practises in All Races of the World.* New York, Falstaff Press, 1933.

Breedlove, S.M. Cellular analyses of hormone influence on motoneuronal development and function. *Journal of Neurobiology,* 17:157–176, 1986.

Breedlove, S.M., and Arnold, A.P. Hormone accumulation in a sexually dimorphic motor nucleus of the rat spinal cord. *Science,* 210:564–566, 1980.

Brindley, G.S. Cavernosal alpha-blockade: A new technique for investigating and treating erectile impotence. *British Journal of Psychiatry*, 143:332–337, 1983.

Bullough, V.L. *Sexual Variance in Society and History.* New York, John Wiley & Sons, 1976.

Carnes, P. *The Sexual Addiction.* Minneapolis, CompCare Publications, 1983.

Cauldwell, D.O. Psychopathia Transexualis. *Sexology*, 16:274–280, 1949.

Chan, S.T.H. Spontaneous sex reversal in fishes. In *Handbook of Sexology* (J. Money and H. Musaph, eds.). Amsterdam/London/New York, Excerpta Medica, 1977.

Clarke, I.J. The sexual behavior of prenatally androgenized ewes observed in the field. *Journal of Reproduction and Fertility*, 49:311–315, 1977.

Coleman, E., Colgan, P., and Gooren, L. The Acault of Burma: Male cross-dressers. Unpublished, 1987.

Crews, D. Functional associations in behavioral endocrinology. In *Masculinity/ Femininity: Basic Perspectives* (J.M. Reinisch, L.A. Rosenblum, and S.A. Sanders, eds.). New York, Oxford University Press, 1987a.

Crews, D. On the origin of sexual behavior. *Psychoneuroendocrinology*, 7:259–270, 1982.

Crews, D. (ed.). *Psychobiology of Reproductive Behavior: An Evolutionary Perspective.* Englewood Cliffs, N.J., Prentice-Hall, 1987b.

De Cecco, J.P. Homosexuality's brief recovery: From sickness to health and back again. *Journal of Sex Research*, 23:106–114, 1987.

DeVoogd, T.J. Steroid interactions with structure and function of avian song control regions. *Journal of Neurobiology*, 17:177–201, 1986.

De Vries, G.J., De Brun, J.P.C., Uylings, H.B.M., and Corner, M.A. (eds.). *Sex Differences in the Brain: Relation between Structure and Function.* Amsterdam/ New York, Elsevier, 1984.

de Waal, F.B.M. Tension regulation and nonreproductive functions of sex in captive bonobos (Pan paniscus). *National Geographic Research*, 3:318–335, 1987.

Dewaraja, R., and Money, J. Transcultural sexology: Formicophilia, a newly named paraphilia in a young Buddhist male. *Journal of Sex and Marital Therapy*, 12:139–145, 1986.

Diamond, M. A critical evaluation of the ontogeny of human sexual behavior. *Quarterly Review of Biology*, 40:147–175, 1965.

Diamond, M. Human sexual development: Biological foundations for social development. In *Human Sexuality in Four Perspectives* (F.A. Beach, ed.). Baltimore, Johns Hopkins University Press, 1977.

D'Occhio, M.J., and Ford, J.J. Contribution of studies in cattle, sheep and swine to our understanding of the role of gonadal hormones in processes of sexual differentiation and adult sexual behavior. In *Handbook of Sexology*, Vol. 7 (J.M.A. Sitsen, ed.). Amsterdam, Elsevier, 1988, in press.

Doehler, K.D., Coquelin, A., Davis, F., Hines, M., Shryne, J.E., and Gorski, R.A. Differentiation of the sexually dimorphic nucleus in the preoptic area of the rat brain is determined by the perinatal hormone environment. *Neuroscience Letters*, 33:295–298, 1982.

Doerner, G. *Hormones and Brain Differentiation.* New York, Elsevier, 1976.

Doerner, G. Sexual dimorphism of the brain: Model for hormone-dependent brain organization. In *Gynecological Endocrinology: The Proceedings of the First International Congress on Gynecological Endocrinology* (A.R. Genazzani, A. Volpe, and F. Facchinetti, eds.). Carnforth, United Kingdom, and Park Ridge, N.J., Parthenon, 1987.

Doerner, G., and Staudt, J. Perinatal structural sex differentiation of the hypothalamus in rats. *Neuroendocrinology*, 5:103–106, 1969.

Doerner, G., Rohde, W. Stahl, F., Krell, L., and Masius, W.-G. A neuroendocrine predisposition for homosexuality in men. *Archives of Sexual Behavior*, 4:1–8, 1975.

Donahue, P. *The Human Animal: Who Are We? Why Do We Behave the Way We Do? Can We Change?* New York, Simon and Schuster, 1985.

Dorland's Illustrated Medical Dictionary, 26th edition. Philadelphia, Saunders, 1981.

Ehrhardt, A.A., Evers, K., and Money, J. Influence of androgen and some aspects of sexually dimorphic behavior in women with late-treated adrenogenital syndrome. *Johns Hopkins Medical Journal*, 123:115–122, 1968.

Ehrhardt, A.A., Greenberg, N., and Money, J. Female gender identity and the absence of fetal gonadal hormones: Turner's syndrome. *Johns Hopkins Medical Journal*, 126:237–248, 1970.

Ehrhardt, A.A., and Money, J. Progestin-induced hermaphroditism: IQ and psychosexual identity in a study of ten girls. *Journal of Sex Research*, 3:83–100, 1967.

Ellis, H. *Studies in the Psychology of Sex*, Vols. 1 and 2. New York, Random House, 1942.

Friday, N. *Forbidden Flowers*. New York, Simon and Schuster, 1975.

Friday, N. *My Secret Garden*. New York, Simon and Schuster, 1973.

Frost, J.J., Mayberg, H.S., Berlin, F., Behal, R., Dannals, R.F., Links, J.M., Ravert, H.T., Wilson, A.A., and Wagner, Jr., H.N. Alteration in brain opiate receptor binding in man following sexual arousal using C-11 carfentanil and positron emission tomography. *Journal of Nuclear Medicine*, 27:1027, 1986. (Abstract)

Gagnon, J.H., and Simon, W. *Sexual Conduct: The Social Sources of Human Sexuality*. Chicago, Aldine, 1973.

Gladue, B.A., Green, R., and Hellman, R.E. Neuroendocrine response to estrogen and sexual orientation. *Science*, 225:1496–1498, 1984.

Goldberg, S. *The Inevitability of Patriarchy*. New York, Morrow, 1973.

Goldfoot, D.A. Sociosexual behaviors of nonhuman primates during development and maturity: Social and hormonal relationships. In *Behavioral Primatology, Advances in Research and Theory*, Vol. 1 (A.M. Schrier, ed.). Hillsdale, N.J., Lawrence Erlbaum, 1977.

Goldfoot, D.A., and Neff, D.A. On measuring behavioral sex differences in social contexts: Perspectives from primatology. In *Masculinity/Femininity: Basic Perspectives*. (J.M. Reinisch, L.A. Rosenblum, and S.A. Sanders, eds.). New York, Oxford University Press, 1987.

Goldfoot, D.A., and Wallen, K. Development of gender role behaviors in heterosexual and isosexual groups of infant rhesus monkeys. In *Recent Advances in Primatology*, Vol. 1, *Behaviour* (D.J. Chivers and J. Herbert, eds.). London, Academic Press, 1978.

Goldfoot, D.A., Wallen, K., Neff, D.A., McBrair, M.C., and Goy, R.W. Social influences upon the display of sexually dimorphic behavior in rhesus monkeys: Isosexual rearing. *Archives of Sexual Behavior*, 13:395–412, 1984.

Gooren, L. The neuroendocrine response of luteinizing hormone to estrogen administration in heterosexual, homosexual, and transsexual subjects. *Journal of Clinical Endocrinology and Metabolism*, 63:583–588, 1986.

Gorski, R.A. Gonadal hormones as putative neurotrophic substances. In *Synaptic Plasticity* (C.W. Cotman, ed.). New York, Guilford Press, 1985a.

Gorski, R.A. Sexual dimorphisms of the brain. *Journal of Animal Science*, 61:38–61, 1985b.

Gorski, R.A. The 13th J.A.F. Stevenson memorial lecture. Sexual differentiation of the brain: Possible mechanisms and implications. *Canadian Journal of Physiology and Pharmacology*, 63:577–594, 1985c.

Gorski, R.A., Gordon, J.H., Shryne, J.E., and Southam, A.M. Evidence for a morphological sex difference within the medial preoptic area of the rat brain. *Brain Research*, 148:333–346, 1978.

Green, R. *"The Sissy Boy Syndrome" and the Development of Homosexuality*. New Haven, Conn., Yale University Press, 1986.

Green, R. and Money, J. Stage-acting, role-taking, and effeminate impersonation during boyhood. *Archives of General Psychiatry*, 15:535–538, 1966.

Greenough, W.T., Carter, C.S., Steerman, C., and DeVoogd, T.J. Sex differences in dendritic patterns in hamster preoptic area. *Brain Research*, 126:63–72, 1977.

Gross, M.R. Sunfish, salmon, and the evolution of alternative reproductive strategies and tactics in fishes. In *Fish Reproduction: Strategies and Tactics* (G.W. Potts and R.J. Wooten, eds.). London, Academic Press, 1984.

Haeberle, E.J. *The Sex Atlas*. New York, Seabury Press, 1978.

Hampson, J.G., and Money, J. Idiopathic sexual precocity in the female. *Psychosomatic Medicine*, 17:16–35, 1955.

Hendricks, S.E., Graber, B., and Rodriguez-Sierra, J.F. Sexual orientation and neuroendocrine response to injected estrogens. *International Academy of Sex Research Twelfth Annual meeting: Abstracts*. Amsterdam, p. 16, 1986. (Abstract)

Herdt, G.H. *Guardians of the Flutes: Idioms of Masculinity*. New York, McGraw-Hill, 1981.

Herdt, G.H. (ed.). *Ritualized Homosexuality in Melanesia*. Berkeley, University of California Press, 1984.

Hirschfeld, M. *Sexual Anomalies: The Origins, Nature and Treatment of Sexual Disorders*. New York, Emerson Books, 1948.

Hite, S. *The Hite Report*. New York, Dell, 1976.

Hoult, T.F. Human sexuality in biological perspective: Theoretical and methodological considerations. In *Bisexual and Homosexual Identities: Critical Theoretical Issues* (J.P. De Cecco and M.G. Shively, eds.). New York, Haworth Press, 1984.

Hutt, C. *Males and Females*. Chicago, Penguin, 1972.

Imperato-McGinley, J., Guerrero, L., Gautier, T., and Peterson, R.E. Steroid 5α-reductase deficiency in man: An inherited form of male pseudohermaphroditism. *Science*, 186:1213–1215, 1974.

Imperato-McGinley, J., and Peterson, R.E. Male pseudohermaphroditism: The complexities of male phenotypic development. *American Journal of Medicine*, 61:251–272, 1976.

Imperato-McGinley, J., Peterson, R.E., Gautier, T., and Sturla, E. Androgens and the evolution of male-gender identity among male pseudohermaphrodites with 5α-reductase deficiency. *New England Journal of Medicine*, 300:1233–1237, 1979.

Jackson, P., Barrowclough, I.W., France, J.T., and Phillips, L.I. A successful pregnancy following total hysterectomy. *British Journal of Obstetrics and Gynaecology*, 87:353–355, 1980.

Jones, H.W., Jr. A long look at the adrenogenital syndrome. *Johns Hopkins Medical Journal*, 145:143–149, 1979.

Jordan, H.W., and Howe, G. De Clérambault syndrome (erotomania): A review and case presentation. *Journal of the National Medical Association*, 72:979–985, 1980.

Kalin, N.H. Genital and abdominal self-surgery: A case report. *Journal of the American Medical Association*, 241:2188–2189, 1979.

Kelly, H.A. *Love and Marriage in the Age of Chaucer*. Ithaca, N.Y., Cornell University Press, 1975.

Klebs, E. *Handbuch der pathologischen Anatomie*. Berlin, A. Herschwald, 1876.

Kolodny, R.C., Jacobs, L.S., Masters, W.H., Toro, G., and Daughaday, W.H. Plasma gonadotropins and prolactin in male homosexuals. *Lancet*, 2:18–20, 1972.

Kolodny, R.C., Masters, W.H., Hendryx, J., and Toro, G. Plasma testosterone and semen analysis in male homosexuals. *New England Journal of Medicine*, 285:1170–1174, 1971.

Krafft-Ebing, R. von. *Psychopathia Sexualis with Special Reference to the Antipathic Sexual Instinct: A Medico-Forensic Study* [Authorized English adaptation of the twelfth German edition, by F.J. Rebman]. Chicago, Login Brothers, 1931.

Lewis, V.G., and Money, J. Gender-identity/role: G-I/R Part A: XY (androgen-insensitivity) syndrome and XX (Rokitansky) syndrome of vaginal atresia compared. In *Handbook of Psychosomatic Obstetrics and Gynaecology* (L. Dennerstein and G. Burrows, eds.). Amsterdam/New York/Oxford, Elsevier Biomedical Press, 1983.

Lightfoot-Klein, H. *Prisoners of Ritual: A Study of Circumcision and Infibulation*. Pub. in process, 1988.

Lindemalm, G., Koerlin, D., and Uddenberg, N. Long-term follow-up of "sex change" in 13 male-to-female transsexuals. *Archives of Sexual Behavior*, 13:187–210, 1986.

Lorenz, K.Z. *King Solomon's Ring*. New York, Thomas Y. Crowell, 1952.

MacLean, P.D. *A Triune Concept of the Brain and Behavior*. The Hincks Memorial Lectures (T. Boag, ed.). Toronto, Toronto University Press, 1972.

Magoun, H.W. John B. Watson and the study of human sexual behavior. *Journal of Sex Research*, 17:368–378, 1981.

Manosevitz, M. Early sexual behavior in adult homosexual and heterosexual males. *Journal of Abnormal Psychology*, 76:396–402, 1970.

Martin, J.T., and Baum, M.J. Neonatal exposure of female ferrets to testosterone alters sociosexual preferences in adulthood. *Psychoneuroendocrinology*, 11:167–176, 1986.

Masica, D.N., Ehrhardt, A.A., and Money, J. Fetal feminization and female gender identity in the testicular feminizing syndrome of androgen insensitivity. *Archives of Sexual Behavior*, 1:131–142, 1971.

McCauley, E., Sybert, V.P., and Ehrhardt, A.A. Psychosocial adjustment of adult women with Turner syndrome. *Clinical Genetics*, 29:284–290, 1986.

McWhirter, D.P., and Mattison, A.M. *The Male Couple*. Englewood Cliffs, N.J., Prentice-Hall, 1984.

McWhirter, D.P., Sanders, S.A., and Reinisch, J.M. (eds.). *Homosexuality/Heterosexuality: Concepts of Sexual Orientation*. New York, Oxford University Press, 1988, in press.

Money, J. Components of eroticism in man. I. The hormones in relation to sexual morphology and sexual desire. *Journal of Nervous and Mental Disease*, 132:239–248, 1961a.

Money, J. *The Destroying Angel: Sex, Fitness, and Food in the Legacy of Degeneracy Theory, Graham Crackers, Kellogg's Corn Flakes, and American Health History*. Buffalo, N.Y., Prometheus, 1985.

Money, J. Endocrine influences and psychosexual status spanning the life cycle, In *Handbook of Biological Psychiatry, Part III, Brain Mechanisms and Abnormal Behavior—Genetics and Neuroendocrinology* (M.M. van Praag, M.H. Lader, O.J. Rafaelsen, and E.J. Sachar, eds.). New York, Marcel Dekker, 1980a.

Money, J. Family and gender-identity/role. Parts I, II, and III. *International Journal of Family Psychiatry*, 5:317–381, 1984a.

Money, J. Gender transposition theory and homosexual genesis. *Journal of Sex and Marital Therapy*, 10:75–82, 1984b.

Money, J. *Hermaphroditism: An Inquiry into the Nature of a Human Paradox*. Doctoral dissertation, Harvard University Library, 1952. University Microfilms Library Services, Xerox Corporation, Ann Arbor, Mich. 48106, 1967.

Money, J. Hermaphroditism, gender and precocity in hyperadrenocorticism: Psychologic findings. *Bulletin of The Johns Hopkins Hospital*, 96:253–264, 1955a.

Money, J. Homosexual genesis, outcome studies, and a nature/nurture paradigm shift. *Endorphins, Neuroregulators and Behavior in Human Reproduction.* Proceedings of the Third International Symposium on Psychoneuroendocrinology in Reproduction, Spoleto, Italy, July 9–12, 1982 (P. Pancheri, L. Zichella, and P. Falaschi, eds.). Amsterdam, Excerpta Medica, 1984c.

Money, J. Linguistic resources and psychodynamic theory. *British Journal of Medical Psychology*, 20:264–266, 1955b.

Money, J. *Love and Love Sickness: The Science of Sex, Gender Difference and Pairbonding.* Baltimore, Johns Hopkins University Press, 1980b.

Money, J. *Lovemaps: Clinical Concepts of Sexual/Erotic Health and Pathology, Paraphilia, and Gender Transposition in Childhood, Adolescence, and Maturity.* New York, Irvington, 1986a.

Money, J. Masochism: On the childhood origin of paraphilia, opponent-process theory, and antiandrogen therapy. *Journal of Sex Research*, 23:273–275, 1987a.

Money, J. Pairbonding and limerence. *International Encyclopedia of Psychiatry, Psychology, Psychoanalysis and Neurology.* Progress Volume I (B.B. Wolman, ed.). New York, Aesculapius Publishers, 1983.

Money, J. Paraphilias: Phyletic origins of erotosexual dysfunction. *International Journal of Mental Health*, 10:75–109, 1981.

Money, J. Prenatal hormones and postnatal socialization in gender identity differentiation. *Nebraska Symposium on Motivation*, 21:221–295, 1974.

Money, J. Propaedeutics of diecious G-I/R: Theoretical foundations for understanding dimorphic gender-identity/role. In *Masculinity/Femininity: Basic Perspectives* (J.M. Reinisch, L.A.Rosenblum and S.A. Sanders, eds.). New York, Oxford University Press, 1987b.

Money, J. Psychologic approach to psychosexual misidentity with elective mutism: Sex reassignment in two cases of hyperadrenocortical hermaphroditism. *Clinical Pediatrics*, 7:331–339, 1968a.

Money, J. *The Psychologic Study of Man.* Springfield, Ill., Charles C Thomas, 1957.

Money, J. *Sex Errors of the Body: Dilemmas, Education, Counseling.* Baltimore, Johns Hopkins University Press, 1968b.

Money, J. The sex hormones and other variables in human eroticism. In *Sex and Internal Secretions*, 3rd edition. (W.C. Young, ed.). Baltimore, Williams and Wilkins, pp. 1383–1400, 1961b.

Money, J. Sexual dictatorship, dissidence and democracy. *International Journal of Medicine and Law*, 1:11–20, 1979.

Money, J. Sexual dimorphism and homosexual gender identity. *Psychological Bulletin*, 74:425–440, 1970a.

Money, J. Sin, sickness or status? Homosexual gender identity and psychoneuroendocrinology. *American Psychologist*, 42:384–399, 1987c.

Money, J. The Skoptic syndrome: Castration and genital self-mutilation. *Journal of Psychology and Human Sexuality* 1(1): 1988, in press.

Money, J. To quim and to swive: Linguistic and coital parity, male and female. *Journal of Sex Research*, 18:173–176, 1982.

Money, J. Treatment guidelines: Antiandrogen and counseling of paraphilic sex offenders. *Journal of Sex and Marital Therapy*, 13:219–223, 1987d.

Money, J. Two names, two wardrobes, two personalities. *British Journal of Sexual Medicine*, 3:18–22, 1976.

Money, J. Use of an androgen-depleting hormone in the treatment of male sex offenders. *Journal of Sex Research*, 6:165–172, 1970b.

Money, J. Vatican sexology. *Free Inquiry*, 7(2):9, 1987e.

Money, J. *Venuses Penuses: Sexology, Sexosophy, and Exigency Theory*. Buffalo, N.Y., Prometheus, 1986b.

Money, J., and Alexander, D. Psychosexual development and absence of homosexuality in males with precocious puberty: Review of 18 cases. *Journal of Nervous and Mental Disease*, 148:111–123, 1969.

Money, J., Alexander, D., and Walker, H.T., Jr. *A Standardized Roadmap Test of Direction Sense*. Baltimore, Johns Hopkins University Press, 1965.

Money, J., and Ambinder, R. Two-year, real-life diagnostic test: Rehabilitation versus cure. In *Controversy in Psychiatry* (J.P. Brady and H.K.H. Brodie, eds.). Philadelphia, Saunders, 1978.

Money, J., Annecillo, C., and Hutchinson, J.W. Forensic and family psychiatry in abuse dwarfism: Munchausen's Syndrome by proxy, atonement, and addiction to abuse. *Journal of Sex and Marital Therapy*, 11:30–40, 1985.

Money, J., Annecillo, C., Van Orman, B., and Borgaonkar, D.S. Cytogenetics, hormones, and behavior disability: Comparison of XYY and XXY syndromes. *Clinical Genetics*, 6:370–382, 1974.

Money, J., and Bohmer, C. Prison sexology: Two personal accounts of masturbation, homosexuality and rape. *Journal of Sex Research*, 16:258–266, 1980.

Money, J., and Daléry, J. Hyperadrenocortical 46,XX hermaphroditism with penile urethra. Psychological studies in seven cases, three reared as boys, four as girls. In *Congenital Adrenal Hyperplasia* (P.A. Lee, L.P. Plotnick, A.A. Kowarski, and C.J. Migeon, eds.). Baltimore, University Park Press, 1977.

Money, J., and Daléry, J. Iatrogenic homosexuality: Gender identity in seven 46,XX chromosomal females with hyperadrenocortical hermaphroditism born with a penis, three reared as boys, four reared as girls. *Journal of Homosexuality*, 1:357–371, 1976.

Money, J., and DePriest, M. Three cases of genital self-surgery and their relationship to transexualism. *Journal of Sex Research*, 12:283–294, 1976.

Money, J., Devore, H., and Norman, B.F. Gender identity and gender transposition: Longitudinal study of 32 male hermaphrodites assigned as girls. *Journal of Sex and marital Therpay*, 12:165–181, 1986.

Money, J., and Ehrhardt, A.A. Gender-dimorphic behavior and fetal sex hormones. In *Recent Progress in Hormone Research* (E.B. Astwood, ed.), Vol. 28. New York, Academic Press, 1972a.

Money, J. and Ehrhardt, A.A. *Man and Woman, Boy and Girl: The Differentiation and Dimorphism of Gender Identity from Conception to Maturity*. Baltimore, Johns Hopkins Press, 1972b.

Money, J., Gaskin, R., and Hull, H. Impulse, aggression and sexuality in the XYY syndrome. *St. John's Law Review*, 44:220–235, 1970.

Money, J., and Hampson, J.G. Idiopathic sexual precocity in the male. *Psychosomatic Medicine*, 17:1–15, 1955.

Money, J., Hampson, J.G., and Hampson, J.L. An examination of some basic sexual concepts: The evidence of human hermaphroditism. *Bulletin of The Johns Hopkins Hospital*, 97:301–319, 1955.

Money, J., Jobaris, R., and Furth, G. Apotemnophilia: Two cases of self- demand amputation as a paraphilia. *Journal of Sex Research*, 13:115–125, 1977.

Money, J., and Lamacz, M. Gynemimesis and gynemimetophilia: Individual and cross-cultural manifestations of a gender coping strategy hitherto unnamed. *Comprehensive Psychiatry*, 25:392–403, 1984.

Money, J., and Lamacz, M. Nosocomial stress and abuse exemplified in a case of male hermaphroditism from infancy through adulthood: Coping strategies and prevention. *International Journal of Family Psychiatry*, 7:71–105, 1986.

Money, J., Leal, J., and Gonzalez, J. Aphrodisiology: History, folklore, efficacy. In *Handbook of Sexology*, Vol. 6: *Pharmacology of Sexual Function*. (J. Money and H. Musaph, series eds.; J.M.A. Sitsen, vol. ed.). Amsterdam, Elsevier, 1988, in press.

Money, J., and Lewis, V.G. Gender-identity/role: G-I/R Part B: A multiple sequential model of differentiation. In *Handbook of Psychosomatic Obstetrics and Gynaecology* (L. Dennerstein and G. Burrows, eds.). Amsterdam/New York/Oxford, Elsevier Biomedical Press, 1983.

Money, J., and Lewis, V.G. Homosexual/heterosexual status in boys at puberty: Idiopathic adolescent gynecomastia and congenital virilizing adrenocorticism compared. *Psychoneuroendocrinology*, 7:339–346, 1982.

Money, J., and Mathews, D. Prenatal exposure to virilizing progestins: An adult follow-up study of twelve women. *Archives of Sexual Behavior*, 11:73–83, 1982.

Money, J., and Mittenthal, S. Lack of personality pathology in Turner's syndrome: Relation to cytogenetics, hormones and physique. *Behavior Genetics*, 1:43–56, 1970.

Money, J., and Norman, B.F. Gender identity and gender transposition: Longitudinal outcome study of 24 male hermaphrodites assigned as boys. *Journal of Sex and Marital Therapy*, 13:75–92, 1987.

Money, J., and Pollitt, E. Cytogenetic and psychosexual ambiguity: Klinefelter's syndrome and transvestism compared. *Archives of General Psychiatry*, 11:589–595, 1964.

Money, J., and Pruce, G. Psychomotor epilepsy and sexual function. In *Handbook of Sexology* (J. Money and H. Musaph, eds.). Amsterdam/London/New York, Excerpta Medica, 1977.

Money, J., and Russo, A.J. Homosexual outcome of discordant gender-identity/role in childhood: Longitudinal follow-up. *Journal of Pediatric Psychology*, 4:29–41, 1979.

Money, J., Schwartz, M., and Lewis V.G. Adult erotosexual status and fetal hormonal masculinization and demasculinization: 46,XX congenital virilizing adrenal hyperplasia and 46,XY androgen-insensitivity syndrome compared. *Psychoneuroendocrinology*, 9:405–414, 1984.

Money,J., and Tucker, P. *Sexual Signatures*. Boston, Little, Brown, 1975.

Money, J., and Walker, P. Psychosexual development, maternalism, nonpromiscuity and body image in 15 females with precocious puberty. *Archives of Sexual Behavior*, 1:45–60, 1971.

Money, J., and Weinrich, J.D. Juvenile, pedophile, heterophile: Hermeneutics of science, medicine and law in two outcome studies. *Medicine and Law*, 2:39–54, 1983.

Money, J., and Wolff, G. Sex reassignment: Male to female to male. *Archives of Sexual Behavior*, 2:245–250, 1973.

Nanda, S. The hijras of India: A preliminary report. *Medicine and Law*, 3:59–75, 1984.

Nanda, S. The hijras of India: Cultural and individual dimensions of an institutionalized third gender role. *Journal of Homosexuality*, 11:35–54, 1985.

Niebyl, J.R. Pregnancy following total hysterectomy. *American Journal of Obstetrics and Gynecology*, 119:512–515, 1974.

Nordeen, E.J., and Yahr, P. Hemispheric asymmetries in the behavioral and hormonal effects of sexually differentiating mammalian brain. *Science*, 218:391–393, 1982.

Norén, H., and Lindblom, B. A unique case of abdominal pregnancy: What are the minimal requirements for placental contact with the maternal vascular bed? *American Journal of Obstetrics and Gynecology*, 155:394–396, 1986.

Nottebohm, F., and Arnold, A.P. Sexual dimorphism in vocal control areas of the song-bird brain. *Science*, 194:211–213, 1976.

Parks, G.A., Korth-Schutz, S., Penny, R., Hilding, R.F., Dumars, K.W., Frasier, S.D., and New, M.I. Variation in pituitary-gonadal function in adolescent male homosexuals and heterosexuals. *Journal of Clinical Endocrinology and Metabolism*, 39:796–801, 1974.

Pauly, P.J. Psychology at Hopkins: Its rise and fall and rise and fall and. . . . *Johns Hopkins Magazine*, 30:36–42, 1979.

Perper, T. *Sex Signals: The Biology of Love*. Philadelphia, ISI Press, 1985.

Phoenix, C.H., and Chambers, K.C. Moderate social restriction during infancy reduces sexual receptivity in adult female rhesus macaques. *Behavioral and Neural Biology*, 36:259–265, 1982a.

Phoenix, C.H., and Chambers, K.C. Sexual behavior in adult gonadectomized female pseudohermaphrodite, female, and male rhesus macaques (*Macaca mulatta*) treated with estradiol benzoate and testosterone propionate. *Journal of Comprehensive Physiology*, 96:823–833, 1982b.

Phoenix, C.H., Jensen, J.N., and Chambers, K.C. Female sexual behavior displayed by androgenized female rhesus monkeys. *Hormones and Behavior*, 17:146–151, 1983.

Plummer, K. *Sexual Stigma: An Interactionist Account*. London, Routledge & Kegan Paul, 1975.

Potts, G.W., and Wootton, R.J. (eds.). *Fish Reproduction: Strategies and Tactics*. London, Academic Press, 1984.

Raisman, C., and Field, P.M. Sexual dimorphism in the preoptic area of the rat. *Science*, 173:731–733, 1971.

Rees, H.D., Bonsall, R.W., and Michael, R.P. Preoptic and hypothalamic neurons accumulate [^{3}H]medroxyprogesterone acetate in male cynomolgus monkeys. *Life Sciences*, 39:1353–1359, 1986.

Reinisch, J.M., and Sanders, S.A. Early barbiturate exposure: The brain, sexually dimorphic behavior, and learning. *Neuroscience and Biobehavioral Reviews*, 6:311–319, 1982.

Reiss, I.L. *Journey into Sexuality: An Exploratory Voyage*. Englewood Cliffs, N.J., Prentice-Hall, 1987.

Rogers, L., and Walsh, J. Shortcomings of the psychomedical research of John Money and co-workers into sex differences in behavior: Social and political implications. *Sex Roles*, 8:269–281, 1982.

Sanders, R.M., Bain, J., and Langevin, R. Peripheral sex hormones, homosexuality, and gender identity. In *Erotic Preference, Gender Identity and Aggression in Men: New Research Studies* (R. Langevin, ed.). Hillsdale, N.J., Lawrence Erlbaum, 1985.

Satterfield, S.B. 14-year experience with surgical sex reassignment. *Abstracts, 5th World Congress of Sexology*, Jerusalem, p. 385, 1981.

Schiavi, R.C., Theilgaard, A., Owen, D.R., and White, D. Sex chromosome anomalies, hormones, and sexuality. *Archives of General Psychiatry*, 1987, in press.

Short, R.V., and Clarke, I.J. *Masculinization of the Female Sheep*. Distributed by MRC Reproductive Biology Unit, 2 Forrest Road, Edinburgh, EHI 2QW, United Kingdom. Undated.

Silverstein, C. *Man to Man: Gay Couples in America*. New York, Morrow, 1981.

Solomon, R.L. The opponent process in acquired motivation. In *The Physiological Mechanisms of Motivation* (D.W. Pfaff, ed.). New York, Springer-Verlag, 1982, pp. 321–336.

Solomon, R.L. The opponent-process theory of acquired motivation. *American Psychologist*, 35:691–712, 1980b.

Somomon, R.L. Recent experiments testing an opponent-process theory of acquired motivation. *Acta Neurobiologiae Experimentalis*, 40:271–289, 1980a.

Stein, K. Interview: John Money. *Omni*, 8:78–88ff, April 1986.

Steinach, E. *Sex and Life. Forty Years of Biological and Medical Experiments.* New York, Viking Press, 1940.

Stoller, R.J. *Sex and Gender.* New York, Science House, 1968.

Stoller, R.J., and Herdt, G.H. Theories of origins of male homosexuality. *Archives of General Psychiatry*, 42:399–404, 1985.

Storms, M.D. A theory of erotic orientation development. *Psychological Review*, 88:340–353, 1981.

Swaab, D.F., and Fliers, E. A sexually dimorphic nucleus in the human brain. *Science*, 228:1112–1115, 1985.

Swaab, D.F., Roozendaal, B., Ravid R., Velis, D.N., Gooren, L., and Williams, R.S. Suprachiasmatic nucleus in aging, Alzheimer's disease, transsexuality and Prader-Willi syndrome. In *Progress in Brain Research*, Vol. 72 (E.R. de Kloet, V.M. Wiegant, and D. de Wied, eds.). Amsterdam, Elsevier, 1987.

Tennov, D. *Love and Limerence: The Experience of Being in Love.* New York, Stein and Day, 1979.

Teresi, D., and McAuliffe, K. Male pregnancy. *Omni*, 8:50–56 and 118, 1985.

Tripp, C.A. *The Homosexual Matrix.* New York, McGraw-Hill, 1975.

U.S. Department of Justice. *Attorney General's Commission on Pornography: Final Report*, two vols. Washington, D.C., U.S. Government Printing office, 1986.

Virag, R., Frydman, D., Legman, M., and Virag, H. Intracavernous injection of papaverine as a diagnostic and therapeutic method in erectile failure. *Angiology*, 35:79–87, 1984.

Wagner, G., and Sjostrand, N.O. Autonomic pharmacology and sexual function. In *Handbook of Sexology*, Vol. 6: *The Pharmacology of Sexual Function* (J. Money and H. Musaph, series eds.; J.M.A. Sitsen, vol. ed.). Amsterdam, Elsevier, 1988, in press.

Ward, I.L. Prenatal stress feminizes and demasculinizes the behavior of males. *Science*, 175:82–84, 1972.

Ward, I.L. The prenatal stress syndrome: Current status. *Psychoneuroendocrinology*, 9:3–11, 1984.

Ward, I.L., and Weisz, J. Maternal stress alters plasma testosterone in fetal males. *Science*, 207:328–329, 1980.

Whalen, R.E., and Edwards, D.A. Hormonal determinants of the development of masculine and feminine behavior in male and female rats. *Anatomical Record*, 157:173–180, 1967.

Wikan, U. Man becomes woman: Transsexualism in Oman as a key to gender roles. *Man* (N.S.), 12:304–319, 1977.

Williams, W.L. Sex and shamanism: The making of a Hawaiian mahu. *The Advocate*, #417, April 2, 1985.

Williams, W.L. *The Spirit and the Flesh.* Boston, Beacon Press, 1986.

Young, W.C. (ed.). *Sex and Internal Secretions*, two vols. Baltimore, Williams and Wilkins, 1961.

Young, W.C., Goy, R.W., and Phoenix, C.H. Hormones and sexual behavior. *Science*, 143:212–218, 1964.

Name Index

Subject Index